The Two-Party System
Nobody Asked For

THE TWO-PARTY SYSTEM NOBODY ASKED FOR

Robert Lockwood Mills

Algora Publishing
New York

Library of Congress Cataloging in Publication Control Number: 2018055728

Names: Mills, Robert Lockwood, author.
Title: The two-party system that nobody asked for / Robert Lockwood Mills.
Description: New York; Algora Publishing, [2019] | Includes bibliographical
  references and index.
Identifiers: LCCN 2018061467 | ISBN 9781628943542 (soft cover; alk. paper)
Subjects: LCSH: Political parties—United States—History. | Two-party
  systems—United States—History. | Democratic Party (U.S.)—History. |
  Republican Party (U.S.; 1854-)—History. | Political culture—United
  States. | United States—Politics and government.
Classification: LCC JK2261 .M56 2019 | DDC 324.273—dc23 LC record available at
https://lccn.loc.gov/2018061467

Printed in the United States

ACKNOWLEDGEMENTS

The author gratefully acknowledges the help he received from the following during the preparation of this book:

Rosie Clifton, his partner for life and best friend, allowed him to poach on her computer because his own machine wasn't up to the task. She also helped get the word out by arranging speaking opportunities and contacting her legion of friends. Andrea Secara, at Algora, demonstrated "Jobesque" patience with an author whose lack of formatting skills, fundamental when converting a computer manuscript into a book, made her job harder. Joyce McIntosh, Jim Marino and the gang at the Sun City Center Writers' Club offered helpful suggestions for humanizing historical figures, thus making the book more readable.

Table of Contents

PROLOGUE

Arguably, 77-year-old men shouldn't write political books. At least, not when the prevailing political atmosphere collides with everything they observed growing up, or were taught in school, or read in a textbook, or heard their Uncle Harry say over Thanksgiving dinner in 1950. Authors are supposed to "write what we know," but the present author admits he doesn't know politics in the 21st century.

That said, someone needs to do something about the status quo. The United States (hereafter, "we") believe we won the Cold War, which back in 1950 had threatened to morph into a nuclear holocaust. We passed civil rights legislation, ending the Jim Crow era, and eventually elected a black man president. We fought a war on poverty, landed men on the moon, provided subsidized medical care to senior citizens and eventually to everyone, created the mightiest military force in history, and saw the Dow Jones Industrial Average rise ten-fold, from 2,500 to 25,000.

For all our successes, where are we in 2018? Half our citizens don't bother to vote. Most that do, vote against candidates, not for them. Our two major political parties control governmental function, yet Congress enjoys a 21% approval rating as of November 2018 (up from 12% in 2017). Democrats hate Republicans, Republicans hate Democrats, and the only thing everyone agrees upon is that government doesn't work. The two-party system just might be the problem.

Nobody seems to like Washington, DC, yet real estate values there are among the highest in the country, which means a lot of people like being in and around a government that most people hate. When the Cold War ended in 1991 with the collapse of the Soviet Union, we were promised a "peace dividend," but expensive military hardware has given way to drones, which enforce a Pax Americana on a world that has grown to hate us. Our debt level (as distinct from budget deficits) is now north of $21 trillion, which begs the question, "What happened to that peace dividend?"

As the debt level rises, neither party wants to deal with it; one party wants new social spending (that can't possibly help), the other cuts taxes (that can't, either) and looks to build a wall from the Pacific Ocean to the Gulf of Mexico, inviting lawsuits going several generations forward from people who don't like the idea of Uncle Sam building a redoubt on their property, all because government isn't enforcing laws that passed back when government functioned.

This book hopes to explain how and why we got to this point. The author is neither a Democrat nor a Republican and thus feels competent to discuss problems that no visible major-party figure has chosen to deal with.

Chapter 1: George Washington Was Prescient

The Father of Our Country balked at the very thought of political parties. His sentiments can be encapsulated into one quote from George Washington's Farewell Address. "Party wrangling agitates the community with ill-founded jealousies and false alarms, (and) kindles the animosity of one part against another."

Washington spoke those words just before leaving office in 1797, after two successive four-year terms as our first president. He had planned to serve only one term, but as his biographer Willard Sterne Randall explains, the president decided another four-year term might serve to prevent a two-party system from developing. It was clear to Washington that a burgeoning political rivalry and turf battle between fellow colonialists Alexander Hamilton and Thomas Jefferson threatened his own non-partisan ideal. Hamilton stood for a central government, empowered by a central banking system. Jefferson favored state and local preeminence over centralized power, further opining that a collision of interests between the residents of population centers and rural communities was natural and desirable.

George Washington vehemently disagreed with Jefferson. One might imagine how their conversation went.

WASHINGTON: "Thomas, we fought a revolution to rid us of tyranny. Now you're suggesting that we continue in a revolutionary context, in the form of a battle between different sectors of the country?"

JEFFERSON: "With all due respect, sir, that will happen in any event. Freedom demands that all citizens be free to pursue their selfish interests."

WASHINGTON: "Inevitably, Thomas, this will lead to chaos. Those selfish interests will take the form of political parties, which will next place their own priorities ahead of the commonweal."

Mr. Randall also reminds us that the United States Constitution, which had been ratified by most of the original 13 colonies even as Washington first prepared to take office in 1789, said nothing about political parties. Our almanacs tell us that Washington belonged to the Federalist Party, but that fact was kept from voters in 1788. No mention of a party appeared anywhere on the ballot, which is exactly as he wanted it.

No mention was made of any candidate for vice president in 1788, either. The Constitutional convention had decided we needed a vice president, but it saw no need to align that individual's political philosophy with that of the president. So, the second-place finisher in the Electoral College became the vice president. If the two men disliked each other, so be it. The same almanacs that refer to George Washington as a Federalist do likewise for John Adams, who finished second and served two terms as vice president (but not as GEORGE WASHINGTON'S vice president, because the two men were never running mates).

Adams made it easy for historians by never eschewing the Federalist party label that Washington had accepted, albeit only through a set of clenched (wooden) teeth. But things got stickier after Adams was elected president in 1796 by a whisker over Thomas Jefferson. Jefferson became vice president, according to the rules, but the author of America's Declaration of Independence wanted nothing to do with any Federalist administration. He kept his distance from Adams, waiting patiently for a second chance to win the big prize, which came in 1800. George Washington had died, but Federalist power broker Alexander Hamilton, who couldn't run for president himself because he'd been born in the West Indies (or was it Kenya?) used his influence with the House of Representatives to help the anti-Federalist Jefferson break an Electoral College tie with Aaron Burr and gain the White House (Adams finished third in the Electoral College).

This episode might stand as the original source of the phrase, "Politics makes strange bedfellows." As George Washington might have warned those involved, had he not died in 1799, this electoral contretemps didn't end with the Electoral College. Four years later, something close to the following was heard: BURR: "Mr. Hamilton, you deprived the country of my services as president. This was an incalculable loss to the people."

HAMILTON: "Mr. Vice President, I acted in accordance with my conscience. Only my conscience guides me."

BURR: "Well, Mr. Hamilton, my conscience requires that I obtain justice on the people's behalf. I will meet you tomorrow at Weehawken. Bring your firearm."

HAMILTON: "I must defend my honor, sir. But I intend to fire my weapon in the air."

Thomas Jefferson's signature achievement during two terms as president (1801–1809) was persuading France to relinquish territorial claims to what became known as the Louisiana Purchase. In this regard Jefferson no doubt benefited from his prior endorsement of the French Revolution, which he watched develop approvingly first hand as foreign minister in Paris in the early 1790s. But historians have noted that the Louisiana Purchase probably violated the U.S. Constitution, and in any case contradicted Jefferson's own philosophical preference for local government over federal authority.

James Madison, primary architect of the Constitution, succeeded Jefferson as president in 1809. George Washington had established a tradition that presidents serve two terms at most, but Jefferson's second term was less successful than his first, so he would have been a poor bet to win a third term, anyway. Madison and Jefferson held differing views toward the presidency and had never been particularly close, but they agreed that anything was better in the White House than a gosh-awful Tory (Federalist) like John Adams, who always favored the British, as had other Federalists who objected to doing business with the French....never mind the reciprocity between the U.S. and France that had prevailed during their respective revolutions. Somehow, word of growing American antipathy toward England had reached London, and before Madison's first term in office had ended, the White House had been set on fire by Tories who had come to resent Washington's treatment of France as a favored trading partner. That's Washington, DC, we're referring to, not George.

At this point in history a two-party system hadn't really developed. Jefferson and Madison were anti-Federalists, but preferred being known as Republicans. The Federalists were on their way out, besides. So, if you check your almanac again, you'll see Jefferson, Madison, and James Monroe listed as Democratic-Republicans.

Democratic-Republicans bore no relationship to today's Democrats and/ or Republicans. Political issues that later came to separate Democrats from Republicans had yet to surface; instead, the government was busy fighting Indians (Native Americans), also affirming North American sovereignty vis a vis European colonialism (Monroe Doctrine), and, hesitatingly, dealing with a problem for which the Constitution had provided no advice whatsoever... human slavery.

This period in history came to be called the Era of Good Feeling. Everyone wanted to get rid of Indians. Nobody wanted Spain to invade North America. England had gone back to minding its own business, while dealing with a monarchy crisis. No need existed for political parties, because everyone seemed to agree with everyone else...except where slavery was concerned. Above the Mason-Dixon line that separates Pennsylvania from Maryland, a broad consensus opposed human bondage. Many states had outlawed the practice within their borders. But the agrarian South was emboldened by the Constitution's silence on the question; and, given that technological advances had enabled a boom economy in its primary export, cotton, preserving slavery became essential to advancing Dixie's economic well-being.

The Missouri Compromise in 1820, which enabled Missouri's admission to the union in 1821, established its southern border with Arkansas as the latitudinal line below which slavery would be permitted nationwide. Above that border, slavery was proscribed everywhere. But because Maine had been admitted at the same time as a free state, the tit-for-tat-styled "compromise" became a violation of its own terms, as Missouri itself permitted slavery.

The issue divided the country geographically, but not necessarily in terms of party labels. Like Jefferson and Madison, Monroe was content to refer to himself as a Republican, when in fact he disavowed partisanship. John Quincy Adams followed Monroe as president, but only after an election in which he had finished behind Andrew Jackson of Tennessee in both the Electoral College and the popular vote. Jackson had a plurality among four candidates, but not a majority in the College, so according to the Constitution, the election went to the House of Representatives, where Henry Clay, primary architect of the Missouri Compromise who had finished fourth (out of four) in the balloting, threw his support to Adams, who was declared the winner.

Jackson was furious. He alleged a "corrupt bargain" between Adams and Clay, in what might have been one of the nation's earliest conspiracy theories, because Adams had chosen Clay as his Secretary of State. A conspiracy was never proven, but Jackson's ire and subsequent election four years later led to the two-party system that George Washington, decades earlier, had warned the country against.

Thanks for nothing, Andrew. Thanks for nothing, Henry. Thanks for nothing, John Quincy. While you were fighting over the 1824 election, new political factions were developing in the country, such that the United States became permanently burdened with a two-party system, one that didn't work any better in 1824 than it does in 2018.

Jackson defeated Adams in 1020. Old Hickory's faction, which emerged as the Democrat(ic) party, inherited the anti-Federalist sentiment of the Jefferson/Madison Republicans. It urged non-renewal (in 1836) of the charter of the Second National Bank, originally the brainchild of (Federalist) Alexander Hamilton and the forerunner of today's Federal Reserve. But even as Jackson's populists claimed the democratic (small d) high ground and swore to return government to the people, Jackson himself adopted a dictatorial posture, declining to make appointments on merit and treating all disagreement with his policies as disloyalty, even as treason. Washington, DC became inundated with Jackson's crudely dressed and unwashed friends from the hinterland, in what became the country's first spoils system.

Jackson called himself a Democrat and kept his friends close by. His enemies, consisting of one-time Federalists, anti-slavery zealots, and Northern mercantilists, were geographically diffused but were united in their opposition to Jackson's version of populism. These anti-Jacksonites adopted the name Whig, which in England had stood for anyone brave enough to speak out against royal prerogatives and risk a permanent vacation in the Tower of London or the removal of his cranium. The Whig moniker suited their primary objective, which was to rid the country of King Andrew I.

The nation now had a two-party system.

CHAPTER 2: A TWO-PARTY SYSTEM THAT NOBODY ASKED FOR

Andrew Jackson won two elections as the founder of the Democratic Party, even though his executive style gave rise to an opposition party, the Whigs, whose members agreed on very little, save that Old Hickory was a tyrant who acted like a king. Jackson's legions, meanwhile, loved Andrew less for his espousal of democratic principles than for his history as an Indian fighter, his triumph at the Battle of New Orleans (after the War of 1812 had ended), and his largesse in rewarding friends with jobs in Washington that they might or might not have otherwise merited.

In other words, the two-party system developed absent any real philosophical gulf separating the respective organizations. A larger gulf existed within the parties, in fact.

Jackson and his first-term vice president, John C. Calhoun, clashed over the nullification question. Calhoun, a South Carolinian, insisted that any state could "nullify" a federally imposed tariff, of its own volition, if the tariff penalized the economy of the state in question. The author imagines their exchange of thoughts on the topic.

CALHOUN: "Mr. President, a tariff war with England will destroy South Carolina's economy. The British are our best customers. They need our cotton for their textile industry."

JACKSON: "Listen up, Bubba. I'm president of the United States, and the president decides tariff policy. The vice president must agree with his decisions. I also decide on my running mates, and you'll be off the ticket in 1832 when I run for reelection."

Calhoun was replaced on the ticket by Martin Van Buren, who became vice president when Jackson defeated Henry Clay. Only 44 years had passed since the first presidential election, but Jackson had succeeded in establishing a custom that the Founding Fathers hadn't contemplated. A presidential candidate has singular authority concerning the vice-presidential nominee of his party. If the candidate asserting that authority happens to be the incumbent president, said authority borders on the monarchical. Contrary to the design of the Founding Fathers, vice presidents now were under the aegis of the president. Van Buren was "Jackson's vice president," and future vice presidents would be described similarly.

It's easy to understand how Jackson got his way...Old Hickory always got his way. It's less clear why the prerogative was passed on to future generations. By our day, it's taken for granted that only the person chosen by a presidential candidate, or his designees, will become the running mate. The president, according to the logic, must be philosophically aligned with the vice president (loyal, in political terms) for the sake of governmental harmony. But looking at the question through a historical prism, we observe how frequently this adjunct to the two-party system has failed to justify the rationale.

Martin Van Buren, recognized by historians as Andrew Jackson's protégé, was elected president in 1836. The Whigs ran several candidates, who split the anti-Democratic vote. This assured Van Buren's election while at once evidencing the Whigs' own lack of homogeneity as a party. Van Buren's chosen running mate was Richard Johnson, a tavern owner from Kentucky who had no real political resume, but who claimed to have fired the shot that killed the hated Shawnee Chief, Tecumseh, 23 years earlier in Canada. Johnson's supporters chanted, "Rumpsey Dumpsey, Rumpsey Dumpsey, Richard Johnson killed Tecumseh." No historical evidence for the claim has ever surfaced. Surprisingly, the rhythmic ditty, despite its pivotal role in American history, was never set to music. If Johnson had killed Geronimo or Sitting Bull instead of Tecumseh, one may wonder how they'd have rhymed it.

Van Buren was impressed by Johnson's "credentials," evidently. But the Electoral College was less impressed, and refused to certify Johnson's election, even as it validated Van Buren's. The issue went to the Senate, as mandated by the Constitution, where Johnson squeaked through. His four years as vice president are forgettable, and notable only in that Jackson's article of faith, that a president may choose his running mate without argument, had failed its first historical test. Future chapters will discuss how vice presidents, presumably chosen for their philosophical compatibility with the president, often are anything but compatible.

The Whig party lacked cohesion, and it might have disappeared into the ether 20 years before its actual demise, except for an accident of history. In 1836 President Jackson had succeeded in preventing the renewal of the Second National Bank's 20-year charter, a hot-button issue. Shortly after Van Buren took over in 1837, the residual turmoil led to a banking crisis, a financial panic and a severe depression that effectively ruined his presidency. Any Whig able to stand on two feet without falling would have been elected by default in 1840, and the new president became aging William Henry Harrison, "Old Tippecanoe," another relic of the Indian wars. Harrison's campaign succeeded in avoiding political issues altogether. "Rumpsey Dumpsey" had been used already, and it didn't rhyme with any Native American Harrison had killed, so the Whigs decided on "Van, Van is a used-up man, Van is a used-up man," and "Tippecanoe and Tyler, too," meanwhile portraying Harrison as the humble resident of a log cabin who drank cider. In fact, Harrison had grown up as the son of wealthy planters who had moved north from Virginia.

Whether the presidential candidate should choose the running mate was still an open question. It worked for Andrew Jackson, but not for Martin Van Buren. In 1840 the Whigs decided that Harrison's partner on the ticket should be Virginian John Tyler, who was in fact a states-rights Democrat, but who provided geographical balance to the ticket (Harrison had long since lived in Indiana).

Harrison caught pneumonia at his inauguration and died a month later. For the second time in four years, the choice of running mate became controversial. Tyler's succession to the presidency was challenged by Congressional Whig leaders Daniel Webster and Henry Clay.

WEBSTER: "Mr. Tyler, according to my interpretation of the Constitution, you are merely the acting president."

CLAY: "I agree, Senator Webster. He's also a member of the opposing party."

TYLER: "Stuff and nonsense. I'm the president. Go back and read the Constitution again, gentlemen."

Tyler won the argument by default. He served out Harrison's term confident of his own entitlement to the presidency, meanwhile lacking the political acumen to persuade others of the same. When he defied the Whig party and advocated the annexation of Texas, the key issue of the day, he had zero chance to be nominated in 1844.

Many historians consider the arguments over annexing Texas to have been a proxy for the slavery question. The Missouri Compromise forbade slave owners from moving farther north than the Missouri-Arkansas border (except to Missouri itself), meanwhile saying nothing about any east-west axis. So, if a slaveholder in Alabama or Mississippi wanted more land, and wanted to take his slaves along, Texas, due west, was fertile ground. But "Manifest Destiny," the banner under which the Mexican War was fought, was a patriotic concept that could be, and was, divorced from calls for abolition. With Tyler's help, Democrat James Knox Polk, a Tennessean who was supported by slaveholders without his having affirmed their priorities, was elected president in 1844. Henry Clay was the loser, for the third time.

By the end of Polk's four years in office a successful Mexican War effort had completed the annexation process. But historians have pointed to the paradox that a hero of that war, General Zachary Taylor, was elected president in 1848 despite the Whig Party's opposition to, and his own reservations, about the war itself. The United States had a two-party system, thanks to Andrew Jackson and his bitter enemies, but it had become well-nigh impossible to separate the parties according to any ideological lines of demarcation. In 1848 Martin Van Buren tried to prioritize the slavery question by running as the candidate of the Free Soil Party. He ran a poor third behind Taylor and Democrat Lewis Cass. Both major parties rested content to kick the abolition question down the frontier highway.

It seemed the Whigs could only win elections by nominating aging war heroes whose political philosophy was so vague as to be irrelevant, and to pair them with much younger running mates from other sections of the country they probably had never met, let alone expressed a preference for. In this sense they departed from the Jacksonian model of choosing running mates, even though that model reemerged and exists today. Taylor died 16 months after taking office, and was succeeded by little-known Millard Fillmore, who had been chosen for vice president as a sop to New York State political boss Thurlow Weed. Shortly after taking office Fillmore signed the Compromise of 1850, which finessed the slavery question again without adding luster to his own historical standing.

In the 1850s Democrats succeeded in temporarily ending the two-party system. Their strategy was to nominate Northern candidates with a South-centric philosophy. Franklin Pierce of New Hampshire wasn't a racist, but his laissez-faire attitude toward states' rights enabled tragedies like the Kansas-Nebraska Act, which combined free-state ideology (Nebraska would bar slavery) with the "popular sovereignty" approach promoted by Stephen A. Douglas, which called for the (sovereign) citizens of Kansas to decide the question for themselves. When Missourians seeking more fertile soil moved westward into Kansas and took their slaves along, It gave rise to open warfare with abolitionists already living there. Popular sovereignty proved to be neither popular or sovereign, "Bleeding Kansas" became an albatross vis a vis Pierce's political stature, and he wasn't nominated for a second term by the Democrats in 1856.

James Buchanan, an aging bachelor who had been seeking the presidency for decades, was fortunate to have avoided fractious domestic issues as Ambassador to the Court of St. James during the Pierce administration. He became the Democrats' nominee. "Old Buck," for his part, maintained that the federal government had no power to interfere with slavery. The Dred Scott decision by the Supreme Court, brought shortly after Buchanan's inauguration in 1857, affirmed his stance and strengthened his resolve to stay above the fray.

The Whigs had disappeared by the election of 1856, having failed in 1852 despite once again nominating a former military icon, 66-year-old General Winfield Scott, who was lovingly known as "Old Fuss and Feathers.". Several new parties threatened the Democrats' dominance, but only two managed to win electoral votes. Republicans, with varying levels of urgency among its adherents, sought to rid the nation of slavery. They nominated John Fremont. The American Party, also known as the Know-Nothings, treated slavery as tangential to a larger question, i.e., "What should we do about all these immigrants [Catholics] who take jobs away from real Americans?" As Buchanan took office, it remained unclear whether Republicans and Know-Nothings would remain fringe parties, or if either group would find a heroic figure like William Henry Harrison or Zachary Taylor.

They didn't know it in 1856, but the two-party system was alive and well. It had only been in hiding for a while.

Chapter 3: A New Two-Party System (That Nobody Asked For)

The Republican Party was formed in 1854. Its second presidential candidate, Abraham Lincoln, became its first president by winning the 1860 election. Few historians have made the comparison, but 1860 was microcosmic of 1836. Except this time, the Democrats lost.

Democrat Martin Van Buren had won back in 1836, largely because the new Whig party was disorganized and nominated several candidates, who divided the anti-Van Buren electoral vote. Lincoln, a one-term Whig Congressman over a decade before, who in recent years had drawn attention through a series of debates with the better-known Stephen A. Douglas, won in 1860 because the Democrats were inchoate. Douglas was officially the Democrats' nominee, having been chosen at a second convention after the first adjourned without picking anyone. But with President James Buchanan's support, a breakaway group of Southern Democrats nominated Vice President John C. Breckinridge. Another faction, calling itself the Constitutional Union party, nominated John Bell of Tennessee. Lincoln won, albeit with less than 50% the popular vote. The seceded Southern states didn't participate in the election, of course, but among those that had remained loyal, none voted for Lincoln. Maryland, a border state that remained loyal to the Union, nonetheless was so resistant to abolition that it gave Lincoln less than 2% of its vote in 1860.

If 1860 was reminiscent of 1836, the 1864 election resembled 1840. In both years the winning candidate's running mate was a member of the opposition party!

The same Democrats who couldn't agree on a candidate in 1860 were united in 1864 behind George B. McClellan, the erstwhile Union general who had clashed with Lincoln over war strategy. Meanwhile no Republican candidate appeared on the ballot, anywhere. Lincoln, the incumbent, ran as the Union party candidate, meanwhile dropping (Republican) Vice President Hannibal Hamlin, who hailed from the strongly pro-abolition state of Maine, from the ticket. Even as William Henry Harrison had become the first Whig president on a ticket with Democrat John Tyler, the first Republican president, Lincoln, dropped the Republican label while running on the Union party ticket with Democrat Andrew Johnson, a strong Union man who had opposed the secession of his home state, Tennessee, but who held firmly to a white supremacist philosophy.

History repeated itself. The first Whig president, Harrison, died a month after being inaugurated in 1841, and Democrat John Tyler took over. The first Republican/Union party president, Lincoln, was murdered a month after being sworn in for his second term in 1865, and Democrat Andrew Johnson succeeded him.

Clearly the two-party system that nobody asked for was becoming a casualty of the parties' own internal contradictions. After Lincoln's murder, the Republican power structure, led by Secretary of State William H. Seward, Secretary of War Edwin M. Stanton (a Democrat who had been James Buchanan's Attorney General), Treasury Secretary Salmon P. Chase (a part-time Republican), and Senators Charles Sumner, Ben Wade and Thaddeus Stevens, was faced with a recalcitrant President Andrew Johnson, who balked at its approach to Reconstruction where the newly freed slaves were concerned. Next, the same party that had won the previous election by dropping a Republican vice president from the ticket and replacing him with a Democrat, now reasserted its Republican bona fides by impeaching the president for having committed the cardinal sin of asking for the resignation of Secretary of War Stanton, the former Democrat, citing Johnson's alleged abrogation of the Tenure of Office Act. This was a clearly un-Constitutional piece of legislation they had managed to implement over Johnson's veto a year earlier, and which since 1868 has been honored only in the breach.

If tape recorders had been invented before 1868, the following conversation between Johnson and Stanton might have been preserved for history's sake:

JOHNSON: "Mr. Secretary, your resignation will be graciously accepted by my office."

STANTON: "Mr. President, I shall remain in my office. Your presidency has been less than legitimate from the outset. In addition, sir, you are a Democrat in a Republican administration."

JOHNSON: "You were a Democrat in the last Democratic administration, Mr. Stanton. And you are now dismissed."

STANTON: "I'm a lawyer, remember that, Mr. President. You wouldn't know to lead if it weren't for your wife's help. My dismissal would be a violation of the Tenure of Office Act."

JOHNSON: "Oh, really? You'll have to impeach me, then."

Republican leaders (known to history as Radical Republicans, or just Radicals) failed by one vote in the Senate to remove Johnson from office. But the political power they wielded had consolidated, nonetheless. Two years before impeaching Johnson, they had attempted to link him to Lincoln's assassin, John Wilkes Booth, supported in the effort by former First Lady Mary Todd Lincoln, who had called Johnson "that miserable inebriate." That effort failed, as did the Radicals' continuing effort to tie Confederate President Jefferson Davis to the assassination. But from their efforts emerged an opportunistic political strategy that became known as "...waving the bloody shirt."

The blood in question was that of Union soldiers who had died on the battlefield. Confederate soldiers had died there too, but the bloody shirt was always dark blue behind the blood. Everyone who had questioned Lincoln's conduct of the war, or who later objected to the Radicals' implementation of punitive measures toward the seceded states, was now branded as a traitor. Every Democrat was included in the calumny, even Northern (Copperhead) Democrats who thought of themselves as loyal Americans but who had earlier objected, on Constitutional grounds, to Lincoln's suspension of the right of habeas corpus during the war, and/or his shutting down of Northern newspapers that had criticized his administration's war strategy.

The bloody-shirt strategy wasn't needed in the 1868 presidential election. War hero Ulysses S. Grant, nominally a Republican but outwardly non-partisan (like Dwight D. Eisenhower 84 years later), rode a tidal wave of personal adoration to the White House. But the bloody shirt did keep Democrats on the defensive for the remainder of the 19th century, and it caused the voting public to overlook scandals that stained the Grant administration almost from the beginning. These included the naïve Grant's unwitting complicity in the cornering of the gold market by Wall Street wheeler-dealers, and Credit Mobilier, a massive swindle that enriched Washington insiders who cashed in on watered railroad stock. Grant's first-term vice president, Schuyler Colfax, was implicated in Credit Mobilier and was dropped from the ticket in 1872. To the public, Grant remained the hero of Appomattox, as if Colfax wasn't *his* vice president.

Democrats couldn't take advantage of the scandals. They were so unsettled that their candidate for president in 1872 was none other than newspaperman Horace Greeley, a life-long Whig/Republican who had committed the unpardonable sin of occasionally criticizing Lincoln's conduct of the war, even as he supported the war effort itself. The bloody shirt was waved at Greeley, too, and Horace not only lost to Grant in a landslide, he died a few weeks later while dodging the crimson spray.

For the next 40 years Republicans persisted in waving the bloody shirt at all Democrats, even after the surviving soldiers in blue and gray, heedless of party labels, had buried the hatchet and greeted one another warmly during Decoration Day remembrances at various gravesites (Decoration Day was renamed Memorial Day to honor the dead of later wars). The strategy worked. A lone Democrat, Grover Cleveland, won election to the White House between James Buchanan in 1856 and Woodrow Wilson in 1912. And Cleveland, at that, was a conservative and a gold bug whose politics more closely resembled that of a Wall Street Republican.

Just as Van Buren had won in 1836 because the Whig vote was fragmented by multiple candidates, and Lincoln had won in 1860 because the Democratic vote was split among three men, so Wilson won in 1912 because incumbent President William Howard Taft, a mainstream conservative Republican, had faced a challenge from former President Theodore Roosevelt. T.R. had sponsored Taft's nomination in 1908, only to become disenchanted with his protégé's refusal to maintain the progressive program T.R. had introduced upon assuming the presidency in 1901 (after William McKinley's assassination). The "Bull Moose" designation on which Roosevelt ran (never an official party name) served him no better than "Free Soil" had helped ex-President Van Buren in 1848, or than "American" (Know-Nothing) had aided ex-President Fillmore in 1856. Even if only to show that presidents lose their appeal after once abandoning their party label (Lincoln being an exception), it finally seemed, by the early 20th century, that the two-party system was here to stay.

It was a chimera. The Republicans took the White House back in 1920, thanks largely to a hangover from the World War, the failure of Congress to endorse the Treaty of Versailles, and a parallel Red scare. The GOP kept it for the subsequent three terms, and they might never have relinquished it were it not for the Great Depression that followed the stock market crash in 1929. Franklin D. Roosevelt was elected in 1932, and re-elected thrice, but his victories were less a matter of partisanship than of economic conditions, combined with FDR's own masterful political tactics, in particular his "fireside chats" on radio, which brought his soothing upper-crust voice into American's living rooms.

Roosevelt's New Deal program fought the economic hardships brought on by the Great Depression, succeeding only after World War Two, which FDR entered only over objections from isolationists in both parties became muted following Pearl Harbor, generated its own economic boom. Less visible at the time was FDR's development of what became known as the New Deal Coalition, a blend of political bedfellows that embraced big-city labor, minorities, and the poor and disadvantaged.

After the war Republicans found it hard to run against the New Deal Coalition without appearing mean-spirited toward the underprivileged. It was tough to oppose Social Security and the G.I. Bill, and even harder to gainsay real prosperity, all of which remained beyond partisan debate. So, the GOP shifted its focus to an anti-Communist witch hunt, a step-grandchild of the Red scare that had followed World War One and had contributed to its 1920 presidential success. The new Red scare, which at its core was based on economic factors but which could be promoted as a fight against "Godless" Communism, drawing in evangelicals, was exacerbated by parallel fears of a nuclear arms race between the United States and the Soviet Union. Two war allies had now turned bitter enemies, in large part for the sake of one political party's own selfish interests and the paranoia it had generated throughout a gullible populace.

Aided by a favorite new toy, the television set, Americans became transfixed as House Un-American Activities Committee (HUAC) hearings portrayed once respected citizens as traitors. President Roosevelt had died just before the war ended, and his earlier downplaying of the threat with dismissive comments like, "I've known a lot of Communists," was now a distant memory. A Red takeover in China in 1949, again based on economic realities but imagined in the West as the triumph of an obscene political ideology, led to a U.S. invasion of Korea, which bordered China but had been divided in half at the end of World War Two by countries that didn't border Korea and had no moral or legal justification for interfering in its sovereignty...the United States and the Soviet Union, who agreed on little else but that Korea had long been under the domination of Japan, a country that had fought 20th-century wars against both.

Senator Joseph R. McCarthy of Wisconsin fanned the flames of anti-Communist paranoia by picking up where HUAC had left off. By the time he was finished he had Americans believing there was a Communist traitor behind every closet door. McCarthy's classic technique was to hold a notepad aloft, curling his face into a wicked sneer and claiming, "I have here in my hand... [a list of suspected Communists]." Nobody ever saw the pad, which for all anyone knew might have been his wife's supermarket list. McCarthy's episodic tirades continued for four years. President Eisenhower, whom McCarthy had cited as "...a conscious agent of the Communist conspiracy," refused to confront his fellow Republican, saying, "I'm not getting down in the gutter with that guy." It appeared that nobody else wanted to, either.

Television has often contributed to cynicism toward politics through its preference for controversy over sober reflection (even controversy for its own sake), as we will discuss in future chapters. But Edward R. Murrow, on the CBS program "See It Now" in 1954, detailed McCarthy's cruelty and the damage it had wrought upon individuals and the governmental process. McCarthy was censured by the Senate, and within three years had died of cirrhosis brought on by alcoholism. His demise surprised nobody who had ever listened as he ranted and raved his way through Senate hearings and press conferences.

It would be nice to say that Murrow's shining moment initiated a trend in the direct of non-partisanship and objectivity in broadcasting. It would be accurate to say Murrow's example remains a remote oasis in a media desert.

CHAPTER 4: THE FABULOUS (?) FIFTIES AND DYSFUNCTIONAL SIXTIES

Older Americans of the author's vintage often look back on the decade of the 1950s nostalgically, even wistfully. It was an era of consistent prosperity, relative peace and quiet (especially after Joseph R. McCarthy's downfall), a well-liked president in Dwight D. Eisenhower who deemphasized partisan politics, and the ascent of traditional (nuclear) "family values," as popularized on television by programs like "The Donna Reed Show," "Leave It to Beaver," and "Father Knows Best." Newsman Tom Brokaw's best seller, "The Greatest Generation," wasn't published until 1998, but it fairly chronicled those men and women who had led the country through the Great Depression and World War II, establishing a template for happy lives throughout the 1950s and beyond.

A closer look reveals a disconnect between American life as portrayed on television and in the pages of *Life* magazine, and the reality of a divided, politically unstable country. Pertinent to this book's theme, the two-party system that still ruled government proved inept at matching political reality to a post-war ideal that still glows, if only in hindsight.

Democrat Adlai Stevenson, a left-of-center intellectual widely appreciated for his altruism and seeming lack of political ambition, was nominated for president in 1952 after President Harry S. Truman declined to run for re-election. But Democrats, still divided geographically between the integrated North and segregated South, chose as Stevenson's running mate John Sparkman of Alabama, best known today for having signed the Southern Manifesto, which objected to the Supreme Court's ruling in *Brown* vs. *Board of Education* and stood four-square behind racial segregation. The Democratic ticket thus paired two men with diametrically opposite social philosophies, in the name of geographic balance. The party evidently hoped to retain the delicate North/South comity maintained by Franklin D. Roosevelt and segregationists in Congress whose support FDR had needed to pass New Deal legislative initiatives. That had always been an unholy bargain based on pure pragmatism, and it didn't work in 1952. The Eisenhower-Nixon ticket won easily.

Not that Dwight Eisenhower and the 1952 vice presidential nominee, Richard Nixon, were well suited to each other. Hardly. War hero Ike maintained a Mr. Nice-guy image with the public, smiling warmly while distancing himself from the rough-and-tumble realities of electoral politics. Nixon, 22 years younger than Eisenhower and far more personally ambitious, had risen to second place on the ticket from a Congressional career that had featured smearing opposing candidates as Communist sympathizers. As a member of the House Un-American Activities Committee, Nixon pursued the one-time fellow traveler Alger Hiss as a dangerous traitor, but the core issue that led to his conviction for perjury was never anything illegal Hiss had ever done, only those whom he had associated with.

During the presidential campaign Nixon faced charges of financial hanky-panky, which he finessed through a televised apologia that came to be known as the "Checkers" speech. Checkers was the Nixon family's pet dog, although Nixon might have saved his own bacon with references to the simple cloth coat his wife wore, a putative testament to their middle-class orientation.

The Stevenson/Sparkman and Eisenhower/Nixon tickets demonstrated that neither party had a uniform ideology. Nothing had changed by 1960, when Democrats nominated John F. Kennedy and Lyndon B. Johnson, joining together a wealthy, Ivy League-educated Catholic liberal from the Northeast with a Texan from the wrong side of the tracks, a graduate of a teachers' college who had opposed civil rights progress as a Congressman.

JFK: "Lyndon, I want you as my running mate."

LBJ: "I accept, Jack."

JFK: "Accept? You were supposed to say 'No.' I only asked you as a courtesy."

LBJ: "Too late now, pal. Besides, a liberal like you could never carry Texas with anyone but me on the ticket."

Political debates, when conducted well, should clearly delineate one candidate's philosophy and positions from those of the opponent. Left-of-center Democrat John F. Kennedy opposed right-of-center Republican

Richard M. Nixon in the first televised presidential debates in 1960. The debates probably won the election for Kennedy, but for reasons having naught to do with political philosophy and everything to do with physical appeal, especially to female voters. From an informational standpoint, the Kennedy-Nixon debates were anything but helpful to the voting public. It was badly misled.

Nobody watching on television knew it, but the anti-Communist ideologue Nixon was then helping the Central Intelligence Agency prepare for an invasion of Cuba, using anti-Castro Cubans together with behind-the-scenes CIA operatives in what later became known as the Bay of Pigs incident. Secrecy was paramount, so when the debate turned to foreign policy and Kennedy criticized the Eisenhower administration for not doing more to prevent a Communist takeover 90 miles off the Florida coast, Nixon couldn't counter the accusation effectively without revealing plans for the invasion, which was unthinkable. Nixon would have loved to conduct the debate off camera, where it might have proceeded as follows:

NIXON: "Listen here, Jack. We're preparing to invade Cuba. It's top-secret. Lay off using Cuba as a political weapon."

KENNEDY: "Allen Dulles told me about it already, Dick. But who are you to criticize someone else's political tactics?"

NIXON: "Would you rather I tell the world about your love life, Jack? It's an open secret in Washington, you know."

KENNEDY: "That wouldn't be a profile in courage, Dick."

The debate is best remembered for non-political factors, Kennedy's movie-star looks and quick wit vs. Nixon's unshaven countenance and overly serious manner. It should be remembered instead for a political role reversal. The liberal Kennedy, who later angered Pentagon hawks with his back-channel diplomacy with Soviet Union Premier Nikita Khrushchev and private concessions during the Cuban Missile Crisis, emerged in the pre-election debates as the more decisive anti-Communist. Nixon, meanwhile, was forced to counter Kennedy's criticism as premature, but without spilling the beans about the upcoming invasion. He was on the defensive throughout. The political weapon he had used to great effect from the start of his political career, accusing others of being soft on Communism, was now being used against him.

Kennedy's presidency ended in a crossfire of rifle shots in Dallas on Nov. 22, 1963. The alleged assassin, Lee Harvey Oswald, was himself murdered two days later by a mob-connected nightclub owner, Jack Ruby, which act led to immediate skepticism that Oswald wasn't the aimless no-account that the government and a compliant media were quick to portray him as. Oswald instead was someone who, if allowed to stand trial, could have implicated others, including political insiders who would now stop at nothing to preserve their anonymity.

Lyndon Baines Johnson, the new president, had a ready answer to the dilemma. He strong-armed a reluctant Supreme Court Chief Justice Earl Warren into heading up a bi-partisan commission, ostensibly to discover the truth behind the assassination and assuage the skepticism. History has shown that the Warren Commission, from the outset, never approached Kennedy's murder as an unsolved crime, instead sought to ratify the government's ongoing description of the dead Oswald as a lone assassin, a perverted version of the truth that served the interests of America's spy network.

The fact that Johnson had staffed the commission with both Democrats and Republicans, which was a pragmatic effort to use bi-partisanship as a cloak for its true objective, was always irrelevant to its eventual conclusions. It was always inevitable that the dead Oswald would be pronounced guilty of murder posthumously, and that no one else was involved in the crime. Johnson, a savvy politician above all else, knew that even faux bi-partisanship could lend credibility to an investigation that desperately needed it. In the final analysis Johnson used the two-party system for his own selfish purposes.

Years after Kennedy's murder it became clear that JFK had planned to withdraw all Americans from Vietnam by the end of 1965, subject only to his continuing in office after the 1964 election. Within days after taking office, Lyndon Johnson reversed JFK's policy, telling intimates he wouldn't be the president who presided over the "loss" of Vietnam to the Communists. None of those intimates had the nerve to ask LBJ how the United States could ever lose something it had never owned.

In a tribute to his skill as a politician, LBJ managed to emerge as the peace candidate in 1964, convincing American voters that Republican candidate Barry Goldwater's hawkish foreign policy could lead to nuclear war. It didn't harm the Democrats' cause that Goldwater faced a challenge from within the GOP from William Scranton, moderate governor of Pennsylvania, who might have been the only legitimate peace candidate. Johnson won an overwhelming victory.

On the domestic front, President Johnson forgot his segregationist past and oversaw a renewal of the civil rights movement that President Kennedy had championed. He also supported JFK's 1960 call for "medical care for the aged." Thus, as part of LBJ's "Great Society" initiative, 1965 became a watershed year, with passage of the Civil Rights Act and the addition of Medicare to Social Security.

Things went downhill from there. Vietnam proved to be a quagmire, costing far more in dollars and American lives than voters had been warned about. The Great Society labored on, leading to a realization that Johnson probably had never acknowledged, that government could afford guns (Vietnam) or butter (social programs) but not both at once. The Social Security trust fund was threatened by longer-term actuarial realities, so rather than reducing benefits or raising the retirement age, Johnson simply merged the fund into general revenues.

With each passing day the Vietnam debacle came to dominate Lyndon Johnson's presidency. College campuses erupted with anti-war demonstrations and draft card burnings. Within his administration, an anti-war faction had developed, apparently including Defense Secretary Robert McNamara, theretofore a believer in the domino theory that had always motivated policy toward Southeast Asia.

Richard Nixon, of all people, emerged from the political shadows, promising to end the struggle in Vietnam with honor and assuring his self-proclaimed "Silent Majority" that he would restore law and order to a fractious country. For his own part, President Johnson faced re-election challenges in 1968 from both anti-war Democrat Eugene McCarthy and Senator Robert Kennedy, who had originally supported the Vietnam initiative but by then had turned against it. This friction led to LBJ's withdrawal from the race. When both Martin Luther King, Jr. and Kennedy were assassinated within months of each other in the spring, it brought the division in the country into focus. Nixon won the presidency he'd long coveted, defeating Vice President Hubert Humphrey, who had been forced through loyalty to "his president" to mute criticisms of the Vietnam policy, while privately maintaining reservations about it.

The two-party system once again had failed the country. Southern Democrats now became Republicans, in accord with Nixon's "Southern strategy," which spoke of law and order but carried an unmistakable undertone of racial intolerance. The "secret plan" to end the war Nixon had promoted proved to be nothing of the sort. Years later it became known that Nixon had privately discouraged North Vietnam from agreeing to any peace initiative until after his election, when presumably they'd have benefited from new negotiations. But Democrats were too factionalized and politically weak to take advantage. Nixon won a second term in 1972 in a landslide, even as the quagmire in Vietnam continued.

CHAPTER 5: OF PARTY BOSSES AND PRIMARY ELECTIONS

Partisan politics in the late 19th century made little .pretense of being democratic. Men like William M. "Boss" Tweed (Democrat) and Thomas C. Platt (Republican), two among many of their ilk, controlled the respective party machines from big-city power bases. They determined the nomination of candidates, allocated patronage, and controlled the pocketbook.

At the dawn of the 20th century, reformers conceived the idea of primary elections. Why allow candidates for office to be chosen behind closed doors with political bosses in charge? Should not voters decide on the nominees? This reform coincided with a progressive movement that swept the country, aided by technological advances like "horseless carriages" and "flying machines," and energized by Theodore Roosevelt, the youngest man in history to serve as president and one who was unafraid to oppose powerful factions within his own party.

The first presidential primary was held in Florida in 1901. Either the Florida reformers forgot that the election was already over (incumbent William McKinley having defeated William Jennings Bryan), or they were getting an early start for 1904. In its egalitarian zeal, however, Florida somehow decided that only registered voters within the respective parties could vote in the primaries, which restriction had the undemocratic effect of disenfranchising close to half the voting public. Meanwhile, Florida's "closed primary" structure strengthened the hold each major party maintained over the democratic process. There are no primaries for Independents or third-party registrants in Florida (or in 13 other states in 2018), notwithstanding the fact that taken together, these constituencies are larger than either Democrat or Republican registrants. The closed primary restriction still prevails in Florida, 114 years after its first implementation.

New Hampshire followed with its first presidential primary in 1920. Possibly because, unlike Florida, they had seen fit to choose the same year in which the election would be held, Granite State reformers effectively provided New Hampshire with a privilege it has never relinquished, i.e., to be the first state on the calendar every four years to hold its primary. New Hampshire guards this franchise so avidly that its legislature passed a law requiring its primary to be held "seven days prior to (the next primary on the calendar, whenever and wherever that is)." This law has nothing to do with democracy and everything to do with the economic benefits to the state of having a horde of politicos and media junkies occupying hotel rooms and eating at New Hampshire's finest restaurants, not to mention that candidates for president, both the announced and the pretending-not- to-be varieties, descend on the area months in advance to "test the waters."

Historians have noted that party bosses were still working hard behind the scenes as late as 1920, when Republicans chose dark-horse candidate Warren G. Harding, following what became known as the "smoke-filled room" deliberation. Harding won the election, as Americans approved of his call for a "return to normalcy" after the Great War and the first Red scare. Unfortunately, Harding's 2-1/2 years in the White House were marked by scandals. The most notorious, the clandestine sale of government property in Wyoming to private interests that became known as "Teapot Dome," happened to implicate the same party bosses who had gathered in that smoke-filled room to nominate Harding in the first place. In retrospect, New Hampshire might have seen it all coming when it held its first presidential preference primary.

If primary elections are more democratic than smoke-filled rooms, they fail to account for unpleasant realities that surround electoral politics. Americans are notoriously lazy about exercising their franchise, with roughly half the voting public staying home during presidential elections, upwards of two-thirds failing to vote in mid-terms, and a still lower percentage participating in primaries. In 2016 Donald Trump gained the Republican nomination by tallying 14 million votes in primaries, which amounted to approximately 6% of all eligible voters. His campaign gained significant momentum in Florida, where Trump won its (closed) primary in an upset over Florida's own not-so-favorite sons, Senator Marco Rubio and ex-Governor Jeb Bush. Primary elections invariably attract the most passionate partisan extremists in both parties. Together with Florida's closed primary status, the clear advantage fell to Trump's tea-party populists vis à vis the supporters of the more mainstream Republicans, Rubio and Bush, who were penalized by their alleged identification with the Washington "swamp" that Trump was promising to drain.

Would Trump have won the Florida primary if Independents and third-party registrants had been allowed to vote, as they're allowed to do in 36 states? It's anyone's guess, but we can posit with confidence that the progressive movement of the early 20th century, that led to the creation of the primary system, never intended for any presidential candidate to be nominated, based on the votes of one-in-sixteen adult Americans.

Creators of the primary election process, quite reasonably, assumed democracy would be advanced by removing decisions from party bosses. But they stopped there. The presidential nominee (his or her advisers, in fact) remained in charge of determining running mates. The public has been allowed no input in deciding which names will be placed on the ballot for vice president, never mind that one or the other will be a heartbeat away from the presidency for the next four years. Only political considerations matter, such as geographic balance (and, more recently, gender balance). It is no longer axiomatic that the presidential nominee decides alone who the running mate will be, albeit he or she would always have veto power over the party's designee. Recent developments have resulted in some odd pairings for voters to contemplate, as discussed in an earlier chapter, none stranger than Donald Trump and Michael Pence.

In 1900 incumbent President William McKinley needed a new running mate, Vice President Garret Hobart having died in office in 1899. Theodore Roosevelt, a progressive who had worn out his welcome with New York State's conservative Republican establishment, was chosen even though McKinley's own political mentor, Marcus Hanna, warned, "Only one life [McKinley's] stands between 'that damn cowboy' [Roosevelt] and the White House." McKinley's murder in 1901 turned Hanna's dire warning into reality, albeit T.R. proved even more popular than McKinley.

Franklin Delano Roosevelt was elected in 1932, following a battle for the nomination with John Nance "Cactus Jack" Garner. The patrician New Yorker Roosevelt and the down-home Texan Garner, placed on the ballot together to create geographic and ideological balance, became a successful team through two elections, only to have Garner balk at a third term in 1940, even as FDR was breaking away from the two-term custom himself. Garner could be heard describing the vice presidency as "not worth a bucket of warm spit." In truth, Garner might have used an unpleasant word that rhymes with "spit," but the point had been made without doing editorial violence to Victorian journalistic standards.

Replacing Garner on the ballot was Progressive Democrat Henry A. Wallace, who proved uncooperative and at once unpopular with mainstream Democrats. He was replaced in 1944 by Harry S. Truman, who didn't want the nomination and accepted it only after President Roosevelt suggested he'd be disloyal to the party if he refused. FDR made the comment in private, of course. Saying it publicly would have meant conceding that vice-presidential nominees aren't chosen for their presumptive executive skills, or even for their ideological compatibility with the president, rather for the electoral benefit to the party itself.

We've earlier noted the odd pairings in 1952, Stevenson/Sparkman and Eisenhower/Nixon. When Nixon rose from the political ashes in 1968 to run for president a second time, his choice for running mate was former Governor Spiro T. Agnew of Maryland. Agnew served as Nixon's combative "bad guy" on the stump, describing young liberals as "nattering nabobs of negativism," an alliteration Agnew borrowed from conservative journalist William Safire and may not himself have even understood. Agnew, who earlier had been thought of as a liberal Republican in Maryland but sounded quite different on the stump, was elected twice with Nixon, but proved to be himself a nabob of something when forced to resign the vice presidency in 1973, under threat of prosecution for corruption while governor.

Republicans seemed to win elections only with oddly paired candidates. Former B-film actor and California Governor Ronald Reagan was nominated for president in 1980 on his second try, on the poorly understood theme of "supply-side economics." The public was desperate for a new economic prescription, after inflation had run amok under Jimmy Carter and interest rates had soared into the stratosphere. Reagan's main competition for the nomination had been George H.W. Bush, a born-again Texan from a blue blood Connecticut family with a lengthy political resume. During the primary campaign Bush described supply-side economics as "voodoo." Then, after accepting the vice-presidential nomination, he decided it was OK after all.

Bush finally reached the White House on his own terms in 1988, teamed with a young Senator from Indiana, J. Danforth "Dan" Quayle, who amused voters with a succession of bizarre quotes including, "It's a terrible thing to lose one's mind, or not to have a mind. How true that is," and, "If we don't succeed, we run the risk of failure." After candidly admitting to fellow Republicans that he "blew it" (by nominating Quayle), Bush proceeded to blow it again in 1992 by keeping Quayle on the ticket. They lost to the Clinton/Gore team.

Walter Mondale, vice president under Jimmy Carter (1977–1981), ran for president in 1984 with Representative Geraldine Ferraro of New York, who became the first woman on a national ticket. They lost to a popular President Reagan, but Mondale did receive credit for breaking through a gender barrier. In 2008, when Republicans faced the first African-American candidate in Democrat Barack Obama, they decided to counter their image as "Caucasian Christian gentlemen" by pairing presidential nominee John R. McCain with a Caucasian Christian woman, Governor Sarah Palin of Alaska. Her GOP bona fides included a call for oil companies to "Drill, baby drill," which cry appealed to everyone in the energy business, but at the same time might have accidentally reminded voters of the calamitous Exxon/Valdez oil spill in 1989, which had occurred just off the shores of Alaska. Ms. Palin also claimed to be able to see the Soviet Union from her home, even though the Palin family lived in Wasilla, Alaska, hundreds of miles from the Bering Strait. The capital city of Alaska where she held forth as governor, Juneau, is almost twice as far from Russia as is Wasilla.

As this is written President Trump, whose extra-marital escapades are legion, and Vice President Mike Pence manage to maintain at least the appearance of cordiality. Pence is a fundamentalist Christian who calls his wife Karen "Mother" and refuses to be in another woman's company if Mrs. Pence is not on the scene. Mr. Trump is something else again when it comes to martial relationships. The president and vice president might stand as the oddest couple this side of Oscar Madison and Felix Ungar.

CHAPTER 6: THE DONALD AND THE ANDREW

This book adopts, as a predicate, that the historical antecedent for Donald Trump's surprising ascent to the presidency is the success of Andrew Jackson, seventh president (1829–1837). It further presumes that Jackson's adoption of the Democrat label, and especially his unique approach to electoral politics, created the two-party system as we understand it today.

The qualification "as we understand it today" is added advisedly. Jackson called himself a Democrat, but the historical record fails to show that he ever asked for votes on a partisan basis. Old Hickory stood for two basic principles that at first blush appear mutually counterintuitive...a strong central government in preference to states' rights, and a "people's" government that distrusts central bankers. The slavery question, which would eventually lead to the creation of the Republican Party, remained in the background during Jackson's presidency, in hopeful reliance upon the Missouri Compromise of 1820. But widespread personal dislike of Jackson, especially in the Northeast, accelerated the growth of the Whig Party, which eventually morphed into Republicanism. Thus, Democrats on one side, and Whig/Republicans on the other created the two-party system, by accident. Nobody ever said, "The one thing this country needs is a system wherein each half of the country loathes the other half."

Donald Trump was elected as a Republican in 2016, even though he had once been a Democrat. He won primaries, in part, by running against the record of the most chronologically proximate Republican president, George W. Bush, meanwhile dismissing brother Jeb Bush, one of several rivals for the nomination, as "low energy Jeb." Trump tapped into a reserve of unvoiced anger in the body politic toward Washington, DC by promising to "drain the swamp" and "make America great again." When coaxed to specify his agenda toward these goals, Trump surprised even mainstream Republicans by risking trade wars through new tariffs, even on the products of our closest allies, and by demanding the construction of a wall extending from the Gulf of Mexico to the Pacific Ocean, the better to protect the country from illegal immigrants and the crime, welfare demands, and disease they supposedly bring from Mexico and beyond.

Trump lost the popular tally to Hillary Clinton by almost three million votes, but his populist rhetoric had registered among enough voters in closely contested Midwestern states to carry him to an Electoral College victory, one he loudly "Trumpeted" in a series of post-election rallies. Meanwhile Trump alleged that widespread electoral fraud had denied him a popular vote win.

To some observers it seemed the two-party system had been on vacation. Trump had survived a series of primaries by denouncing mainstream Republicans like Jeb Bush, Marco Rubio, and Governor John Kasich of Ohio with one pithy insult or another, and by departing from Republican orthodoxy by denouncing free trade principles and taking a nativist position on immigration. Meanwhile Hillary Clinton's path to the Democratic nomination had met resistance from an independent socialist running as a Democrat, Senator Bernie Sanders of Vermont. Sanders campaigned to her political left by calling for free college education, universal health care, and a rescission of the Supreme Court's bizarre Citizens United decision, which had declared corporations to be people and their deep-pocketed campaign contributions to be the equivalent of speech (and thus protected under the Bill of Rights).

Had the two parties been replaced by four? Pundits observed the emergence of both left-wing and right-wing populism. Political wags suggested the ideal ticket in 2016 might have been Trump-Sanders or Sanders-Trump. Both had been born and raised in New York, and neither man allowed undue politeness to intrude upon his blunt verbalisms. But otherwise, no two more dissimilar men ever occupied the same political stage. In the Senate, Trump's provocative rhetoric encountered censure from mainstream Republicans Bob Corker (TN) and Jeff Flake (AZ), who announced their pending retirements, and Ben Sasse (NE). Meanwhile House Speaker Paul Ryan offered tepid support for Trump's initiatives while also deciding to retire. Democrats, meanwhile, hoped to reclaim control of the House in 2018, even as a faction of younger party members sought to replace aging Rep. Nancy Pelosi as their leader. Pelosi's defenders protested that opposition to her was gender based; after all, why didn't the same opposition prevail versus Senate Minority Leader Chuck Schumer, who is roughly the same age as Pelosi?

Alas, the two-party system is alive and well as we speak. Save for the few dissenters cited here, and in the face of burgeoning non-partisan initiatives such as the Serve America Movement and Unite America (see later chapter for details), Republicans on Capitol Hill rallied around President Trump, no doubt recognizing that a unified party was necessary to maintaining majorities in the House and Senate. Democrats cloaked their internal divisions in unified opposition to what they saw as the most loathsome of Trump's conduct, viz., offending our closest European allies with tariff threats and hostile rhetoric, separating immigrant children from their parents at the border crossing with Mexico, and especially Trump's seeming affection for Russian President Vladimir Putin, who remains a wild card figure in Special Prosecutor Robert Mueller's ongoing investigation of suspected Russian interference (in Trump's behalf) in the 2016 election.

Where Mueller is concerned, all Democrats (and some Republicans) favor emergency legislation to protect him from being fired. President Trump hasn't made that explicit threat, but his ongoing accusations that Mueller is conducting a "witch hunt," together with the firing of Attorney-General Jeff Sessions and the demotion of Deputy Attorney-General Rod Rosenstein, to whom Mueller was reporting, have led pundits to predict that Mueller's days might be numbered. Other pundits have suggested that firing Mueller would, in and of itself, be obstruction of justice, after which Congress would have to decide if, 1) the pundits were correct, and 2) if so, whether obstruction of justice met the Constitutional requirement for impeachment, "high crimes and misdemeanors."

Andrew Jackson's election in 1828 derived from public backlash against the "corrupt bargain" between John Quincy Adams and Henry Clay that Jackson claimed had brought Adams to the White House four years earlier, despite the fact of Jackson's having won more popular votes and more electoral votes than Adams. The furor over the election wasn't partisan at all, rather an expression of an American preference for fairness and a distaste for political chicanery. Adams later adopted the Whig label when he returned to Congress as a representative from Massachusetts, but in 1824 he ran as a National Republican, at least according to latter-day historians who have assigned him that label. In fact, in that election year the United States was still non-partisan in practice and in spirit. Even in 1828, when Jackson obtained revenge for 1824, party labels took a back seat to stylistic differences between two men from disparate backgrounds who clearly detested each other.

Abolitionists met at Ripon, Wisconsin in 1854 to form the Republican party, in collective opposition to entrenched Democrats who had avoided confronting slavery in the name of states' rights, and to replace a Whig Party that had lost all relevance. Party leaders Henry Clay and Daniel Webster had died in 1852, and the Whigs had run out of Indian fighters and Mexican War heroes to offer as presidential candidates. Back in 1832, despite the absence of party cohesion and the lack of a dominant issue to run on, Whigs had nominated Clay, in opposition to an entrenched incumbent, Andrew Jackson of Tennessee.

It could be argued that the Whigs were never politically relevant, given that their most respected statesmen, Clay and Webster, tried but failed to reach the White House on policy grounds, while grizzled war veterans like William Henry Harrison and Zachary Taylor did succeed, but only by deemphasizing political issues in favor of sloganeering.

The two-party system thus developed not in fealty to any opposing political themes, instead in collective opposition to the status quo. In 2018, the country has returned to its roots. If Andrew Jackson returned from the grave and met Donald Trump at the White House following his election, one might imagine their conversation to have proceeded as follows:

JACKSON: Thank you for placing my bust in your office, Mr. President. It looks perfect.

TRUMP: I've always been one of your admirers, Andy. I hated reading about when you were impeached. Sad.

JACKSON: You might be confusing me with Andrew Johnson, Mr. President. But that bust does look like me, so it's OK.

TRUMP: What about that scar on your head, Andy? Did some bimbo scratch you in the heat of passion?

JACKSON: No, Mr. President. That came from a scalping in one of the Indian wars. Can't remember which one. By the way, what kind of animal is a bimbo? I've never heard of them.

TRUMP: It's OK, Andy. What Indian wars are you talking about? Do you mean that war between India and Pakistan? I'm going over there to fix that, once and for all. The guys in charge over there are good friends of mine. I'll fix it, for sure.

JACKSON: I'll be leaving now, Mr. President. Good luck. It's tough to tell your friends from your enemies in this job.

TRUMP: Everybody loves me, Andy. They know I'm making America great again.

Chapter 7: Media (Plural Noun) Vs. Media (Singular Noun)

In colonial times, citizens seeking guidance regarding political questions had a limited number of big-city newspapers to rely upon. Folks in rural areas experienced politics through word of mouth, making rumor and fact indistinguishable from each other. In the mid-19th century, following the invention of the telegraph, daily and weekly newspapers proliferated, with Horace Greeley and William Lloyd Garrison, and later Joseph Pulitzer and William Randolph Hearst among others, shaping public opinion from ivory towers in New York, Boston, and San Francisco.

Journalism moguls enjoyed unusual power and influence due to the absence of competing media. Greeley even became the presidential nominee of the Democrats in 1872. Hearst, originally a Californian, was elected to Congress from New York, then announced his candidacy for president. He came fairly close, finishing second in the balloting for the 1904 presidential nomination at the Democratic convention.

Magazine publishing also grew in popularity and influence in the post-Civil War period, as German immigrant cartoonist Thomas Nast mocked New York's Tammany Hall politicians through the pages of *Harper's Weekly*, and Victoria Woodhull advanced the nascent women's movement in *Woodhull and Claflin's Weekly*. Together, newspapers and magazines constituted the media in the 19th century, albeit the word "media" itself didn't appear in the American lexicon until more than a century later. Today it's typically misappropriated as a singular noun, and sometimes used pejoratively by politicians, as in "The media is [*sic*] the enemy of the people."

Donald Trump might have been the first to publicly castigate the media as (an) enemy, but he shouldn't be singled out as a critic. Abraham Lincoln became so frustrated by newspaper criticism of his Civil War strategy that he sent soldiers to shut the offending papers down, even as he struggled to maintain the favor of loyal Republican Horace Greeley at the *New York Tribune*. Henry Ward Beecher, beloved theologian and brother of *Uncle Tom's Cabin* author Harriet Beecher Stowe, who was later identified by biographer Debby Applegate as *The Most Famous Man in America* (Doubleday, 2006), was himself a victim of crusading feminist Woodhull in 1873, who told readers in her journal of his extra-marital affair with Elizabeth Tilton, his parishioner and wife of his pastoral associate Theodore Tilton. The aforementioned publishers, Pulitzer and Hearst, taunted William McKinley over his hesitation in declaring war with Spain in 1898, boosting circulation in their respective New York dailies with headlines like "Remember the Maine," which removed all doubt in the public mind that the destruction of a US battleship in Havana harbor had been a deliberate act of provocation. Without waiting for the results of an investigation he had ordered to weigh the facts, McKinley capitulated.

The late 19th century has been called "The Gilded Age," so identified by Mark Twain (1835–1910), Missouri-born storyteller and social commentator par excellence whose life span closely tracked the growth of the print media but ended before the emergence of radio and television. Twain was beloved for his humor and irreverence, as reflected in quotes like "Get your facts first, then you can distort them as you please," and "Patriotism is supporting your country all the time, and your government when it deserves it." Twain's influence developed through the printed word only.

Meanwhile, his later counterpart from the heartland, Oklahoman Will Rogers (1879–1935), known for saying, "Everything is changing. People are taking comedians seriously and politicians as a joke," and "I don't make jokes, I just watch the government and report the facts," took advantage of radio, first in 1926 and in 1930 with his own weekly program. At one point, on the defensive for allegedly infusing his opinions with partisanship, Rogers famously countered, "I don't belong to an organized party. I'm a Democrat." The self-deprecating tenor of that remark reminded historians of Abraham Lincoln's rejoinder when Stephen A. Douglas accused him of being two-faced during their debates. "With a face like this, who would want a second one?"

Will Rogers died in a plane crash in 1935, before television superseded radio as a broadcast medium and long before social media began to supplant television. Yet from the public's warm acceptance of both Rogers and Mark Twain as fonts of political wisdom, one may infer that *style, more than timeliness and urgency* (two articles of faith that motivate journalists), invades the public consciousness in a lasting fashion. Humor registers with voters, where stridency repels them.

Contrast the mildly self-deprecating humor and "above the fray" neutrality of Twain and Rogers with the acerbic proselytizing found in current broadcasting from partisan commentators on both the left and right, who seem to care more deeply about being right than being objective. They're also more concerned with unanimity of thought among their listeners than they are with acknowledging that any given hot-button issue might contain nuance or complexity. In the case of television, nuanced or complex issues typically can't be resolved in the time allotted before the next commercial message.

The pattern might have begun with radio's Rush Limbaugh, who beginning in 1988 welcomed call-ins to his program from sycophants who, provided they praised his commentary effusively enough, were awarded with the sobriquet "ditto-head." If Limbaugh's broadcasting career had begun only four years earlier, "ditto-heads" might have served to contemporaneously validate the "group think" concept, which derived from George Orwell's 1952 book, "1984." Orwell forecast that in the future (circa 1984) uniformity of thought, not scholarly exchanges of opinion, would be desired and rewarded. He might have sold more books in the end by naming it "1988."

In Journalism 101, contrariwise, students are taught that objectivity is intrinsic to good reporting. Clearly objectivity collides with group think, as Orwell must have understood. No ditto-head would be caught dead including a compromising notion in any phone call to Rush Limbaugh, lest the conversation be short-circuited and the truant caller left to mourn his heresy while failing to become a ditto-head. Likewise, at political websites like *RawStory* and *Huffington Post* (left-wing oriented) and *Breitbart* and *InfoWars* (right-wing), one's blogging credibility is assessed according to a scorecard that measures "up votes" and "down votes," as tallied on the computer screen for all to see. Woe unto anyone who earns a down vote, a fate to be avoided at all costs. A down vote only registers as such if the offending comment isn't stricken, prior to its publication, by a stern site monitor who remains on the lookout at all time for "trolls." In the argot of the blogosphere, a troll is someone who visits political sites with a predisposition to cause trouble, and probably is being paid for his troublemaking by a partisan billionaire somewhere who might be described as an "uber-troll." George Soros and the Koch brothers, who are often cited as imaginary financiers of trolls, would fit that description.

The present author visits both left-wing and right-wing sites, and is proud to admit that he has been called a troll at both. Why George Soros would be paying Bob Mills to invade Breitbart, while at once the Koch brothers have Mills on the payroll to bother people at RawStory, is left to partisans to compute. Note well, "troll" is the mildest invective an invading heretic will be called. Often "troll" is bypassed in favor of "moron," "libtard," or "right-wing nut job (RWNJ to texters)." Not infrequently an offended ditto-head will post something like, "Your a moron," a grammatical construct that leaves little doubt who the real moron is, but ends the debate nonetheless.

Television has developed a way to remain true to an objectivity standard, or at least appear to do so, while retaining loyalty from an audience that has long since ceased to covet balanced reporting and prefers down-and-dirty cat fighting. As with group think, this has been an evolutionary process. Call it the "staged confrontation" method, the same approach that governs professional wrestling.

Beginning in 1966 William F. Buckley, Jr., sardonic author and self-styled scourge of all left-wing apostates, hosted "Firing Line," a lively (but always civil) exchange of views on public television with Buckley's friends on both sides of the political aisle. Included regularly were intellectuals like John Kenneth Galbraith, an economist whose political views ran in the opposite direction from Buckley's, but who absorbed the host's gentle barbs with unfailing courtesy, which Buckley reciprocated. For all his argumentative talent, Buckley dependably retained an aristocrat's capacity for highbrow self-effacement, as best exhibited during his half-serious campaign for mayor of New York City. In response to a reporter's (serious) question, "What will you do first, if you're elected?" Buckley replied, "I'd demand a recount." Even his enemies smiled. Unlike today's television pundits, Buckley took life seriously without taking himself as seriously.

"Firing Line" was intellectually gratifying, but from the outset it had been designed to reach an audience that appreciated civil discourse. As the fractious decade of the '60s'60s passed into the '70s and '80s, this audience shrank. More heated arguments were called for, so in 1982, "The McLaughlin Group," hosted by John McLaughlin, made its debut. The format was similar, but McLaughlin himself lacked Buckley's gentle touch, thus the program appealed less to the "Firing Line" audience than to viewers who tuned in to root for somebody, not unlike spectators at sporting events.

The connection is never acknowledged by broadcasting executives, but beginning with "The McLaughlin Group" and accelerating as television networks became progressively more corporate through mergers and acquisitions (thus more bottom-line oriented), public-issue programming (other than on public broadcasting channels) became less civil and was in fact more like professional wrestling, wherein a "good guy" faces off against a "bad guy" while the crowd cheers wildly and rules of engagement are ignored lest they intrude upon the "action." Thus, networks could piously claim they were honoring journalistic requirements for balance, e.g., left-wing vs. right-wing, Democrat vs. Republican, while privately enjoying the growing advertising revenues as viewers tuned in to "root" for their ideological favorites in the debate.

This trend expanded exponentially as Internet websites vied with television for audience. Not inhibited by any journalistic rules and with no self-imposed regulations save the right to erase messages they dislike, RawStory and Breitbart (herein used as proxies for all sites on the political left and right) present every issue as if part and parcel of a political campaign. Every subject is viewed through a partisan prism and accompanied by unflattering photos of a bête noire from the opposing side (imagine the villain at a wrestling match) and introduced by headlines that might or might not reflect the content of the article. During the 2016 campaign, for example, a story about Hillary Clinton would be accompanied by a photo of her grimacing in disgust, while on RawStory Donald Trump might be seen in full-throated anger at someone (unidentified) who had ticked him off.

Even newspapers with a pronounced liberal or conservative bias would never disparage a public figure by using an unflattering variant of his or her name. On social media and at liberal Internet sites, however, we see First Lady Melania Trump identified as "Melanoma" and the president as "Dumpf," while on conservative sites "Obummer" is used to belittle President Obama. Senator Elizabeth Warren (D-MA), who said she had Native American blood but was derided with the moniker "Pocahontas" by a skeptical President Trump, is now called "Faux-a-hontas" at Breitbart, as if to settle the question of her ancestry beyond cavil.

Did competition for attention among newspapers, broadcast media and the Internet eradicate civility and moderation in public discourse? Or did the power of the two-party system, combined with extreme partisanship on both sides, compel the media to lower standards? It's a chicken-and-egg question that few have even tried to answer, let alone settled.

Chapter 8: Rules of the (Political) Game

The print and broadcast media aren't solely, or even primarily to blame for a dysfunctional United States Congress that enjoys a whopping 12% approval rating at this writing. Facebook, Twitter, and other social media aren't responsible, either. As discussed in the last chapter, television does seek controversy, often controversy for its own sake, to boost ratings and fatten advertising revenues. At the end of the day, however, the fault lies with the denizens of Capitol Hill, who devise their own rules of engagement. These rules benefit the Democratic and Republican parties themselves (especially the party in power), while doing nothing to relieve partisan gridlock or advance the quaint notion that Senators and Congresspeople are hired by the public to do the public's business, for the public's benefit only.

Before we examine some of these peculiar rules, let's look at history. The first Rules Committee on Capitol Hill was established at the beginning of the first Congress, April 2, 1789, *before anyone had ever heard of a political party*. The committee outlined the Speaker's duties and responsibilities, set rules for debate and the passage of bills, and a week later determined the makeup of various committees and set the duties of a Sergeant-at-Arms and a Clerk. These rules seemed sensible enough, bothered nobody, and prevailed until 1883, five decades after the two-party system that nobody had ever asked for came into being, with Andrew Jackson on one side and Whigs on the other.

Most Americans are unaware that the Speaker of the House need not be a member of Congress, or even a member of any political organization. The two major parties dominate politics so thoroughly in 2018 that a non-partisan House Speaker is unthinkable.

But who decided that when the residents of a sovereign state see fit to elect an Independent like Bernie Sanders (Vermont) or Angus King (Maine) to the Senate, as they have done in preference to both the Democrat and Republican candidates, that the preferred candidate of the voters would next have to caucus within a party establishment that the voters had just rejected? Sanders and King caucus with Democrats, even though they were elected in preference to a Democratic candidate. Then they must sit with the organization whose candidate they had just defeated. How democratic (small d intentional) is that? In a sports contest, an umpire or referee enforces rules previously established by a higher authority, like the commissioner of the league. Two teams in competition are never allowed to set their own rules of engagement during a game, yet that's exactly how the United States Congress functions. There's no umpire and no referee. Individual members answer to the public on Election Day, but the two parties themselves are answerable to nobody.

Who decided to reward the loss of cognitive function that inevitably strikes octogenarians by establishing the seniority system, one that awards the greatest influence and privilege to those who have served in Congress the longest, and are therefore closest to mental impairment? This arrangement (it doesn't deserve to be called a system) would never be tolerated in the corporate world, where retirement ages are often mandated. It isn't tolerated on America's highways, where senior-age drivers are required to take tests to renew licenses. But since 1911 the seniority arrangement has been taken for granted. It has been rationalized as necessary to maintain non-partisanship, according to a prevailing need (in 1911) to diminish the solitary power of House Speaker Joseph Cannon, whose long-standing rule would appear to have mitigated *against* a seniority system. As a given, one must be either a Democrat or Republican to gain standing in Congress in the first place (see preceding paragraph), so how in the name of Boss Tweed does a seniority system promote non-partisanship?

Joseph Cannon was hardly an exception. Speakers wield extraordinary power, with or without a seniority system. George W. Bush's administration invaded Iraq on false pretenses, suborned torture in violation of international treaty covenants (and lied about it), and spied illegally on American citizens, in the name of combatting terrorism (and lied about it). A strong case existed for impeachment of President Bush and Vice President Dick Cheney, but Speaker of the House Nancy Pelosi (D-CA) decided impeachment was "off the table," because she alone had determined that an impeachment effort would probably fail, and more particularly would give Republicans an issue to run on at the next mid-term election.

The question for a concerned citizen to ask was never, "Is Ms. Pelosi's logic sound?" Rather, "If impeachment remains the public's only Constitutional protection against a law-breaking president, who gave Nancy Pelosi the right to unilaterally decide, for purely political reasons, that the matter could not even be discussed on the floor?" Nobody outside the halls of government has ever asked for the Speaker of the House, who is elected by the residents of a single Congressional district (out of 435), to enjoy that kind of unchallenged authority. Congress alone makes its own rules, which also include allowing a single Senator to place a "hold" on a nominee, even a nominee that no other Senator objects to, thereby preventing that individual's name from reaching the floor. One Senator out of a hundred can overrule the other 99.

Former Representative David Jolly (R-FL) received quite a shock upon first arriving in Congress a few years ago. As a freshman, he was obliged to attend the usual indoctrinatory meetings, at one of which he was told that a precondition of his remaining in good standing with the party leadership (with all that implies regarding committee assignments and future financial aid) would require that he spend at least 40% of his working hours on the telephone, raising money. Congress is in session about half the year, so a member who spends 40% of his or her time in fundraising is spending only 20% doing the public's business. In exchange for this slavish devotion to duty, members of Congress enjoy six-figure salaries, a large staff, Cadillac benefits, and a lifetime pension that vests after exactly two years in office.

Where does the money raised by Jolly and his colleagues go? To public works? Back to the citizens whose tax dollars keep Congress in session? Of course not. It goes to the Republican and Democratic National Committees, which reallocate it according to political exigencies. Typically, the money finances television advertising that tells us how awful Candidate X's opponent is, meanwhile saying little or nothing about Candidate X, for whose benefit the "opposition research" has been conducted.

The present author is a registered Libertarian. He registered first as an Independent upon moving to Florida in 2006 from Connecticut, then changed to the Libertarian Party before the 2016 election. Like Florida, Connecticut is a closed primary state, so your obedient servant was forced to register as a Democrat to vote for Ned Lamont, who in 2006 opposed incumbent Democratic Senator Joseph I. Lieberman, someone he regarded as irreparably compromised by commitments to insurance and accounting company lobbyists and the defense industry. For the record, Lamont won the primary in an upset. Then, Lieberman ran as an Independent in November and won re-election, capturing votes that otherwise would have probably gone to the Republican candidate because of said Republican's lamentable personal history (no further comment is offered in the interest of civility).

Since 2006, the Democratic Party has decided it owns me. On a daily basis my inbox is inundated by demands (as distinct from polite requests) for money, in behalf of the party itself and/or for candidates in far-distant places like North Dakota and Nevada. When I go to the snail-mail box, inevitably a plea for funds highlights my status as a "good Democrat" (I was never even a bad one) whose support is urgently needed in behalf of protecting wildlife in Alaska, or saving some marsupial from extinction, or electing a candidate to Congress who would guarantee to protect all those entitlements that I hold dear but which are threatened by those awful Republicans. In addition to hourly demands for financial contributions, I'm asked to sign Michelle Obama's birthday card (she never sent me one, so I demur) and to sign an e-card thanking Associate Justice Ruth Bader Ginsburg for always voting the way Democrats want her to vote on their most sacred issues, and for not retiring from the court.

James Carville, long-time spokesman for liberal causes, once appealed for support with conventional courtesy, in keeping with his gentlemanly Southern roots. The bald eagle of the political battlefront now dispenses with protocol and sends fundraising messages as follows: "Listen up, Robert. I'm telling you to donate ____ to ____. Right now!"

That is not an exaggeration. My message to James is, "You'll grow a full head of hair and change parties before any Democrat you endorse sees a penny from yours truly."

CHAPTER 9: ATTACKING THE TWO-PARTY TRUST

During Mark Twain's Gilded Age of the late 19th century, and especially before passage of the Sherman Antitrust Act in 1890, free-market capitalists including John D. Rockefeller, Andrew Carnegie, Cornelius Vanderbilt and J. Pierpont Morgan built empires by combining separate companies they owned into "trusts," thus dominating the market for their products or services. (Disclosure: J.P. Morgan was a second cousin of the author's great-grandmother.)

Trust-busting President Theodore Roosevelt lamented these "malefactors of great wealth," and though Teddy left office in 1909, momentum from his progressive crusade led to the break-up of Rockefeller's Standard Oil trust. Deemed by the Supreme Court a violation of the Sherman Antitrust Act, the trust was divided into separate companies in 1911. The progressive movement also led to the passage of the Clayton Antitrust Act in 1914, the purpose of which was to prevent anti-competitive conduct from morphing into trusts.

Mature schoolchildren understand the principle behind antitrust enforcement. The economic health of the country depends on competition, and corporate consolidation, by definition, reduces competition. In many cases the combined companies use their financial might (often employing an inflated stock price as a substitute currency, so they can maintain their cash position) to buy out the competition, enriching both the smaller company's stockholders and whatever investment banking firm arranged the deal. Typically, the merger or acquisition is trumpeted in the financial press as economically beneficial to both companies through cost efficiencies (often involving massive layoffs of personnel), and the story is accompanied by photos of the respective company leaders smiling and shaking hands.

Don't believe the financial press. Almost all mergers benefit one company to the exclusion of the other, and many are initiated by the "M. & A." (Mergers and Acquisitions) divisions of investment banking firms, because the fees for handling the mergers pay for Rolls Royces and yachts for the investment bankers themselves. Consider that since the 1980s, American Telephone & Telegraph (Ma Bell) has been broken apart with the assistance of investment bankers, and later put back together again while the same people earned a second huge fee for recreating the original entity. Humpty Dumpty should have been so lucky.

Energy giants Exxon and Mobil merged in 1998, forming the third-largest company in the world. Some critics asked, "Doesn't this violate antitrust laws?" It did seem as if an elephant had mated with a mastodon. But others defended the merger by insisting that antitrust enforcement, in a global economy, penalizes those companies burdened by laws like the Sherman Act, which was passed decades before technological advancements led to the development of multi-national companies. In any event, even though Exxon Mobil became the world's largest oil company, it didn't create a monopoly. Competition is still intense in the energy business.

What about our political system? If it's healthy for dozens (or even hundreds) of companies to compete for business, shouldn't the marketplace for ideas be similarly large and diverse? Is the Democrat/Republican duopoly inevitable, or is there hope for a new arrangement that honors independence of thought?

Author Joseph Epstein thinks so. In a recent Wall Street Journal opinion piece, Epstein cited Republicans in his home state, Illinois, for asking (by mail) if he planned to register with the GOP in the coming mid-term election, and proceeding to ask for personal data including his age, income, and whether he owned his home or not. Epstein tossed the offending mailer into the trash, but emphasized that he hasn't voted for a Democrat for president in 42 years, and even then hadn't considered himself as a bound member of any party.

Epstein's non-partisan bona fides are on display in the article. "One party lashes you to the moral certainty of Elizabeth Warren, the other to the overconfidence of John Kasich, who, if pressed, will tell you that as governor he wiped out the Islamic State in Ohio." Epstein continues by remarking that party membership often requires supporting people you wouldn't want to meet for lunch (Mills: "Amen to that."). He confesses to not having voted for president in 2016, being loath to choosing between "a thoroughgoing vulgarian [and one] whose ideas had already been shown to be either insipid or inimical."

Joseph Epstein doesn't lay out a specific alternate to the two-party system in the brief Wall Street Journal piece, but possibly his upcoming book, *Charm: The Elusive Enchantment* will have more to say in that regard. Meanwhile Ron Fournier, president of the Michigan-based public relations firm Truscott Rossman, suggests that Nov. 6, 2018 might become "Independents Day."

Fournier was once a political reporter in Washington whose writings reflected the public's disenchantment with the two-party system. Perhaps making his wish the mother to the thought, Fournier predicted the ascent of a new third party, or at least a "white knight" candidate whose loyalty was to the country, not a party. Fournier now says he was "...chasing a unicorn when I should have been herding reindeer." Still, he's a believer, and cites the 40 percent of voters who identify as independent of Democrats and Republicans, which in more than half the states is a larger percentage than either major party can boast. He compares this hopeful fact with the stark reality that only two members of Congress (Sanders and King) are independent, likewise a mere 27 out of 7,137 state legislators nationwide.

Fournier is now a spokesman for the Unite America Institute, whose goal is to facilitate independent candidacies. Toward that end the group targets certain states where a handful of independents might create what he calls "disproportionately influential governing conditions." The Unite America Institute finds that in the United States Senate and in 31 state legislatures, five or fewer independents could tip the balance of power, and the institute is providing campaign assistance for these potential difference makers. The first Unite Summit, held in August, 2018, in Denver, saw over 200 candidates and strategists gather to plan strategy for November.

David Wasserman, House editor for The Cook Political Report, cites an anomalous imbalance that could affect the two major parties in the mid-term elections, one he says "...could produce extremely divergent results — and make Congress even more toxic and adversarial in 2019." Wasserman could have added that such toxicity would likely strengthen any non-partisan movement that is now in its nascent stages, such as Unite America and Serve America Movement (SAM). He points to the strong possibility of a divided Congress (Democrats capturing the House, Republicans keeping control in the Senate), adding that "...both parties could claim a mid-term mandate — and reinforce their stubbornness."

Wasserman imagines a Democratic House majority owning the subpoena power to investigate everyone in the Trump administration, then exercising it to the frustration of President Trump himself. Meanwhile the Republican Senate would be rubber-stamping Trump's appointees under Wasserman's scenario. Further exacerbating the divide between extremists in both parties would be the likelihood that moderates who might otherwise "work across the aisle" would be the most likely to lose their seats, which in turn would intensify public dissatisfaction with both parties and energize a third-party movement for 2020 (the author's conclusion, not Wasserman's).

When the Founding Fathers created a bicameral Congress, they effectively overrepresented sparsely populated states at the expense of those with population centers. Consider that California and Wyoming each have two Senators. This is a built-in advantage for Republicans, whose victory margins are greatest in (red) states like Wyoming, Utah, and Montana, while California and New York are dependably blue but have the same two Senators apiece. Any non-partisan initiative, therefore, would do well to concentrate its efforts on purple (swing) states like Florida, Pennsylvania, Michigan and Wisconsin, where Congressional representation is significant and where a small percentage of independents can be expected to make a difference. It would seem Unite America has already taken this proposition to heart.

CHAPTER 10: FAILED THIRD PARTIES IN HISTORY

Challenges to the two-party system, historically, have never addressed the legitimacy of the two-party structure itself, which remains immune from attack. Instead, third parties have sought to meet specific political goals through renegade candidacies, and/or to ride the crest of a new political wave, like abolition or progressivism.

In making this distinction, the author's stated assumption, that the two-party system began with the rise of Andrew Jackson, in opposition to a fragmented Whig Party, still prevails. Prior to Jackson's rise to the presidency in 1828, the United States had, beginning in 1788, what could be described as a "no party system," when George Washington was elected on ballots that cited no party identification. Beginning in 1800 with Thomas Jefferson's election, the country could be said to retain a "one party system." Jefferson declared himself to be a Republican, and he's called a Democratic-Republican in the history books, but in truth he was an anti-Federalist who believed in the supremacy of local government, albeit the Louisiana Purchase in 1803, the ultimate big-government achievement, belied that stance.

The author can't prove it, but he holds to a belief that "Democratic-Republican," the party identification used by historians to categorize Jefferson, James Madison, and James Monroe politically, was adopted *after the fact* of these presidents' lives, in an effort to avoid their having to use "Republican," which might have suggested some connection with the current GOP. Using Democratic-Republican was a convenient defense against being accused of partisanship on the part of historians by later partisans. There's nothing in the historical record to suggest that any of these men called himself a Democratic-Republican, or that such a designation even existed during their lifetimes.

Jackson protégé Martin Van Buren was elected as a Democrat in 1836, but lost favor with the party after an unhappy four years in the White House, one marked by an economic depression, and a failed bid for reelection in 1840. His political appetite remained strong, however, and he appeared on the ballot of the Free Soil Party in 1848. The majority of Free Soilers, unlike Van Buren, were Whigs, dissatisfied with the party's ambivalent stance on abolition.

Inspired by the Wilmot Proviso, a quixotic if unsuccessful effort to limit the expanse of slavery into new territories acquired through the Mexican War, "conscience Whigs" broke off and formed the Free Soil Party, the campaign of which had the unintended effect of strengthening the two-party system. Van Buren captured 10% of the popular vote nationwide, which wasn't enough to earn him even one electoral vote, yet it might have sufficed to deprive Democrat Lewis Cass of the electoral votes of several battleground states in the Northeast and enabled Zachary Taylor's election. Taylor was a nominal Whig, a Mexican War hero who, like a young Whig Congressman named Abraham Lincoln, had expressed reservations concerning the war that brought him fame, even as his victory extended the life of a factionalized party that would disappear within six years of his election. The two-party system was alive and well, even if tainted with schizophrenia.

Van Buren's candidacy stands as the first example in history of the "spoiler effect" in electoral politics. Absent the Free Soil Party's emergence, Democrats very probably would have kept the White House in 1848, given that (Democratic) President James Knox Polk, who declined to run for reelection for reasons of health (Polk died months after leaving office), had presided over the annexation of Texas and prosecuted a successful war with Mexico. Collectively, historians have rated Polk's presidency as "near great," yet the candidate of a dying Whig party prevailed in the next election, if only because the Free Soilers probably "spoiled" the party by drawing off votes that might otherwise have gone to Democrat Cass.

The spoiler effect is always conjectural. Who knows for a fact that the votes Van Buren won in 1848 would have otherwise gone to the Democrats? Maybe those voters would have stayed home. Maybe they'd have voted for Taylor. It's guesswork. But without question, the conjecture by itself serves to perpetuate the two-party system, because losing candidates attempt to discredit third parties as merely "spoilers" and question their legitimacy. Others decry voters who "threw away" their franchise by voting for a third-party candidate with little or no chance to win. These lamentations all carry a vague suggestion that only Democrats and Republicans have a right to appear on a presidential ballot.

This phenomenon was visible in 2000, when Democrat Al Gore won the popular vote against Republican George W. Bush but lost in the Electoral College because third-party candidate Ralph Nader, reputed as a critic of Corporate America, drew off Democratic votes in Florida, enough to elect Bush (with the Supreme Court's able assistance). It happened again in 2016, when Hillary Clinton tallied almost three million more votes than Donald Trump but lost narrowly in key Midwestern states where third-party candidates Jill Stein (Green Party) and Gary Johnson (Libertarian) siphoned off votes and helped Trump carry those states and win in the Electoral College.

The anger from disappointed Democrats, as directed at Nader, Stein, and Johnson, was real (although Johnson had been a Republican governor of New Mexico and might have drawn as many votes from Trump as from Clinton). Visit a left-leaning political website and you'll observe not only that third-party candidates are blamed for the failure of a Democrat to win, but third-party voters are excoriated as well, for enabling those candidates to be spoilers. The present author, who voted for Nader in 2000 and Johnson in 2016, has been described at RawStory in terms not suitable for publication, merely because he refused to vote for the lesser of two evils. A typical exchange follows.

ANGRY DEMOCRAT: You got your way, you %#&&@&#. You helped elect Trump by voting third-party.

MILLS: No, I voted for Gary Johnson because I disliked Trump, and disliked Hillary Clinton as well.

ANGRY DEMOCRAT: I can't stand you @#@&@#@ third-party creeps.

MILLS: What is so sacred about the two-party system? (no response from angry Democrat)

Another version of the spoiler argument proceeds as follows: "People who vote for a third-party candidate are wasting (or throwing away) their vote," because it's a mathematical certainty that no third-party candidate can win. It really isn't a certainty, because political upsets do happen (see chapter on a Minnesota election). But the "wasted vote" argument is specious. It would apply equally to Republican voters in Massachusetts and Rhode Island, and Democrats in Nebraska and Utah, where their preferred candidate is as certain to lose the electoral votes of the state as any third-party candidate would be. Nobody accuses those voters of spoiling anything. The argument is a passive (but effective) defense of the two-party system, which begs the follow-up question, "What has that system ever done to deserve it?"

In 1856, ex-President Millard Fillmore accepted the nomination of the American Party, better known in history books as the "Know-Nothings." The name didn't suggest a lack of scholarship on the part of its fractious membership, rather it referenced its defensive response to questions about the party's xenophobic anti-immigration platform, i.e., "I know nothing about (any anti-Irish bigotry)." Fillmore carried only one state, Maryland. Given that the Whig Party had vanished into the ether, and that Republicans were new to the political wars and were virtually invisible below the Mason-Dixon Line, Democrat James Buchanan's victory was inevitable. The American Party disappeared quickly after 1856, but it remains an example of a one-issue party that can coalesce around an objectionable yet populist concept (Irish immigrants taking jobs from "real" Americans) while piously labeling themselves the American Party. Fillmore didn't cover himself with glory by running as its candidate.

The word "populist" is used, probably too liberally, to describe politicians who purport to represent the "people" against a tyrannical central government. In 1892 an actual Populist party emerged, energized by frustration with "sound money" policies in Washington that penalized agricultural interests in the heartland. Populist candidate James B. Weaver garnered 22 electoral votes, running far behind the winner, Democrat (and former President) Grover Cleveland, a "gold bug," and incumbent President Benjamin Harrison (likewise a sound-money advocate). The Populists did succeed in presaging the progressive movement of Theodore Roosevelt's era, but it also highlighted the strength of the two major parties, because in 1896 William Jennings Bryan of Nebraska incorporated the Populists' opposition to tight money as the Democratic candidate. Bryan advocated free coinage of silver, most dramatically in his memorable "Cross of Gold" campaign speech.

Even as Whigs evolved into Republicans in the 1850s, Populists merged into Democrats in the 1890s. The fact that Bryan's cry, "Mankind will not be crucified on a cross of gold!" contradicted the governing philosophy of incumbent President Cleveland, a sound-money Democrat, must have confused the electorate and helped Republican candidate William McKinley, who won the election easily in the wake of a severe recession that prevailed throughout Cleveland's second (non-consecutive) term. McKinley hadn't been hampered by intra-party squabbles over monetary policy. Yet four years later, Bryan was again carrying the Democratic banner without forfeiting his progressive ideals. The populist movement that had inspired his candidacy in 1896 had become a Democratic movement, at least in terms of party identification. The Populist Party became invisible.

McKinley's murder in September 1901, by an anarchist who forswore all political power as tyranny, elevated Theodore Roosevelt to the presidency. T.R.'s magnetic personality disguised the fact that his progressivism (recognition of labor unions, internationalist foreign policy, trust-busting) ran counter to Republican orthodoxy. Traditional Republicans, and especially party leaders, recoiled in horror to hear Roosevelt describe the giants of industry as "malefactors of great wealth," but in the Belle Epoque, a time marked by explosive industrial growth (automobiles, airplanes, radio, films), relative peace, and sunny optimism toward the future, young "Teddy" transcended partisanship. He declined to run again in 1908, and his chosen replacement on the Republican ticket, William Howard Taft, was elected over Democrat warhorse William Jennings Bryan, who no longer preached from an easy-money pulpit. Easy money didn't blend well with Bryan's evangelical brand of Christianity, so Bryan instead pursued an equally ineffective strategy of campaigning against Social Darwinism, which held that only the rich can survive, and they always do, on the backs of the poor and middle class.

Roosevelt was still only 54 years old in 1912, and he was vigorous enough to have recently returned from a highly publicized safari in Africa in behalf of *National Geographic Magazine*, a venture which resulted in the deaths of hundreds of big animals and was followed by a ticker-tape parade in New York to celebrate his triumphal return. When he wasn't killing rhinoceroses and hippopotami and claiming that the mass slaughter somehow benefited the planet, T.R. was keeping a close and jaundiced eye on politics. He had grown frustrated with President Taft's unwillingness to continue the progressive agenda he had followed as president. So, convinced that his personal popularity would supersede partisan labels, Roosevelt ran for president again, this time as the self-styled "Bull Moose" candidate.

T.R. first tried to garner the Republican nomination, even in the face of Taft's desire for a second term. Evidently, he had underestimated the entrenched power of the party establishment, which honored the old canard, "Now is the time for all good men to come to the aid of their party." Slaughtering defenseless animals in Africa might have excited crowds on Broadway who had never seen a rhinoceros, dead or alive, but it didn't count for much with the GOP's permanent base, Wall Street capitalists and small-town businessmen. The party establishment gave the 1912 nomination to Taft, finally paying T.R. back for having referred to Rockefeller, Morgan, et al. as "malefactors of great wealth." The Republican elephant never forgets.

Roosevelt campaigned hard, even after taking a bullet in the chest from a would-be assassin in Milwaukee. But charisma couldn't compensate for the fact that Republicans were divided, and Democrat Woodrow Wilson seized the progressive mood of the electorate and won the election. It passed notice at the time, but the two-party system, ostensibly a vehicle for voters to differentiate between candidates, had now become so firmly entrenched that Republican Roosevelt and Democrat Wilson, merely eight years apart, had each run successfully...as a progressive! Incumbent Taft, meanwhile, ran a poor third in 1912, and even though he'd represented one of the two major parties, he had in fact been the "spoiler" candidate by drawing Republican votes away from the more colorful Roosevelt. T.R., who never lacked for self-esteem, must have imagined that Taft had drawn votes away from him.

Episodically throughout the 20th century, third-party candidates appeared on presidential ballots, but their ineffectiveness served only to reaffirm the supremacy of a two-party system that nobody had asked for. Socialist Party candidates Norman Thomas and Eugene V. Debs, Progressive Robert M. LaFollette (1924 version progressivism), "Dixiecrat" J. Strom Thurmond, Progressive Henry A. Wallace (1948 version), and Independents George Wallace (no relation to Henry, in fact not even close) and Ralph Nader (no relation to anyone) attracted regional or special-interest support. Occasionally a third-party candidate captured a few electoral votes (Thurmond and George Wallace). Still, their renegade parties never threatened the established order.

Only in 1992, when multi-millionaire businessman H. Ross Perot ran as the Reform Party candidate, did the media pay close attention. Even then, it was Perot's quirky mannerisms and his reliance on a variety of confusing charts, not his pleas for more efficient government, that attracted the television cameras. Perot won 19% of the popular vote nationwide, but zero electoral votes. Republicans complained that he had drawn votes from President George H. W. Bush and enabled Bill Clinton's election (the spoiler argument again), but Perot's campaign had emphasized the failure of presidents in *both parties* to conduct the public's business in the public interest.

The author worked for Perot's campaign in 1992. He believed then, and still believes, that Perot, far better than other third-party candidates, personified the need for a new approach to electoral politics in the good old U.S.A.

CHAPTER 11: ALL POLITICS IS LOCAL, AND OTHER MYTHS

The author lived in Connecticut before moving to Florida in 2006. An abiding memory of his life in New Canaan was the town's ongoing effort to run its affairs on a non-partisan basis, in the spirit of George Washington's animus toward political parties and Thomas Jefferson's preference for separating local government from centralized authority.

The effort was sincere but very difficult to achieve in New Canaan, because of an overwhelming Republican advantage in registration (better than two to one vs. Democrats). The town did require bi-partisan representation on its Board of Selectmen, which created an appearance of neutrality, but only within a Republican-Democrat paradigm. There was no room for a third party in town — bi-partisanship is one thing, tri-partisanship is another. When Connecticut's governor in the 1990s, Republican John Rowland, visited New Canaan from Hartford at election time one year, he preached the gospel, "All politics is local." Meanwhile Rowland, at the request of a photographer from the New Canaan Advertiser, posed for photos with the GOP candidate he was then endorsing for First Selectman (mayor), who won overwhelmingly. All politics is local, one assumes, but only until the governor from up-state takes it upon himself to proselytize a community's voters in behalf of one national party or the other. In fact, Rowland was wasting his time at the taxpayers' expense. Republicans didn't need anyone's help to win an election in New Canaan, Connecticut in the 1990s. They still don't.

Really, what New Canaan needed was never bi-partisanship, nor a third party, but *non-partisanship*. Is there any Republican or Democrat way to run a school system or fire department? Does politics on the national level have anything to do with repairing roads, collecting garbage, or setting speed limits on local streets? The statement, "All politics is local" has a familiar ring, and Thomas Jefferson certainly would have approved. But a casual student of American history knows that the two-party system arose and evolved around national issues only, as discussed earlier — the fight over a central bank, westward expansion, and later slavery vs. abolition, still later tariff/trade and labor/management issues. So how did we arrive at the point at which the governor of a state urges voters in a local community to pick the candidate of his own party, someone the governor has never met and will never see on a typical business day?

Trial attorneys are taught never to ask a question of a witness unless they know the answer in advance, and smart-alecky authors follow the same discipline. The above question requires a lengthy answer, one the author already knows.

In its purest form, politics is public service. Ideally, a politician is motivated not by personal ambition, rather by a desire to serve, and for a specific time period only. A public servant should crave neither power nor personal enrichment. If a politician in 1800 said, "I'm resigning my position to spend more time with my family," it conformed to the public service ideal. It was believed. Today that statement translates as, "I'm about to get canned from my job, so I'm quitting to make it appear as if leaving were own my idea." In the 21st century, political figures are assumed to be ambitious.

"All politics is local" was a fact of life in the 18th century. Before train and automobile travel, one's daily routine was limited to the home front. Neighbor helped neighbor, particularly in rural areas, and a town government consisted of the best-known and most trusted members of the community. In the 19th century the country expanded westward, and horizons widened. An Abraham Lincoln could be born in a log cabin in 1809 in Kentucky, move to Indiana and eventually to Illinois, become a lawyer and local politician, relocate to Washington, DC as a Congressman for two years, enrich himself representing railroads back in Chicago, and after the invention of the telegraph enabled a surge in newspaper publishing, attract nationwide attention as a debater. Twelve years after leaving Washington following a single Congressional term, Lincoln would become the 16th president.

Lincoln was a sincerely motivated politician, but at once was an intense partisan (first as a Whig, eventually as a Republican) who was driven by a determination to rise from poverty and anonymity, and one whose wife might have been more ambitious for him than he was for himself. Abraham Lincoln could fairly be described as the historical bridge between the non-partisan phrase, "All politics is local," and the antonymous axiom, "Now is the time for all good men to come to the aid of their party."

But even in Lincoln's day it would have been unthinkable for the governor of a state to visit a local community and involve himself in its political affairs. Even presidential candidates remained at home in election years. The familiar "front porch campaign" of a Rutherford B. Hayes, a Grover Cleveland or a William McKinley emphasized the altruism that was expected of public servants in the 19th century. The cost and difficulty of travel was a handicap, but it wasn't determinative. An operative phrase (one rarely heard in the current environment) was, "The job seeks the man." Blatant ambition was a no-no in the post-Civil War years. More typical was the self-effacing attitude of iconic General William Tecumseh Sherman, who dismissed speculation that he was seeking the White House by saying, "If nominated, I will not run. If elected, I will not serve."

In the 20th century automobile and airplane travel invited more ambitious candidates and more aggressive campaigning. Meanwhile radio, and later television brought a candidate's message into the living room, even as the candidate was speechmaking thousands of miles away. But touring the country for months on end is still expensive, and television spots cost big bucks. If Candidate Jones didn't happen to be independently wealthy, someone had to help defray the cost of spreading the candidate's message far and wide.

The Democratic National Committee had been founded in 1848, the Republican National Committee in 1856. Each consisted of exactly one individual in each state, and raising money wasn't part of said individual's job description.

As the costs of campaigning grew over the years, both committees necessarily had to grow commensurately to pay the bills, lest the other gain an advantage. Most corporations were run by Republicans, and their shareholders were predominantly Republican, so the GOP sought, and drew in, corporate money. Then the Tillman Act was passed in 1907, which forbade it. But well intentioned as it was, the act contained no effective enforcement mechanism, so corporate money flows continued, even after the passage in 1910 of the Federal Corrupt Practices Act, which required candidates for the House of Representatives to reveal the source of all contributions.

As labor unions gained power and influence in the early 20th century, Democrats saw them as a potential countervailing source of campaign funds, thereby neutralizing the Republicans corporate-money advantage. This leveled the playing field, at least until the Taft–Hartley Act in 1947 banned unions from supporting candidates directly. Officially, both national committees acknowledged the laws against corporate and union contributions, but nobody was fooled. Big money flowed from behind the curtain into their respective coffers, such that in 1971 the Federal Election Campaign Act was passed and signed by President Richard Nixon. It was amended in 1974, when the Federal Election Commission was created.

Congress was paying lip service to election integrity, creating at least the appearance of a level playing field. But the only two teams on that field remained the Democrat Laborers and the Republican Plutocrats. Independently wealthy businessmen H. Ross Perot, who ran on a Reform Party ticket in 1992 and 1996, and Steve Forbes, who sought the Republican nomination in 1996 and 2000 on a platform of tax reform, could afford to finance their own efforts. But neither had the support of a Goliath like the RNC or DNC. The major party organizations relied on their established sources in the corporate and labor fields to raise money as always, but also mined data about voters' preferences. Their respective data banks guided their candidates' campaigns with a sophistication that transcended dollars.

Then came the Citizens United decision in 2010. The Supreme Court decided that corporate campaign contributions were the equivalent of free speech, and thus protected from regulation by the First Amendment to the Constitution. Effectively, all bi-partisan efforts since 1907 to get big money out of politics had been neutered by a single court ruling.

This was a huge break for the Republicans, of course, but by 2010 Democrats had mastered the technique of reaching individual donors on-line. While the GOP cultivated corporate America, Barack Obama drew in enough, five and ten dollars at a time, to offset big-money fundraising of his Republican opponents in 2008 and 2012. Democrats still hope to overturn Citizens United someday, but the SCOTUS remains under Republican control as of this writing, meaning the Democrats will have to fight the battle with other weapons.

CHAPTER 12: A COURT RULING WORSE THAN CITIZENS UNITED?

Non-fiction authors are expected to spend more time doing copious research than in typing words onto a computer, if they expect their efforts to be praised by the literary community. That's fair enough, but sometimes an item falls into the author's lap, as if his stars were aligned that day according to some heavenly astrological paradigm.

On a Saturday in late summer 2018, during the preparation of this book, the *Tampa Bay* (Florida) *Times* carried a story with the following headline: NONPARTISAN VOTE PLAN HALTED. Beneath the headline appeared a photo of a smiling judge, one whose name the author is withholding for His Honor's own protection. The judge's cheerful countenance belied the gravity of his ruling.

It seems an effort had been undertaken to conduct upcoming elections for the offices of sheriff, property appraiser, and tax collector in Hillsborough County on a non-partisan basis. That seemed sensible enough. Partisan politics need never intrude upon the daily responsibilities of these public servants, who are expected to keep the peace, value property, and collect taxes according to legal guidelines and independent of political considerations. There's no Democrat or Republican way to handle these duties that anyone has successfully outlined. The remedial plan was for a referendum on Election Day, whereby the public could decide whether to adopt the proposal or reject it.

Apparently, the originator of the plan had been a Republican, because when the idea was advanced, the Democratic Executive Committee sued Hillsborough County and the Supervisor of Elections. The DEC's argument was to the effect that the plan, even though its stated objective had been to allow citizens to decide the plan's viability through a referendum on Election

Day, would negatively affect "voter engagement," and as such, amounted to voter suppression. Seriously, folks.

Enter Judge _____, who cited a precedent from another Florida county, where an appellate court had decided it was *unconstitutional* to make elected positions non-partisan. The appellate court had thereby sided with a sheriff, a tax collector and a property appraiser in that county who had insisted on the right to run for office as Democrats, because they'd been elected that way previously. The County Commission that earlier voted 5–2 to initiate the change was overruled, thus pleasing the two Democrats on the panel who had constituted the minority.

Unconstitutional? One shudders to imagine what George Washington, who cherished the non-partisan ideal up to his dying day, would have said in response to that ruling. One can imagine what James Madison, father of a United States Constitution that never mentioned any political party, might have thought. Three public servants sue to protect their right to run as partisans for non-partisan offices, and a court decides in their favor on Constitutional grounds? Granted, the Republicans on the County Commission who promoted the idea might have been motivated by something other than a spirit of non-partisanship, themselves. In fact, you can bet on it. Voters are often lazy, and to the extent that some pull a lever according to party labels, without considering the merits of the individual candidates, it's to the advantage of an incumbent (in this instance, three Democrat incumbents) to maintain that party identification. The newspaper article suggested that the matter was still at issue and might eventually reach the Florida Supreme Court, but whether it does or not, the ultimate victor will be the two-party system itself. If the Supreme Court upholds the precedent, Democrats win. If it decides otherwise, Republicans win. The two-party system is always a zero-sum game.

Lost amid the partisan squabbling is the fact that the voting public was denied (on constitutional grounds!) an opportunity to decide if candidates for public service may be allowed to present themselves to the voters on their own merits. "No," the court said, a partisan label must be attached to each candidate's name, because that's what another court already decided.

If all politics is local, the two Republicans competing for the Florida gubernatorial nomination haven't been told (incumbent Rick Scott is barred from running by term limits and is running for the U.S. Senate). The ex-Congressman and ex-Agriculture Commissioner Adam Putnam, who was the early favorite for the nomination, is opposed by Rep. Ron DeSantis, who responds to every question about Florida's needs with a reminder that he's been endorsed by President Trump. The president spends weekends in the state and maintains a golf handicap there, but otherwise has no visible stake in the race for governor. The president's endorsement has forced Putnam to plead that he's a Trump fan, too. Meanwhile issues that will confront the next governor, including secondary education, highway congestion, flood insurance, protecting wetlands, and offshore drilling in the Gulf of Mexico, none of which directly connect to the president, aren't being discussed. When the eventual nominee faces his Democrat opponent, it's close to certain that he won't succeed merely by citing the president's endorsement. Trump carried Florida in 2016, and he remains very popular within the party, but he's decidedly unpopular among Democrats and Independents.

Florida is a purple (swing) state, although Republicans have done well in recent years, and the outcome of the Senate race between incumbent Democrat Bill Nelson and Republican Governor Scott could determine which party controls the Senate for the next two years. It's that close. One would expect President Trump to be focusing on that race, but he's been relatively quiet in support of Scott, yet vocal in support of gubernatorial candidate DeSantis. This is especially interesting because Scott, like Trump, came to politics as a billionaire from the business world, but also because their histories in business were marked by scandal and controversy. Or maybe it's just a matter of the president's preternatural craving for approval, which DeSantis has provided in spades. Scott has maintained a distance from the president.

The torrential flood of advertising from both parties continues unabated. The volume testifies to the fundraising skill of two national committees, who first raise money institutionally to cover the cost of television ads, radio spots, and mailing pieces, then spend it on urgent messages telling us how awful the other party is. These are supplemented by on-line messages, which cost a pittance to prepare and send, and thus the parties reiterate their urgent pleas to an absurd degree. It seems a new poll is taken daily (we never know by whom), and it indicates that "Candidate _____ is now trailing Opponent _____!" Worse yet, "Opponent _____ has been receiving billions from [gasp] Sugar Daddy _____, and only if good Democrats like you, Robert [sic], don't step up to the plate now, [our] Candidate _____ might lose!"

Another tactic employed by both major parties is the survey questionnaire. "You've been selected, Robert, to answer the following questions..." (questions like, "Do you trust Donald Trump?") Whatever answers are provided, the survey segues into another urgent plea for money. Still another approach is to tell Robert that he, among all the "good Democrats" in Sun City Center, Florida, has been chosen to host the "2018

Sun City Center Democratic Victory Campaign," which would, if he were to accept the designation, inevitably lead to an extended gripe session about the Republican-dominated legislature in Tallahassee, but accomplish nothing otherwise. Editor's note: The 2018 Sun City Center Democratic Victory Campaign never existed.

This isn't to pick on Democrats. As described in an earlier chapter by author Joseph Epstein, Republicans are no less shameless in their greed and in their capacity for oversimplifying complicated issues. But just imagine for a moment if non-partisan interests enjoyed an unlimited budget to advertise for non-partisan solutions to national problems that remain unsolved, in large measure because of a duopoly that limits political discourse to irascible comments about the other side.

Not only does all the money flow to the two parties, but a court in Florida has now decided that the United States Constitution requires that party labels must appear alongside candidates' names on Election Day. When said Constitution was written and ratified by the states, however, there was no such thing as a political party. One wonders at what later time in history an unknown amendment was added that validates the court's decision.

Chapter 13: Voter Fraud, Electoral Fraud, and Fraudulent People

American history is replete with disputed elections, especially presidential elections. In 1800 a tie in the Electoral College led not only to a fractious debate and resolution in the House of Representatives, but also to the death, in a duel four years later, of a Founding Father who sought to mediate the dispute, Alexander Hamilton by name, at the hands of a notably sore loser, Vice President Aaron Burr (see earlier chapter).

In 1824 the second-place finisher in both the Electoral College and the popular vote, John Quincy Adams, was elected by the same House of Representatives. The hotly disputed outcome led to the creation of a new political party, led by the 1824 victim, Andrew Jackson, and ultimately to a two-party system that nobody wanted or asked for. If Jackson had won in 1824, a two-party system might not have developed until decades later, if at all.

In 1876 the losing candidate, Samuel Tilden, led in the Electoral College by 19 votes, and led in the popular vote as well, but a total of 20 electoral votes from three states was in dispute. This was during Reconstruction, and after much debate, lasting almost until Inauguration Day, 1877, an electoral commission made up of eight Republicans and seven Democrats decided to award all 20 disputed electoral votes to Rutherford B. Hayes, who was (surprise!) the Republican candidate. Throughout his four years in office, Hayes was referred to in the press as "Rutherfraud" or "His Fraudulency." He declined to run for a second term in 1880, and most historians believe that was part of a sub rosa agreement with Democrats, who otherwise wouldn't have accepted the outcome of the election. Hayes also withdrew Northern troops from the South, ending Reconstruction. That was also thought to have been part of the bargain.

In 1888, incumbent President Grover Cleveland (Democrat) led Republican Benjamin Harrison in the popular vote, but the outcome in the Electoral College hinged on late returns from New York, where at the eleventh hour, a surprising swing to Harrison gave him the state's electoral votes, and the election. Inexplicable swings in vote tallies from large cities have been commonplace since before 1888, so nobody should have been shocked. And when Harrison piously claimed from his front porch in Indianapolis, "Providence has granted us the victory," a behind-the-scenes operative in New York who worked for the Republicans but who disliked Harrison personally, Matthew Quay by name, replied, "Tell that S.O.B. that providence didn't have a damn thing to do with it."

Fast forward to 1960. John F. Kennedy edged out Richard M. Nixon in both the Electoral College and popular vote. Meanwhile the Democratic (Daley) political machine in Chicago, which had ties to former Ambassador Joseph P. Kennedy, the candidate's father, and had owned a long-standing reputation for political hanky-panky, was accused of fraudulent hijinks that enabled Kennedy to carry Illinois. It was widely accepted as true, especially after JFK himself, speaking to a post-election dinner audience, joked, "I asked my father not to have Mayor Daley steal even one more vote than was necessary." Very funny, Mr. President. We always loved your sense of humor.

By the time the 2000 election rolled around, technological advances in election machinery had rendered paper ballots obsolete. Instead, most precincts nationwide used electronic voting machines that sped up the voting process. The companies manufacturing the equipment must have had fast-talking salespeople, because it quickly became evident that while the machines did keep the lines moving, they were susceptible to hacking by any clever and badly motivated technician. Votes for Candidate A could be "flipped" to Candidate B with an automatic flick of a switch, either by advance manipulation of votes at the polling site itself, or later, when votes from various precincts would be collected and computed by a tabulator.

The 2000 election was notable for an untoward situation in Southeastern Florida, where confusing balloting equipment resulted in votes intended for Democrat Al Gore somehow being tallied for conservative minor-party candidate Pat Buchanan. This led to a televised spectacle, with election officials measuring so-called hanging chads to determine a voter's true intent. The TV drama made front-page headlines, but the decisive fraud had happened months earlier, when the Republican-controlled state government succeeded in barring thousands of otherwise qualified voters from registering, mostly minority voters who would have been expected to vote for a Democrat. Florida voters, who seem to tolerate wrongdoing as if it were authorized by the state constitution, were so upset that Secretary of State Katherine Harris, who had led the registration purge, was soon elected to Congress.

If 2000 was bad, 2004 was worse. The present author traveled at his own expense from Connecticut to Florida to volunteer as a poll watcher in behalf of a non-partisan coalition. He hadn't been at the polling site for even an hour when he heard a woman scream, "I voted for Kerry, but the machine said I voted for Bush." At that moment it seemed to be an innocent error, but soon, reports from throughout Florida and Ohio detailed widespread vote flipping from Kerry to Bush, thus dramatizing the ease with which an electronic voting machine can be corrupted. In Ohio, it turned out that Wally O'Dell, C.E.O. of one of the companies that had manufactured the faulty machines, was a Republican operative who had promised to deliver Ohio's electoral votes to Bush. He succeeded.

The author observed another clever tactic at the polling site in 2004 that helped the Republicans retain the White House. As with vote flipping, it was prevalent in Ohio as well as in Florida. The allocation of voting machines to various precincts is implemented under the aegis of the state government, which in both states just happened to be Republican-controlled in 2004. And, in both states, Democratic-leaning districts were provided with so few machines that long lines resulted. Voters were often forced to choose between voting and returning to work on time. In Republican-leaning districts, more than enough machines were on hand and the voting process proceeded smoothly.

If anyone still doubts that the 2004 election was stolen, consider that a mathematically prohibitive 6-1/2% discrepancy prevailed between the tabulated vote and exit poll results. The chance that a candidate leading in the popular vote by 3-1/2% (Bush) could trail in the exit polls by 3% (Kerry led there) is on the order of one in several trillion.

The mainstream media are often cited, not without justification, for undue partisanship. *The New York Times*, which President Trump often belittles inaccurately as the "failing *New York Times*," has been derided as blatantly left-wing-oriented by Republicans for decades. Interesting, then, that the same *New York Times* dismissed widespread claims of election fraud in 2004 out of hand in a front-page article. Several weeks later, however, the paper dramatized election fraud in the Ukraine with front-page photos and banner headlines, two days running, of angry citizens who swarmed the streets of Kiev in protest in below-freezing temperatures. Effectively, the

Times was editorializing on its front page, to the effect that election fraud only exists outside the borders of the United States.

The author's point isn't to demonize Republicans, either. There's little doubt that both sides cheat, and because "the other side is doing it," neither side calls it cheating, merely a necessary response to maintain equilibrium. Because the two parties maintain a death grip on all political activity in the United States, close elections going forward will be decided in favor of whichever party is more adept at manipulating election equipment and/or preventing qualified voters from registering.

Following the 2004 debacle in Ohio, an official challenge to the result was brought forward, but not by the same Democrats who had been victimized. John Kerry threw in the towel immediately, notwithstanding a flood of complaints. No, it was the Green and Libertarian parties who stood up for election integrity by lodging the protest. They lost the fight, of course. Third parties almost always lose.

Senator Barbara Boxer (D-CA) wasn't satisfied. She lodged her own protest on the Senate floor, which attracted exactly zero votes in support. Newly elected Senator Barack Obama (D-IL), when asked if he would support Boxer's protest, refused to do so and added contemptuously, "Get real. There was fraud on both sides."

Yes indeed, Mr. Obama. And by your standard election fraud must be OK, provided both sides are doing it. We do get it. Four years later the young Senator ran successfully for president. We may conclude that during the interim, Democrats had taken steps to counteract election fraud, preventing a repeat of 2000 and 2004 and helping Senator Obama become President Obama.

But what of the future? It doesn't look good for public confidence in elections. Donald Trump won an Electoral College victory in 2016, even while complaining that massive fraud in California and elsewhere had denied him a popular vote majority. He drew almost 3,000,000 fewer votes than Hillary Clinton nationwide, but President Trump would have us believe that margin was achieved fraudulently. He ignores (or can't comprehend) the self-evident truth that if Democrats had set out to rig the election, they would have flipped votes in battleground states that went to Trump by slim margins, rather than building up unhelpful popular vote pluralities in California and New York.

No, Mr. President. Hillary Clinton won the popular vote. But many people who lived through 2000 and 2004 believe your extravagant complaint, not surprisingly. Here's what you can do to help, though, now that you're our president. Attack all election fraud. Don't pretend that only Democrats do it.

Don't pretend that the only issue is people voting illegally, when that's been checked out and found to have been a minor problem. Deal with electronic vote fraud, which is easy to execute and difficult to detect. Restore faith in our elections. And please encourage all states to fairly and honestly register voters. Thank you in advance, Mr. President.

Chapter 14: How Television, Blogs, And Social Media Affect Politics

The author stopped watching television about 15 years ago, in disgust. The last straw was having to put up with Public Broadcasting's "Washington Week in Review," which at the time was taking up the debate over the invasion of Iraq. Except the program didn't discuss the invasion itself, only the subsequent political ramifications.

The Bush administration labeled the bombing of Baghdad "Shock and Awe." The premise for a sneak attack that killed innocent Iraqis as they slept in their beds, which was reminiscent of the Japanese attack on Pearl Harbor in terms of its execution, was to punish Iraqi leader Saddam Hussein, who wasn't touched by any bomb during Shock and Awe. Allegedly, Saddam was still in possession of weapons of mass destruction (WMD) that he had (supposedly) cleverly hidden from United Nations inspectors. "Washington Week in Review" didn't deal with the moral questions surrounding the attack, or try to determine whether WMD really existed, and if so, what an appropriate response should be. After all, this was the "*Washington* Week in Review." The entire program was devoted to insider politics in Washington, DC, the geographic center of the universe to all pundits who work there. Exclusively, the program highlighted the problems Democrats in Congress were then having in trying to decide whether to support a Republican administration's act of (undeclared) war. The bombing itself wasn't mentioned, let alone whether "Shock and Awe" was an appropriate name. It was almost as if the subject matter under discussion were the assassination of John F. Kennedy, and all anyone talked about on air was the weather in Dallas.

The program probed the question, "What would happen, politically, if Democrats supported the invasion, then no WMD were found?" And, "What if a majority of Democrats called the invasion unjustified, only for WMD to appear?" Did the fact that the party was divided on the Iraq issue suggest internal political weakness that might carry over to the next election? How might Democratic leaders in the House and Senate deal with internal disagreements? A Republican president had launched a unilateral attack on a foreign country with which the United States was not at war, an attack that no Democrat had called for and one based on dubious intelligence reports (later proven false). The televised "review" of that act by pundits in Washington was devoted entirely to whether the opposition party could resolve disagreement among its own members, and the political consequences that might accrue from a failure to do so.

I had watched Fox Network once or twice but quickly determined that its commentators weren't bringing news developments to viewers objectively, rather acting as a propaganda vehicle for the Republican Party. Fox promoted itself with the phrase, "We report, you decide." In fact, Fox had already decided every issue it reported on, and its reports were, to be polite, out of balance.

A neighbor in Connecticut who hosted an informal political salon (left-wing oriented) invited me to view a documentary titled "Outfoxed," based on the observations of two ex-employees of Fox Network. It described how, at the top levels of Fox every morning, its executives decided in advance what issues would be highlighted that day, and how a chosen issue *du jour*, e.g., the invasion of Iraq, would be presented on the air. Commentators were then required to discuss the issue with the same bias that went into its selection that same morning.

Fox Network's audience is predominantly middle-aged and older men who vote Republican. These viewers had complained for years, not without reason, about a liberal bias throughout the mainstream media. The liberal orientation was manifested by an emphasis on identity politics, on favorable coverage of the Clinton administration, and before that, perceived one-sided coverage of the failed Supreme Court nomination of Robert Bork, and an overemphasis on the Iran Contra scandal that caused problems for President Reagan. Some Fox viewers still harbored a belief that a liberal media had been responsible for the downfall of President Nixon. It didn't matter that most major decisions about news selection and coverage at Fox were being made by Roger Ailes, a former Republican party strategist who specialized in ruthless tactics. Ailes simply transferred the same cutthroat politicking that worked on the stump to the television business, and his behind-the-scenes strategizing pleased an audience that had long hoped for a network with a conservative perspective.

Critics of Fox pointed to the perceived arrogance and lack of objectivity of featured commentators Bill O'Reilly, Sean Hannity, and Tucker Carlson. Absolutely no one was neutral about Fox Network.

President Donald Trump, before and especially since his election, has declared war on the media, converting "media" into a singular noun and describing it as an "enemy of the people." Making media an "it" isn't just grammatically inept, it has the subtle effect of ascribing to all media a single viewpoint. i.e., bias against Trump. If "media" meant all sources of news (which it does), then it would be harder to claim all of them are his enemies.

In terms of televised media, his animus extends to every network except Fox. Trump is so hostile toward rival networks that he erupted in anger one day when first lady Melania Trump, forgetting the rules, chose to tune in to CNN while riding with the president on Air Force One. Trump has contrived the term "fake news," which in his argot refers to TV networks and newspapers that cite any facts that happen to conflict with his selective version of the same facts. The fact that said media are acting in accordance with their historical role as watchdogs is irrelevant to the president, who judges all reporting according to a single criterion, i.e., whether or not the coverage is favorable toward him personally.

Fox Network's viewers see it as truthful, and all other networks as "fake." Critics of Fox see it as right-wing extremism in the guise of news reporting. Fox, in turn, sees those critics as left-wingers who can't get over the fact that Donald Trump won the 2016 election and Hillary Clinton didn't. It would be easy to assume from the network broadcasting wars that everyone is an extreme partisan. Yet based on party registrations, almost half of all voters belong to neither the Democrat nor the Republican party, and many of those who do belong to one or the other hold moderate positions on most issues. Presumably, moderates and centrists seek news broadcasting that isn't constantly trying to win an argument. But as discussed in an earlier chapter, truly unbiased coverage would collide with every network's love of confrontation. Centrism makes for boring television.

It isn't a stretch to posit that all coverage of public issues on network television caters to extremists in both major parties, at the expense of everyone else. The author decided in 2003 that this wasn't about to change, and gave up watching the boob tube, except for sports events. To the extent that things have changed, it has been for the worst.

As this chapter was being prepared a new controversy was raging in the body politic. Social media sites Facebook and Twitter, the latter being President Trump's vehicle of choice in venting against the Mueller investigation, media coverage of everything connected with it, and all "fake news," have decided to ban certain hyperbolic commentary in the interests of decency and good taste. As private companies, they're well within their legal rights to regulate anything and everything that enters their universe, but it's close to certain that right-wing interests will conflate such regulation into a First Amendment issue. Already those same interests have complained bitterly about colleges that canceled speaking engagements planned for conservatives like author Ann Coulter, rejecting the schools' excuses that such appearances would create an untenable danger in terms of security.

Facebook and Twitter don't face the same security risks, but are understandably anxious about privacy issues that have arisen from their data mining, and about possible federal legislation aimed at remediating those issues in the public interest. During the 1990s, when technology firms ruled supreme and the stock market rose to unprecedented levels, Scott McNealy, chairman of Sun Microsystems, responded bluntly, "You have no privacy, anyway," when questions were raised about just how much publicly held companies should know about people's private lives. McNealy shrugged off criticism of his comment and rested comfortably in his position atop a Fortune 500 company that had been in existence only since 1982.

For the record, the author shuns Facebook and Twitter as well as television, except when his grandchildren post photographs of their most recent activities. He believes in privacy, but his grandchildren are the smartest and best looking in the world, as everyone on Facebook well understands. He knows anything negative about them is fake news.

Chapter 15: Bucking the Two-Party System

Third-party candidates for high office have a hard time. As discussed earlier, regardless of their policy positions and irrespective of their qualifications, they inevitably confront attacks from Democrats and Republicans both as "spoilers," as if an independent or minor-party office seeker must be insincerely motivated and has entered the race only to prevent one of the major-party candidates from winning. Voters who choose a third-party candidate are often derided for "throwing away" their vote, typically by frustrated supporters of a losing candidate who assumes that votes for the third-party candidate would have gone to their choice if it weren't for the stubbornness of the third-party voter.

On rare occasions a major-city newspaper will endorse a third-party candidate for president. In 2016 the Chicago Tribune did recommend the Libertarian ticket of (former governors) Gary Johnson and William Weld. But a more familiar approach for newspapers that wish to express dissatisfaction with major-party candidates, one taken every four years by USA Today and the Wall Street Journal among others, is to make no recommendation. A few daily newspapers, unhappy with the choices offered in 2016 yet unwilling to endorse a third-party candidate, recommended "anyone except Donald Trump" or "anyone except Hillary Clinton." If nothing else, these sources at least validated the proposition that most people vote against, not for, a candidate.

It's possible, though impossible to prove, that no presidential election in history presented voters with two more unwelcome major-party candidates than Donald Trump and Hillary Clinton. Despite this, and notwithstanding his endorsement by the Chicago Tribune and eight other daily newspapers, Libertarian Johnson garnered only 3.3% of the popular vote. Green Party candidate Jill Stein, who has been vilified by angry Democrats as a spoiler ever since, received a mere 1.07%. Mr. Trump won the election even though his immediate Republican predecessor as president, George W. Bush, refused to vote for him, almost no daily newspapers endorsed him, and influential Republicans in the media like Bill Kristol and George Will derided his candidacy. Ms. Clinton won the popular vote by almost 3,000,000, albeit many liberal Democrats who favored Bernie Sanders, and who were angered by the perceived favoritism of the Democratic National Committee toward the winner (which furor led to the resignation of committee head Debbie Wasserman Schultz), stayed home or wrote Sanders' name in.

It isn't a stretch to argue that the 2016 presidential election represented a defeat for traditional Republicans, a defeat for all Democrats, yet a victory for the two-party system itself. Neither major-party candidate was the incumbent, both carried high negative ratings in every poll, yet the two most successful minor-party candidates, together, received less than 5% of the popular vote. A comparison with 1992 is striking, because Gary Johnson and Bill Weld were both established political figures (two-term state governors), while Ross Perot had zero political experience. Perot drew 19% of the vote and Johnson/Weld drew barely over 3%.

As a registered, dues-paying Libertarian, the author receives a monthly bulletin from the party. It bursts with optimism toward the future, as validated by its success in gaining ballot access in all 50 states and an occasional victory in a state or local election. Its 2016 convention in Orlando was well attended. Yet missing from the written copy is any strategy for overcoming a two-party duopoly that survives and flourishes, even as more than half the public has disapproved of Donald Trump's presidency since his inauguration, and only 12% approve of a Congress comprised of 532 major-party members and exactly two Independents (who must caucus with Democrats).

As with Green Party members, Libertarians are sincerely motivated and willing to donate time and money. Most vote *for* their chosen candidates, as opposed to voting *against* someone else, and are less likely to stay home on Election Day than are registered Republicans and Democrats.

As accurately reflected in a message being circulated on-line by a neighbor of the author's in Florida, Libertarians want to keep "Republicans out of their bedroom, and Democrats out of their wallet." They're tolerant on social issues, e.g., gay rights and marijuana for medical use, conservative on government spending (too extravagant, to put it mildly), and decidedly opposed to the notion that the United States is responsible for policing every uprising in every country on the planet. Libertarians emphasize civil liberties and are offended whenever government violates the privacy of citizens in the guise of combatting terrorism.

As this chapter was being written, primary elections were being held. In the Florida governor's race, Republicans chose Ron DeSantis, a right-wing disciple of President Trump. Democrats picked an African-American, Jacksonville Mayor Andrew Gillum, an unapologetic left-winger endorsed by Bernie Sanders. Voters emphatically rejected Adam Putnam, a former high-ranking Republican Congressman from the political mainstream, and Gwen Graham, a middle-of-the-road Democrat and daughter of former Governor and Senator Bob Graham. Both Putnam and Graham were well financed, better known throughout the state than DeSantis and Gillum, and were clear favorites for the nominations when the campaign began.

The outcome confirmed an assumption that extremists in both parties are the most likely to turn out to vote on primary day. Barring a miracle, either DeSantis or Gillum will be Florida's next governor, having been duly chosen by partisans even though both hold to positions well outside the mainstream. Most voters are neither far to the right nor far to the left, but in a closed primary state like Florida, independents and third-party voters, who better reflect majority opinion throughout the state, have no say in the matter. Can it truly be said that the Libertarians and Greens are "fringe" parties, when the country has become so polarized? Would it be "throwing one's vote away" to choose a Libertarian candidate, in preference to an extremist from the right or left? Could such a voter be called a "spoiler" for selecting the candidate in the race whose views mostly closely reflect mainstream thought?

The outcome in Florida also dramatized a new phenomenon. President Trump's glowing endorsement of DeSantis far outweighed Putnam's diverse political resume and strong financial position, with Republican voters. Senator Sanders endorsed Gillum and appeared personally in his behalf. Yet going forward, neither Trump nor Sanders will be directly involved in the affairs of the state. Neither man has a stake in whether Florida's schools improve, or if the traffic congestion on Interstate 4 between Tampa and Orlando will be ameliorated by a new rail system. Yet regardless of who wins in November, the involvement of Donald Trump and Bernie Sanders will have had more to do with the outcome than any policy position taken by a candidate of either party.

Primary elections came into being during the Progressive Era of the early 20th century, as a (small-d) democratic way of taking the nominating process away from party bosses and transferring it to "the people." But in Florida and 13 other closed-primary states, "the people" consist of registered members of the Democrat and Republican parties only. Third-party registrants and independents pay the same taxes they do, but being excluded from the primary process, they are denied full representation in the democratic process. When the actual election is held in November, registered Democrats may vote Republican and registered Republicans can vote for the Democrat, and they often do exactly that. On primary day, however, they're confined to the candidates of their own party.

Would Donald Trump and Bernie Sanders have involved themselves in Florida's gubernatorial primary process if non-affiliated voters had been eligible to vote? It's guesswork, but the author's guess is that they'd have stayed home. DeSantis and Gillum appealed to the extreme wings of their parties, right and left; had independents and third-party members been allowed to vote, Putnam and Graham would almost certainly have won their primaries, and Trump and Sanders, were they to have interfered, would have suffered a loss of prestige as unsuccessful Republican and Democratic kingmakers.

CHAPTER 16: THE ENDORSEMENT GAME

Endorsements have become firmly entrenched into America's political system. Candidates boast in their campaign ads that they're "...endorsed by ____ [somebody popular]." Since the 19th century newspapers have regularly recommended candidates for office, but their choices have often been attributed to an existing liberal or conservative bent on the part of the editorial staff, and so, attract attention only when their recommendation comes as a surprise.

When a candidate seeks a recommendation from another politician, the candidate hopes to bask in the reflected glory of the (presumably) more popular endorser. Nobody seeks an endorsement from someone less worthy of respect.

In a polarized electoral climate like that of 2018 CE, Ron DeSantis, candidate for the Republican nomination for Florida's governor, benefited from President Trump's endorsement and earned the nomination over the better known and better financed candidate, Adam Putnam. DeSantis understood that primary voters are the most rabid and partisan within a party, and that President Trump evokes great loyalty from Republicans who fit that description, so DeSantis spoke of little else during the primary campaign except that he was the president's favorite in the race. Most Democrats loathe Trump, but Democrats can't vote in a Republican primary in Florida. Non-affiliated voters can't, either.

But for DeSantis to win in November, he'll need more than the votes of rabid Republicans (a future chapter will reveal the outcome). The endorsement of President Trump will have the opposite effect with many independent voters, and DeSantis probably can't win in a purple state like Florida without a generous share of independent votes.

This is boilerplate political talk. Behind the maneuvering and the photo-ops that portray smiling politicians with their endorsers, typically with their hands raised together in "victory," lies an unsolved riddle. "Why should it matter to any voter whether Candidate X has the support of Politician Y?" A corollary question follows: "Did Candidate X make a promise to Politician Y in exchange for the endorsement?" Even absent a quid pro quo agreement between X and Y, any voter relying on someone's endorsement in casting a ballot has effectively sacrificed the franchise by placing it in the endorser's hands.

Occasionally we read of an endorsement that seems to violate partisan protocol. Rand Paul, Republican Senator from Kentucky and son of former Texas Congressman and third-party candidate for president, Ron Paul, has recommended Gary Johnson, Libertarian Party candidate for president in 2016, for Senator from New Mexico in 2018, in preference to the Republican candidate. Johnson is popular in the state, having served two terms as (Republican) governor, but Paul's endorsement would appear to have little to do with Johnson's popularity and everything to do with political philosophizing. In making the endorsement Paul cited Johnson's fiscal conservatism as governor, which fits with his own preference for limited government. Certainly, Paul's decision has nothing to do with partisanship, because of the real likelihood that Johnson will siphon votes from the Republican for the benefit of the Democrat (the "spoiler" effect). If the Democrat were to win the New Mexico race because of Johnson's candidacy and Paul's endorsement, it might capture control of the Senate for the Democrats, which would certainly make Paul a pariah within his own party (if he isn't already).

Third-party candidates are always underdogs, but Gary Johnson might well pull an upset. Congress had a 12% approval rating at the last report, suggesting the public will be in the mood for fresh blood on Capitol Hill. If Johnson were to win, he would become the only registered Libertarian in the Senate. By definition, and by the body's rules (see earlier chapter), a Senator may not caucus alone. Presumably Johnson would caucus with the Republicans, his former party and the party whose candidate he would have just defeated.

Rand Paul, like Donald Trump, is a polarizing figure. Few voters, and even fewer pundits, are neutral about him. But his worst enemy would concede that Paul is consistent in his (small l) libertarian views, especially his aversion to a hemorrhage of government outlays that has led to a debt load of over $20 trillion and growing, a problem neither major party has been willing to address. When he was governor of New Mexico, Johnson needed to concern himself only with that state's financial affairs, but as a U.S. Senator and colleague of Rand Paul's, he could make a real difference by helping to stem runaway federal spending. The author believes Paul deserves credit for courageously placing the country's financial health ahead of the monkey-see, monkey-do partisanship that voters have come to expect from Washington politicians. In November we'll learn if New Mexico's voters feel the same way.

It might be impossible to know when a candidate first asked another politician for an endorsement. Before the ascent of political parties, it would have been contrary to custom, even distasteful to many. We might imagine the following conversation from 1796, as George Washington was completing his second and final term as president, and Vice President John Adams was running for president against Thomas Jefferson.

JOHN ADAMS: Mr. President, I'll be seeking the presidency this year, and I'd appreciate your endorsement.

GEORGE WASHINGTON: My what? Listen here, Mr. Adams, I would never tell anyone else how to vote.

ADAMS: Sir, I'm afraid my opponent, Mr. Jefferson, is a Francophile.

WASHINGTON: What of it, Mr. Adams?

ADAMS: We know of the ongoing friction between France and England. Do we dare insult our British friends?

WASHINGTON: They might your friends, Adams. They certainly aren't mine.

ADAMS: I hope I'll have your vote, Mr. President. I've been honored to serve with you for the past eight years.

WASHINGTON: You might have it. I haven't decided yet. Besides, my vote is my business, and not yours.

Three decades after this imaginary conversation, the two-party system came into being. Even then, intra-party rivalries were more common than allegiances. Andrew Jackson and John C. Calhoun ran successfully together in 1828, but if Calhoun harbored thoughts of a future presidency, his hopes were dashed when he called for the right of states to nullify federal laws. "Nullification" might seem radical by 21st-century standards, but states' rights were taken for granted in the early 19th century. Thomas Jefferson and James Madison supported nullification in principle.

Political endorsements were rarely sought or noticed at a time when campaigns were run from someone's front porch, when the telegraph was the most sophisticated means of communication, and long before newsreels and television brought candidates to life for the public. When candidates for president succeeded based on their military heroism (Jackson, W. H. Harrison, Taylor, Grant, Hayes), or through maneuvering by political bosses at convention time (Polk, Pierce, Buchanan, Lincoln, Garfield, B. Harrison, McKinley), endorsements were superfluous, even harmful if the public sensed the endorsement had come at a price.

Then came the 20th century. Primaries gradually replaced smoke-filled rooms during the candidate selection process. Months ahead of the first primary, wannabe candidates abandoned their front porches and scoured the country, seeking endorsements from former presidents and honored statesmen, sitting governors, corporate executives, labor leaders, minority spokespeople, women's rights advocates, bar associations, the gun lobby, senior citizens' groups, religious leaders, environmental experts, show business figures, academics, professional athletes and coaches, children's advocates, medical experts, law enforcement professionals, and literally anyone and everyone whose recommendation might matter to the person living next door.

But asking for votes one at a time was costly and inefficient. Inevitably, the phrase "special interests" replaced the public interest in the political lexicon. "Vote for _____ if you believe in [a woman's right to choose, the right to bear arms, saving the whale, a strong military, etc.]." Persuading groups that you represented their interests (even to the exclusion of someone's else's interests) meant possibly earning thousands of votes in one fell swoop.

Then came the next step in a descending spiral of political gamesmanship, i.e., persuading these same groups that the favored candidate's opponent was its mortal enemy. "Do you realize that _____ voted against _____ in Congress, eight times?" This approach is based on "opposition research," and approximately since the 1980s, finding the best "op researchers" has meant producing the most convincing negative ads on television.

Both parties do it, of course. Negative advertising, as the preferred and dominant political tactic, can be traced to the Democrats' (successful) 1987 anti-confirmation effort against Supreme Court nominee and Constitutional literalist Robert Bork, which resulted in a negative vote in Congress after Bork had expressed reservations about earlier court decisions regarding civil rights. The GOP, with an elephant that never forgets, retaliated during the 1988 presidential campaign with a TV ad, blaming Democratic candidate and former Massachusetts Governor Michael Dukakis for the early release of convict Willie Horton, who then committed another violent crime. The fact that an earlier Republican governor had introduced the program under which Horton was released wasn't mentioned. The name of the game is winning. Democrats succeeded in keeping Bork off the Supreme Court, but George H. W. Bush defeated Dukakis for the presidency.

Residual disgust with the 1988 presidential campaign might have contributed to the relative strength of Reform Party candidate H. Ross Perot in 1992, who received 19% of the popular vote nationwide. If Gary Johnson wins a Senate seat this year, it will mean one fewer Republican or Democrat out of 100 Senators, not a significant difference unless Johnson's election results in a 49-48-3 distribution in the Democrats' favor (with Johnson joining Sanders and King as unaffiliated members). But it might significantly influence future campaigns, in that third-party candidates would be encouraged to run and, with a reasonable chance of winning, might earn greater financial backing.

A Johnson victory in New Mexico could also affect the opposition-research tactics of major-party candidates. Running negative television ads against _____ (one's major-party opponent) won't have the desired impact when third-party candidate _____ becomes the beneficiary of the negativity.

CHAPTER 17: OF SENATE RULES AND SUPREME COURT NOMINATIONS

As discussed in an earlier chapter, Congress sets its own rules, which work to the advantage of whichever major party is in power at the time a given rule is applied. Not to belabor an analogy to baseball, it's as if the team in first place in the standings gets to decide who will umpire the games, what the size of the strike zone will be, and in whose stadium the games will be played.

The incongruity of allowing a competitive body to set its own rules, and to break them whenever it serves the purposes of whichever party is ahead in the competition, is best illustrated when a presidential nominee is voted on. Before leaving office in 2016, President Barack Obama nominated Judge Merrill Garland, considered to be a moderate, to fill a Supreme Court seat left vacant by the death of (conservative) Justice Antonin Scalia. Garland seemed well qualified, based on his legal acumen and experience. Republicans controlled Congress, however, and Senate Majority Leader Mitch McConnell decided not to allow hearings on the nomination, defending his decision by reminding everyone that a presidential election was coming up later in the year, and that "voters" should decide on Scalia's replacement. By "voters," McConnell meant the new president, as chosen by the voters, and the fact that Hillary Clinton received the most votes on Election Day didn't matter in the end.

Nothing in the Constitution, or even in precedent, justified McConnell's blatantly partisan act. But Republicans privately gloated that turnabout is fair play. When Democrats controlled the Senate, (then) Majority Leader Harry Reid had used his power, and a parliamentary tactic, to allow a simple majority to enforce cloture (end of debate), amending an existing rule that had always required a three-fifths (60%) vote to end a filibuster. Before Reid acted, Democrats were able to muster a majority, but less than 60%, so Reid served the short-term interests of his party while establishing a new precedent that Republicans were delighted to use in their own behalf by blocking Garland's nomination.

As this is written the Senate is considering President Trump's nominee for the same vacancy, Judge Brett Kavanaugh. Under the precedent set by Harry Reid, a simple majority of the Senate will suffice to enforce cloture. and the same narrow majority will advise and consent to Kavanaugh's appointment once a vote is taken. Democrats, knowing they're outnumbered, are trying to delay a vote by insisting on the right to examine a massive array of documents that might or might not pertain to Kavanaugh's qualifications for the court, but in any event will take at least until Election Day to fully peruse. Meanwhile activists representing a cross-section of special interests near and dear to Democrats are disrupting the hearings with vocal outbursts.

The commotion over Kavanaugh's nomination is taking place in a noisy milieu, chaotic even by Washington's standards. A new book titled *Fear*, authored by Bob Woodward, erstwhile investigative journalist for the *Washington Post* who helped end Richard Nixon's political career, relies on inside-the-White House sources to document President Trump's wildly erratic behavior. The book soared to the top of the best-seller list on day one. Meanwhile, *The New York Times* departed from custom by printing an anonymous Op-Ed column from a White House insider, possibly one of Woodward's sources, that told of Trump's volatile temperament, but assured the reader that there were "adults in the room," working hard to restrain the worst impulses of a childish chief executive. Trump, meanwhile, provides credence to the internal criticism by decrying leaks as treasonous acts, proving he, as did Nixon, places a higher value on loyalty to him personally than to any higher calling.

Since time immemorial, presidents have complained about "leaks" that reflected badly on them. But when a president wants to plant a thought in the public mind, without the public's being aware of its source, it's OK to leak it.

For once the media need not create controversy to attract audiences. Calls for impeachment fill the air, and the same Republicans who pursued Bill Clinton for years until his overactive libido finally caught up with him, a group that included the current Supreme Court nominee, Kavanaugh, now protest that Democrats are compromising the national interest, even behaving treasonously, in their animus toward Donald Trump. Can anyone say, "Whose foot is wearing the shoe?"

Let's take a flight of fancy and suppose that a higher authority, e.g., a select group of politically unaffiliated Americans, were entitled to devise rules for all government functionaries to abide by. If this group followed the examples set forth by George Washington and like-minded Founding Fathers, it might include the following provisions, not necessarily in order of priority:

1) The House Speaker and Senate leader must not be members of any organized political party.

2) If Congress can't agree on these leaders, an unaffiliated rule-making group will choose them.

3) No member of Congress, while on the job, may engage in any fundraising efforts whatsoever.

4) All national political committees are to be abolished permanently.

5) The Electoral College is abolished, and presidents are chosen by popular vote.

6) Primary elections are open to every voter, without regard to party, and all are held on the same day.

7) Political advertising on television may not cite any political party, under penalty of censorship.

8) No member of Congress may serve as a lobbyist at any time after leaving Congress.

9) Corporations and labor unions are permanently barred from making political contributions.

10) Supreme Court justices must retire at age 75.

11) Every citizen is entitled to the same health-care benefits enjoyed by members of Congress, at the same cost.

12) Presidents (four years) and Senators (six years) are limited to one term only (no pension).

13) House members are limited to two two-year terms (no pension) and must live in their district throughout.

14) With Congress subject to term limits, the seniority system will disappear.

15) No campaign activities are allowed by or for any candidate more than 90 days before an election.

The author believes that implementing the above reforms would bring politics and public service under one umbrella, and that a failure to implement them would work only to the advantage of organized political parties and individuals who enter politics to enrich themselves. "Career politicians" would vanish from the scene. Political endorsements would be limited to genuinely felt preferences, with no quid pro quos attached. With all campaigns limited to 90 days, polls would disappear through irrelevance, and the influence of special-interest groups will diminish in favor of the "greater good for the greatest number" paradigm. Shorter campaigns will also greatly reduce opposition research, because less time would be available to gather dirt on an opponent, leading to citizens voting *for* candidates rather than *against* them. Primary elections would be held 30 days after the 90-day campaign period commenced, and would be held simultaneously throughout the country.

A paradox frequently cited by political pundits is that Congress owns a pathetically low approval rating from the public, yet incumbents are re-elected over 90% of the time. With the word "incumbent" removed from the lexicon by term limits, all candidates would compete on a level playing field. The power of incumbency would disappear, as would the seniority system, which rewards the onset of senility. Presumably Congress would regain a measure of popularity.

The greatest change would occur on television. Candidates would be judged on their own merits, not according to which party they belonged to or who had endorsed them. Networks would be judged on their objectivity and accuracy, not on how many viewers agree with their point of view. Negative ads would be a thing of the past. With partisanship out of the picture, no candidate could be successfully portrayed in a commercial as the "puppet" of a party leader, because the leaders would be, by rule, non-partisan. Wealthy individuals would have an advantage, in that they wouldn't need financing from any party, but a 90-day limit on campaigning would lessen the effect.

CHAPTER 18: WALL STREET AND THE TWO-PARTY SYSTEM

The author spent 28 years as a broker with Wall Street firms (1973–2001). A great majority of people he worked with were Republicans, which is something of an oddity considering history. The stock market, on average, has behaved better when a Democrat occupied the White House.

Stockbrokers live on commissions, and their incomes necessarily fluctuate with the vagaries of the market. The life isn't for everyone, and brokers pride themselves on a level of independence and self-sufficiency that sets them apart from the crowd. A broker's preference for Republican ideology is based less on the fiscal conservatism of a William McKinley or Calvin Coolidge than on the sunny optimism of a Ronald Reagan, and on the conviction that the economy is not a zero-sum game, rather one that allows unlimited growth potential in return for hard work.

Contrariwise, when a stockbroker hears a Democratic politician talk about "working people," he thinks of labor bosses and guaranteed benefits. When he hears the same politician advocate for the poor, the broker thinks of high taxes, welfare benefits, and a culture of victimhood, all of which are anathema to someone living on commissions and stock profits. His liberal-minded college professor might have explained that labor unions grew out of the abuses of laissez-faire capitalism that marked the Gilded Age of the late 19th century, and that only labor unions and a progressive movement enabled collective bargaining, and in turn workmen's compensation and later, the Social Security system. "That's history," thinks the broker. "I'm on my own now, and I don't need any help. Just cut my taxes, please."

A broker must pass a difficult exam before registering with a New York Stock Exchange member firm. The test has nothing to do with picking stocks, and a great deal to do with the stock market's regulatory history.

The aspiring broker must be current on the Securities Act of 1933, the Securities Exchange Act of 1934, and the Investment Company Act of 1940. The candidate must have more than a surface knowledge of taxation, tax avoidance, estate law, accounting rules, and laws governing pension funds and mutual funds.

The author passed the test on his first try in 1973, but the truth is that nothing on the test intruded upon his Wall Street life at any time thereafter. The New York Stock Exchange is a strict regulator, and those who repeat the kinds of sins that led to the Great Depression, and that led subsequently to the above-mentioned regulatory acts in response, are dealt with by the exchange in a process that lacks the safeguards a defendant enjoys from the criminal justice system. Registering with a member firm carries with it the tacit understanding that the exchange, not the member firm, is the instrument of discipline. There's no presumption of innocence, no formalized legal process, and no higher "court" a disciplined broker may appeal to.

Several of the author's colleagues were forced out of the business for relying on inside information, in one highly publicized case because the broker was relaying information to his clients that he himself truly believed wasn't inside information, but merely advice (tips) from an outside source whose record for picking stocks was exceptional. It turned out that the source was itself relying on inside dope, and that's why its record had been so good. All brokers who relied on that source and bought the same stocks for their clients, whether they bought them for their own accounts or not, were told, "You should have known the information was private." For not knowing, many were discharged from their firms and banned from Wall Street for life. The New York Stock Exchange is a law unto itself.

All that said, most brokers never encounter discipline from the New York Stock Exchange. Picking a bad stock isn't a punishable offense, albeit after several bad picks in a row, the client might punish the broker by closing the account. It's when a broker tries too hard to please a client, and relies on inside information, that the exchange steps in.

Brokers can also be punished for recommending "unsuitable" stocks to a client. For example, Broker Uptick (not a real person) says to a widow in her 80s, living on Social Security, that she could make a killing overnight by buying Whizbang.com (not a real company). She takes his advice and buys the stock. If it goes up, all well and good. If it tanks, the firm might be forced to pay restitution to the woman, and the broker might be looking for a new job, because stock recommendation must suit the profile of the client in terms of age, marital status, and risk tolerance.

The most impactful change on Wall Street between 1973 and 2001 occurred under a Democratic president, Jimmy Carter. Before 1977, member firms like Merrill Lynch, the author's employer at the time, established their own minimum commission levels, emphasis on "minimum." There was no such thing as a commission discount, regardless of the amount of business a client transacted. The Carter administration thought this was an example of undue regulation on the part of investment firms, as distinct from exchange oversight or government regulation. So, consistent with a deregulatory philosophy that one normally associated with Republicans, it decreed that henceforth, minimum commission levels would be outlawed.

This was good news for stockbrokers, not such good news for their firms. Merrill Lynch balked at first by attempting to hold to its commission schedule, but the free market took over. Competing firms raided Merrill Lynch's staff, promising new recruits that they could exercise their own discretion regarding commission discounts, and further that if the transferring broker convinced his best clients to open accounts with the acquiring firm, a healthy recruiting bonus would be added to the package. Discount brokers like Schwab and Quick & Reilly emerged as added competition, offering active traders deep discounts from prior levels. Years later firms like Ameritrade offered even larger commission discounts for clients who traded on-line without the need for a broker.

Almost overnight in the late 1970s, Wall Street began to resemble major league baseball, which had then recently entered the age of free agency. Like ballplayers leaving the team that scouted and trained them, to sign elsewhere for big bucks, stockbrokers availed themselves of their own (employment) free market. Eventually Merrill Lynch was forced to play by the new rules, and itself became an aggressive recruiter of rival firms' best producers. Its chief executive at the time of the transition was Donald T. Regan, a hard-nosed businessman whose name would soon arise in a political context.

Jimmy Carter's administration had introduced revolutionary change to Wall Street, but it was less successful where the economy was concerned. Inflation reached double digits, and as the cost of living soared, so did short-term and long-term interest rates. Businessmen couldn't borrow at affordable rates, and mortgages were out of the reach of many new home buyers, devastating the construction business. Distracted by Middle Eastern turmoil and lacking the political know-how required for success in Washington, Carter failed to stem the inflationary tide.

Ronald Reagan offered a dose of Republican medicine for the country's ailments in 1980, and those most deeply affected by the economic malaise, financial professionals prominent among them, heeded Reagan's prescription of more passive government. Reagan won in a landslide, and prominent among his earliest presidential appointments was Merrill Lynch's Donald Regan, who became his chief of staff. Mr. Regan's autocratic manner had inspired grudging respect at Merrill Lynch, where subordinates wouldn't challenge him. But it didn't sit well with First Lady Nancy Reagan, who did, so he didn't stay long in the White House. Regan did remain in the administration, as Secretary of Treasury.

The Federal Reserve Banking System has been in effect since 1913, and for the most part has avoided becoming a political football. Andrew Jackson succeeded in his opposition to central bankers, but in the decades afterward a series of financial panics (one beginning mere weeks after Jackson left office in 1837) led to the Federal Reserve as we know it today. Crucial to its efficiency has always been its independence from partisan politics, something that seemed impossible to achieve in Andrew Jackson's day, even if Jackson's hostility was based more on mistrust of Eastern bankers than rigid partisanship.

Runaway inflation in commodity prices, together with skyrocketing long-term interest rates, forced Paul Volcker, a holdover from the Carter administration as chairman of the Federal Reserve, to tighten credit shortly after the 1981 inauguration through the "Fed's" open-market operations, allowing short-term rates to rise, narrowing the "yield curve" and throwing the economy into a severe recession. To his credit, President Reagan didn't interfere, and although Wall Street went into crisis mode for a while in 1981, his administration's patience was rewarded when interest rates declined as a result of the recession.

The stock market began a historic rally in August 1982, one that most stockbrokers didn't see coming. Suddenly all was well in the financial district, and the precious independence of the Federal Reserve Bank had been preserved.

Volcker retired in 1987, and was replaced by the scholarly economist Alan Greenspan, a lifelong Republican whose monetary theories derived from University of Chicago's conservative guru Milton Friedman, and whose libertarian disdain for government regulation matched President Reagan's. Shortly after taking over, Greenspan faced a market crisis in October 1987 that befuddled even the more experienced market observers and brokers.

Commodity futures contracts had been a staple of markets in Chicago and New York since the 19th century. Their purpose was to balance supply and demand for agricultural products such as wheat and corn. If a farmer attempted to sell his product immediately after harvest, the huge volume offered for sale would necessarily depress prices. So, creative minds in the mid-19th century devised contracts that promised to deliver a given commodity at a future date, with the prices set above cash levels to allow for the cost of storage, plus an interest factor. Because speculators were willing to gamble on price fluctuations, they provided the demand to offset the farmer's supply. The markets, which operated under different regulatory authority than did stocks and bonds, proved to be efficient.

In the 1970s someone in Japan with an equally creative mind decided that a futures market in stock indexes could balance supply and demand, also. There's no harvest season for a common stock, thus no real economic need for stock index futures has ever existed. But institutional investors holding large positions in growth stocks liked the idea of hedging those positions, by selling futures contracts whereby they promised to deliver the underlying stocks at a future date. Meanwhile aggressive traders in Japan, of which there are legions, took the opposite side of the transaction, achieving great leverage through the relatively small margin payment required.

Japan attracted the world's attention with index futures. By the time the Volcker-induced recession had reached its nadir in 1982, futures contracts on the Standard and Poor's 500-stock and 100-stock indexes had come into being, but so stealthily as to attract almost zero notice in the financial press. When the stock market began its rally that August, buyers of futures contracts climbed on board to the sound of one hand clapping. As the contracts spurted higher, arbitrageurs simultaneously sold the futures while buying the underlying stocks, locking in an immediate profit on the price spread and providing needed liquidity to a new market.

Most stockbrokers celebrated the market rally, even without understanding what was going on with index futures. Brokerage firms allowed only commodity specialists to handle transactions in index futures, so other brokers with little or no exposure to commodities were left to enjoy the ride without being onboard themselves. In addition to index futures, index options were created, which brought in traders who couldn't afford to play the futures game but would buy an option contract for a modest sum that provided almost the same leverage.

Things went well on Wall Street for five years, until a shocking collapse that began late on a Friday in October and continued into the following Monday. On Friday, index futures contracts, futures options and stock options happened to expire at the same time (the name "Triple Witching Day" was coined to celebrate the occasion, with no sense of irony, because Wall Street has none), meaning that institutions holding large, heavily leveraged positions were scrambling to close those positions together. It happened that many traders had sold "naked" puts (unsecured option contracts to sell stocks), never anticipating the kind of decline they were witnessing. They were caught in the maelstrom.

Index futures and futures options weren't well understood, even after five years. The financial press scrambled to educate the public, but without much success. Fortunately, Chairman Alan Greenspan understood what was going on, and provided liquidity for the stock market from his recently acquired seat at the Federal Reserve Bank. Greenspan became an overnight hero when the market quickly stabilized, and his continued penchant for holding down short-term interest rates pleased Wall Street no end. His popularity continued to grow during the 1990s, when the market was so strong, fueled largely by a boom in "dot.com" stocks, that tax receipts from realized short-term capital gains and a boom in corporate profits meant the federal government was able to declare an actual surplus by 1998.

Chairman Greenspan left his desk in 2006. His disdain for market regulation might have contributed to the financial collapse that followed shortly after his departure, in that undue real estate speculation had resulted from the packaging and resale by brokerage firms of mortgages whose underlying quality was extremely poor, yet had been rated highly because the fact of their bundling cloaked the weak financial condition of the borrowers at the end of the money chain. The real estate market collapsed in 2008, and the residual damage to the overall economy no doubt contributed to the election of the first African-American president, Democrat Barack Obama.

After taking office President Obama presided over a rescue plan for the economy. The most partisan Democrats hoped he'd punish Wall Street titans for their clear misconduct, but Obama took the high road and even included Wall Street executives in the recovery plan. Lehman Brothers, an old-line firm that had declared bankruptcy in September 2008, wasn't rescued. Bear Stearns, another highly leveraged firm, had been sold to J.P. Morgan/Chase for $2 per share. Citicorp, on the other hand, was judged "too big to fail" and was included in the rescue.

The president signed the Dodd-Frank bill into law in 2010. It sought to remedy the kinds of abuses that led to the 2008 collapse, yet as this is being written Dodd-Frank itself has come under intense criticism because its restrictions, which apply to all banks without regard to size, are said to impact smaller financial institutions with shallower pockets, disproportionately. Christopher Dodd and Barney Frank are Democrats, and what at first seemed to be a non-partisan rescue for the economy is now emerging as a spitting contest between the two major parties. Once again, the public interest is being subordinated to the selfish ambition of Republicans and Democrats.

CHAPTER 19: THE TWO-PARTY SYSTEM AND THE FIRST
AMENDMENT

If a third party is ever to gain the recognition that is now enjoyed by a duopoly of the major parties, it might be that a consistent faithfulness to the Bill of Rights, specifically to Amendment One, holds the key to its success. As things stand, many Democrat and Republican politicians believe in free speech and free association, but only in conformity to their fixed ideologies.

Amendment One: "Congress shall make no law respecting an establishment of religion, or prohibiting the free exercise thereof; or abridging the freedom of speech, or of the press; or the right of the people peaceably to assemble, and to petition the Government for a redress of grievances." That's pretty clear language. Interpretations of the language by interested parties, however, vary according to the motives of those doing the interpreting.

When African-American football players exercise their right to "petition for a redress of grievances," in particular perceived abuses of power by police toward African-American crime suspects, by refusing to stand when "The Star Spangled Banner" is played before a National Football League game, they are attacked by a Republican president as "S.O.B.s," and by bloggers on conservative sites as overpaid, spoiled brats who should leave the country. President Trump would subordinate the players' First Amendment rights to a higher calling, i.e., *fealty to Donald Trump's own view of what constitutes patriotism*. The "overpaid spoiled brat" who initiated the controversy, quarterback Colin Kaepernick of the San Francisco 49ers, has forfeited a multi-million-dollar annual paycheck to make a political point. His identification by Trump as one disloyal to the country has resulted in a de facto refusal to hire him as a player, by teams worried about their bottom lines. Kaepernick's argument, meanwhile, has registered only with those who share his outlook on police and race. The 1ˢᵗ Amendment is no longer an absolute. It is a political football, figuratively and literally.

When a spokesperson for conservative Republican causes, the author Ann Coulter, wished to speak on a college campus, the threat of violence against her prompted the University of California/Berkeley to cancel her invitation rather than taking steps to guard against violence. Self-proclaimed white nationalist Richard Spencer, who heads the National Policy Institute, has been barred from several campuses for the same (announced) reason, and has been condemned by Democrats (and some Republicans) as a neo-Nazi who engages in "hate speech." Spencer was blamed for the violence that erupted in Charlottesville, Virginia in August 2017, even though no direct evidence connected him to any specific violent act.

Nobody has ever successfully defined hate speech or "hate crimes," yet in most jurisdictions so-called hate crimes carry greater penalties upon conviction that do "ordinary" crimes. Hate-crime laws presume that the authors of the applicable criminal code are competent to read the mind of someone accused of a crime that hasn't occurred yet, and further that between two acts of violence, both punishable as assault, one is somehow less serious than the other if the assailant in question didn't really hate the person being assailed.

Colin Kaepernick, Ann Coulter, and Richard Spencer represent widely disparate political philosophies, yet they share a valid grievance. One political element or another has sought to *abridge their freedom of speech* in support of its own agenda.

When the Bill of Rights was amended to the Constitution, the phrase "freedom of the press" referenced newspapers and journals only. If the Founding Fathers had foreseen radio, television, the Internet and social media, presumably they would have proscribed all interference with "freedom of the media." Because the Constitution was prepared at a time when political parties were unknown, the authors couldn't have anticipated that one's allegiance to press (media) freedom would someday be governed by one's partisan preference.

President Trump has declared war on the media as "the enemy [*sic*] of the people." He is unwilling to honor its historical role as a watchdog over government, meanwhile personalizing all criticism of him with ad hominem attacks on his critics. He created a term now in widespread use, "fake news," to describe any media coverage that calls his veracity into question or otherwise embarrasses him. When a disgruntled member of his own team authored an anonymous editorial in *The New York Times*, detailing his erratic behavior, he erupted in anger. As we speak, his supporters are focusing not on the content of the editorial itself, instead are converting the issue into a "Whodunit?" Upon discovering who it is that done it, presumably they will proceed to shoot the messenger.

The president and his most ardent supporters believe in what they've labeled a "deep state," a nebulous alliance of Washington insiders whose agenda isn't clearly delineated but which controls government from the shadows. It acts to the frustration of those who seek to "drain the [Washington] swamp," the same swamp President Trump referenced to good effect during his campaign. The deep-state concept, though it's invisible to the naked eye, validates the president's paranoia to his legion of supporters. Once its existence is accepted as fact, there's no limit to how often it may be used as a political weapon.

If a deep state exists, presumably it would include organizations that prize secrecy above all other virtues. The Central Intelligence Agency, National Security Agency (often mocked as "no such agency" because of its initials and its obsession with secrecy), Army Intelligence, and Navy Intelligence operate in a netherworld where so-called classified information is sacred and one's security clearance, or lack of same, is a tacit measurement of one's worth to the state. Since the CIA in particular has been associated with a variety of illegal acts, including the operation of secret prisons and extraordinary rendition, torture of prisoners, and drone attacks on targets of its own selection, the deep-state concept carries a ring of credibility. But President Trump's acolytes associate the deep state only with its effect on his presidency, as if to suggest it came into being on the date of his election and only for the purpose of discrediting him personally.

The deep-state idea is further validated by the willingness of CIA officials to blatantly lie about whatever it is that they're doing at a given moment. These lies are told in the name of honoring a blood oath of loyalty to the organization itself, almost as if our national security infrastructure were an extension of organized crime, and the words "classified" and "omerta" were interchangeable. When it was revealed that the CIA had kept a 201 file on Lee Harvey Oswald, "lone assassin" of John F. Kennedy, after denying any association with Oswald for decades, it affirmed the merit of the 1970s efforts of Senators Frank Church (D-ID) and Richard Schweiker (R-PA) to hold the organization to account. If Democrats and Republicans could ever again reach the same kind of bi-partisan cooperation that prevailed back then, Americans might know enough about the deep state to reject it as a political weapon.

Freedom of the (media) should require that all newspapers and broadcasters voluntarily refrain from using political buzzwords and phrases that have been contrived by single-issue pressure groups to advance their agendas. A discussion of the abortion question shouldn't be limited to preserving a "woman's right to choose," albeit the National Organization for Women would aver that the issue begins and ends there. Demands for greater gun control shouldn't become a simple matter of "the right to bear arms," as the National Rifle Association would have it. The phrase "working people" should include all working people, not merely those who belong to labor unions, and no media outlet should ever use the phrase "voter fraud" (people voting illegally) without acknowledging questionable tactics by Republicans that restrain the minority vote, and the ease with which electronic voting machines can be hacked so that votes are "flipped" from one candidate to another.

True freedom of the media would be a boon to the development of third parties, through the elimination of political language that is chosen by extreme elements within the two major parties, then filtered through the print and broadcast media. If "a woman's right to choose" and "the right to bear arms" are acceptable phrases to define an issue, even though they present only one side, then "deep state" and even "fake news" become acceptable.

Chapter 20: God, the Media, and the Two-Party System

It bears reemphasizing that the Bill of Rights antedated the formation of all political parties. If the framers could have imagined the political landscape that exists in 2018, its chosen language, "Congress shall make no law respecting an establishment of religion, or prohibiting the free exercise thereof..." might instead have appeared as, "No political constituency may act to conjoin church and state, nor suggest that church doctrine is binding upon common law, nor may any such law intrude upon one's freedom to abide by said church doctrine."

In other words, the church should stay out of politics, and politicians should leave the church alone. But as Moses never said when God exhorted him to lead his people out of Egypt, "Easier said than done, O God." To believe in the separation of church and state is one thing, to pretend that laws haven't already been passed because of someone's literal interpretation of Biblical commands is another.

Example: The Hebrew Bible (Old Testament to Christians) teaches that acts of sodomy are sinful, and laws have been passed in various states to affirm this teaching. But freedom of association, as affirmed by the Bill of Rights, must apply to heterosexuals and homosexuals alike, assuming only that homosexuals have an equal claim to citizenship. Sodomy laws, by definition, are applied only against homosexuals.

Example: The Biblical exhortation, "An eye for an eye, a tooth for a tooth," was meant to limit punishment for misdeeds to a proportionate response, i.e., an adulteress should not be stoned, and a petty thief should not suffer dismemberment of the hand. Instead lawmakers have often interpreted the phrase to the contrary, "Make sure the punishment is sufficient to recognize the severity of the offense and to deter future miscreants." One result of this misinterpretation has been that life sentences have been given to drug addicts who deal in drugs to support their habits, while violent crimes are punished with shorter terms.

The justice system might better be governed by a different Biblical citation, "Vengeance is mine, saith the Lord." Better still would be forbidding the application of Biblical language upon secular law.

Example: According to the New Testament, when Jesus was asked if Jews should pay taxes to their Roman occupiers, He held up a coin bearing the image of Julius Caesar and replied to the questioner, "Render unto Caesar what is Caesar's, and unto God the things that are God's." Clearly, Jesus was calling for a separation of church from state. Christians may tend to include in such separation a support for continued exemption from taxes for church property. Secular humanists and other non-Christians interpret Christ's words to mean the opposite, that taxes must be paid irrespective of religion. They point to the wealth of the Roman Catholic Church, and of many Protestant megachurches, as proof that exempting church property from taxation is unjust.

The two-party system seldom dealt with church/state issues before the current era. Thomas Jefferson, a Deist, managed to rewrite the Holy Bible while creating his own version, "The Philosophy of Jesus of Nazareth." The "Jefferson Bible" dealt with Jesus as He was seen by His first century contemporaries, not as imagined by later theologians, as the Son of God and as His co-equal in a Holy Trinity. Nothing Jefferson wrote or said about religion affected his historical standing then or since, because he wrote it long after his presidency ended. Had he written his own bible while at once holding office as the representative of a major political party, he would have reaped the scorn of the opposition party for having imposed a religious viewpoint, however secular in content, upon state affairs.

Abraham Lincoln's religious beliefs have been debated by historians. He never joined any church, but his few recorded comments on religion suggest his awareness of a higher power. Lincoln's skill at deflecting questions about God is manifest. At the height of the Civil War Lincoln was asked, "Is God on our side?" meaning the side of the men in blue. He answered, "Sir, my concern is not whether God is on our side. My greatest concern is always to be on God's side, for God is always right." Lincoln understood that the brutal conflict had driven families apart. It had caused many devout citizens in the North and South to question their own faith in God, but Lincoln refused to allow God to become a political weapon.

The efforts of a Republican clergyman to influence the 1884 presidential campaign backfired on the GOP candidate, James G. Blaine, and became a warning to all future candidates for office against enlisting, or even accepting, the support of religious figures. Shortly before Election Day, Rev. Samuel D. Burchard spoke to his congregation in New York City, forgoing a theological message while urging parishioners not to support the (Democratic) party of "Rum, Romanism, and Rebellion." "Rum" stood for a stereotype of Democrats as alcoholics, "Romanism" referred to (lowly) Catholic immigrants who were taking jobs away from "real" Americans, and "Rebellion" spoke to the GOP's ongoing effort to "wave the bloody shirt" and portray all Democrats as after-the-fact Confederate sympathizers. Burchard's sermon was highlighted in New York newspapers, copies of which were then distributed throughout working-class, ethnic neighborhoods in the city that leaned Democratic and were likely to take offense. The backlash against Burchard's use of a religious platform to advance nativist politics enabled Democrat Grover Cleveland to carry New York State by a whisker and with it, the Electoral College. If it were not for Burchard's lapse in judgment, Republicans very probably would have maintained uninterrupted control of the White House from 1861 until 1913.

Most clergymen during the post-Civil War period were Republicans, including Henry Ward Beecher. But Beecher, whose fame had been tarnished by the Elizabeth Tilton affair in the 1870s, had turned away from partisan advocacy by 1884. He bucked the tide and quietly supported Cleveland. Politicians and preachers kept their distance from one another during campaigns after 1884, no doubt daunted by Burchard's experience. Evangelist Dwight L. Moody (1837–1899) and Episcopalian Phillips Brooks (1835–1893) achieved wide fame and popularity without being associated with political issues or cultivating political leaders. Temperance advocate Carrie Nation (1846–1911) destroyed saloons with her hatchet in the name of God, but because temperance was a non-partisan issue, Carrie didn't cross paths with political leaders of her era.

Many prominent politicians during the late 19th century were devout Christians. James A. Garfield belonged to the Disciples of Christ sect, Benjamin Harrison and William Jennings Bryan were Presbyterians, William McKinley a Methodist, yet all kept their religious faith separate from politics. The pattern continued into the early 20th century, when the progressive movement, incompatible on its face with all doctrinaire ideology, including faith-based, dominated political discourse.

The advent of radio in the 1920s brought religion to the masses for the first time. An aging William Jennings Bryan put politics aside in favor of broadcast appeals, in favor of creationism versus the teaching of evolution. His stalwart (or misguided) defense of Biblical inerrancy as both prosecutor and witness at the 1925 "Monkey Trial" of science teacher John Scopes in Dayton, Tennessee, captivated a nationwide radio audience as it widened a geopolitical gulf between the Bible Belt and urban America. That gulf was further expanded on air by journalist H.L. Mencken at the time (Mencken covered the Monkey Trial on radio, mocking it as "...the greatest story since the Resurrection"). The religious and cultural divide still exists, and now extends to politics. Evangelist Aimee Semple McPherson (1890–1944) expanded her following and captured souls via radio during the decade. But the first clergyman to mix politics and religion on the radio to great (though controversial) effect might have been Monsignor Charles Coughlin (1891–1979), a Canadian-born Roman Catholic based in Michigan.

Father Coughlin's radio career began in the 1920s, when he confined his broadcasts to Catholic teachings. After the onset of the Great Depression, he blended social commentary with the word of God. A supporter of Franklin D. Roosevelt and the New Deal at first, and a vehement critic of nativist, anti-Catholic organizations like the Ku Klux Klan, Coughlin turned against FDR in the mid-1930s. His on-air manner became openly hostile toward the administration. Coughlin's commentary blended anti-socialist, Fascist-sounding dogma with anti-Semitism, even as the Nazi threat loomed in Europe. Coughlin, whose audience was estimated to be in the tens of millions, also proselytized for the America First Committee, which maintained an isolationist posture toward involvement in European skirmishing. The AFC included among its membership aviation icon Charles Lindbergh, Senators Burton K. Wheeler (D-MT), David I. Walsh (D-MA), and Gerald P. Nye (R-ND), and two future presidents, fresh from their college campuses, John F. Kennedy and Gerald R. Ford.

The outbreak of World War II curbed Coughlin's influence. His broadcasting career was over, but a new era had begun. In 1950 a young Baptist preacher named William Franklin Graham, Jr. (1918–2018) founded the Billy Graham Evangelistic Association and began radio broadcasts of "The Hour of Decision," exhorting listeners to make the decision in that hour to follow Christ. Meanwhile Graham led revival crusades at venues from Los Angeles to Moscow, crusades that would eventually be televised. A registered Democrat, Billy Graham didn't shy from appearing political, and although a Southern-born Baptist, he spoke out forcefully in behalf of racial integration. Meanwhile he formed friendships with Presidents Eisenhower, Johnson, and Nixon, even as he opposed John F. Kennedy's election in fear that as president, the Roman Catholic JFK might defer to the Vatican's authority on public issues.

Protestant clergyman Dr. Norman Vincent Peale (1898–1993) rose to prominence from the pulpit of the Marble Collegiate Church in New York City. Peale appeared on radio as early as 1935 in "The Art of Living," and later was seen on television, but was best known in the 1950s for authoring The Power of Positive Thinking, a book that blended religion with an optimistic outlook on life and became a best seller. Peale was also positive in thinking that Adlai Stevenson, Democratic candidate for president in 1952, was unqualified for the office because he had been divorced. Peale endorsed Dwight D. Eisenhower, thereby accelerating a departure from the Victorian Era notion that religion and politics must remain segregated.

Norman Vincent Peale was attracted to prominent people, and vice versa. He joined Julie Nixon, daughter of his close friend Richard M. Nixon, and David Eisenhower, grandson of the president, in matrimony. Donald Trump's first marriage began at Marble Collegiate with Dr. Peale presiding. It can't be said that Peale or anyone else in attendance that day envisioned a future Trump presidency, so performing that ceremony shall remain, in the context of this volume, a non-political act on the Dr. Peale's part.

Perhaps owing to the success of Billy Graham's televised crusades, other Protestant preachers followed with regularly scheduled programming on television. Marion "Pat" Robertson (born 1930) began "The 700 Club" in 1966, and it remains on the air today, with Robertson holding forth at age 88, his messages always closely allied with conservative Republican political orthodoxy. Robertson bristles at being called a "televangelist," insisting on the more scholarly sounding "religious broadcaster." Always controversial, Robertson once referred to non-Christians as "termites," and connected several Protestant sects with the Antichrist. Robertson insists that the United States was found as a Christian nation. His quixotic run for the 1988 Republican presidential nomination ended ingloriously.

Televangelist and author Robert H. Schuller (1926–2015) began his "Hour of Power" program in 1970. Less politically strident than Robertson, Schuller's messages emphasized individual striving for goodness, as also expressed in his book, "Tough Times Never Last, but Tough People Do." Schuller's telecasts emanated from the Crystal Cathedral in Garden Grove, California, a structure his ministry built and to which he invited celebrities to testify to their Christian beliefs. After leaving the air in 2010, Schuller's ministry encountered financial problems, and the Crystal Cathedral was sold to the local Catholic diocese.

Jim Bakker (born 1940) and his (then) wife Tammy Faye Bakker began televising "The PTL (Praise the Lord) Club" in 1974. It became a regular fixture on afternoon television before leaving the air in 1989 in the wake of rape accusations against Bakker, which were followed by the discovery of massive financial irregularities involving PTL and Heritage, USA, a religious theme park in South Carolina. Bakker went to prison and his marriage to Tammy Faye ended. Evangelist Jimmy Swaggart (born 1935), a passionate preacher affiliated with the Assemblies of God ministry who often shed tears while proclaiming salvation to audiences, first appeared on television in 1971. His broadcasts ended in 1988 after Swaggart confessed to associating with prostitutes. He then was defrocked by the Assemblies of God hierarchy.

Along with Billy Graham, Jerry Falwell (1933–2007) could be called the spiritual father of televangelism. At age 22 Falwell founded the Thomas Road Baptist Church in Lynchburg, VA, which became his base for a radio and television ministry, The Old Time Gospel Hour. In 1971 Falwell founded Liberty University, also in Lynchburg, and in 1979 began The Moral Majority, an unapologetic blending of religion with politics. Far more willing than Graham to make enemies and stoke controversy in behalf of Christianity, Falwell attacked a woman's right to choose (he saw it as the right to kill babies), belittled gays and lesbians, and promoted prayer in public schools, all the while reminding Americans of the evils of (godless) Communism. His advocacy was welcomed at first by Republican politicians, but the Moral Majority lost credibility in the late 1980s in the wake of the scandals surrounding Bakker and Swaggart, and its life ended. Its credibility was partially restored a decade later, after Bill Clinton was impeached for lying under oath about his relationship with Monica Lewinsky.

If politics and religion make a witch's brew, it might be time for a new Volstead Act. A flood of accusations of sexual harassment against prominent politicians and show business personalities, called the MeToo phenomenon, has invited sanctimony from the religious right and hypocrisy from the left. The Moral Majority is alive and well, at least in spirit, while Republicans and Democrats each claim to be holier than thou.

Chapter 21: Of Dinos and Rinos

A "DINO" isn't a baby dinosaur. A "RINO" isn't a small rhinoceros. These are political acronyms, used by the most partisan Democrats and Republicans to belittle not the opposition, but the more moderate members of their own parties. The phrases "Democrat in Name Only" and "Republican in Name Only" reflect a widening gulf within each party, which is self-evident. Less obvious is that they show the huge ideological chasm between the parties, because both have surrendered control of the political dialogue, if not their party's leadership, to left-wing and right-wing extremists.

As suggested in an earlier chapter, it often seems as if the two-party system in the United States has yielded to a four-party alignment. On the Democratic side, young voters, unafraid of being labeled "liberal" or even "Socialist" by Republicans, have combined with Bernie Sanders' loyalists to promote their favorite liberal causes: preservation of the Affordable Care Act, a $15 minimum wage, free tuition at community colleges, stronger gun-control laws, a tougher regulatory stance toward Wall Street firms, and greater awareness of global warming and renewed support for the Kyoto Protocol. Within this group one finds strong, but not unanimous, sympathy for impeaching President Trump.

More moderate Democrats (DINOS to the extreme element), a group including Congressional leaders Chuck Schumer, Nancy Pelosi, and Dianne Feinstein, along with Hillary Clinton, ex-President Obama and ex-Vice President Biden, emphasize broader goals. All hope to preserve the Affordable Care Act (the hated Obamacare, to Republicans). They oppose any interference with a woman's reproductive rights and any Supreme Court effort to overturn Roe v. Wade. They agree with the left-wingers on gun control measures, but are cautious about costly commitments like free college tuition, and extremely cautious about impeachment, not necessarily because a case doesn't exist for removing President Trump from office, but because (as of September 2018) Special Prosecutor Robert Mueller has yet to report on his findings. Also, the Democrats' leadership avoids impeachment talk out of a reluctance to give Republicans an issue for the mid-terms.

Republicans, of course, would have us believe that no distinction exists between extreme liberal and moderate Democrats. All GOP candidates for office profess that every Democrat is wedded to an extremist agenda, and that moderates are only pretending to be moderate as an election strategy; after which, if elected, they will capitulate to the ultra-liberal Congressional leadership. The Republican approach consciously overlooks the obvious, that the Democrats' leadership is less ambitious than the young-lion extremists regarding a left-wing program. The Republican argument would prove valid if younger and more liberal Democrats were to succeed in capturing party leadership from Schumer and Pelosi, but that cannot occur before the November elections, and may never occur.

Republicans are also divided, if less so than Democrats. Traditional Republican doctrine, around which the party was unified during the Reagan Era and before the onset of Tea Party Republicanism, calls for low taxes, limited government spending, minimal regulation, and a rigid anti-Communist posture backed by an iron-clad national defense establishment. There were no RINOs (Republicans in name only) when Reagan was in office, and relatively few during the Bush 41 and Bush 43 incumbencies.

Democrat Bill Clinton captured the White House in the 1992 election, in part because incumbent President George H. W. Bush failed to keep a promise sacred to Reagan Era Republicans. He raised taxes. Clinton also benefited from the collapse of the Soviet Union in 1991, which diluted the standard anti-Communist message of the GOP. Democrat Barack Obama was elected in 2008, in part because the previous president, George W. Bush, allowed government spending to get out of hand (largely because of an invasion of Iraq, the aftermath of which became a colossal mess), and also because his laissez-faire attitude toward Wall Street irresponsibility led to a banking crisis and a collapse in real estate values during his last year in office.

The failures of the Bush (fils) administration cast doubt within the GOP over the tactics of political tactician Karl Rove, who had once been fired by Bush (père) but had somehow worked his way back into favor within the party hierarchy. Rove proved to be a genius at stealing elections, but less successful in his desire to remake the party according to a William McKinley-like paradigm, combing fiscal restraint and muscular foreign policy, to which Rove appended outreach to a rapidly growing Hispanic population. Hispanics are predominantly Roman Catholic, believe in family values and, as Catholics, share with conservative Republicans an abhorrence of abortion.

Rove's model couldn't prevent the ascent of Obama. Enter Tea Party Republicans like Senator Rand Paul (KY), Representatives Michele Bachmann (MN), and Steve Scalise (LA), who, motivated by a desire to return the party to orthodox Republican conservatism, established their own caucus in 2010. The Tea Party moniker didn't sit well with the party establishment, however. It sounded too radical. Mainstream Republicans preferred to simply unite with the fractious group in opposition to anything and everything Barack Obama proposed, most especially the Affordable Care Act. "Obamacare" horrified libertarian-minded Republicans by including a mandate to purchase coverage, and after the bill was passed by Congress, it horrified all Republicans when it was approved by the Supreme Court. Chief Justice John Roberts, normally a reliable conservative to the GOP, cast the deciding vote in favor of the ACA. His reasoning was that the mandate to buy insurance amounted to a tax, and thus passed Constitutional muster. Congress may tax the public, but it may not abrogate its Constitutional rights.

Mainstream Republican Senator John McCain (AZ), a foreign-policy hawk but moderate on social issues, had been nominated in 2008. With the economy in chaos and a Republican in the White House to receive the blame, he lost. In 2012 former Massachusetts governor Mitt Romney, with a similar platform to McCain's, was nominated, as the Tea Party faction failed to offer an electable candidate as an alternative. Romney should have won, and probably would have won, but for a tape-recorded speech in which he suggested that 47% of the American people were living off the government. This notion didn't sit well with retired folks who had paid into Social Security for 40 years, nor with veterans who (unlike Romney himself) had served their country in uniform and had earned Veterans Administration benefits.

By the time the 2016 election rolled around, both parties remained divided. Former Senator and Secretary of State Hillary Clinton was the choice of mainstream Democrats, and of the Democratic National Committee. Senator Bernie Sanders (VT), backed by the most liberal Democrats and many younger voters, won several primaries, but Ms. Clinton won the nomination in the end, in part because the Democrats' rules allowed for so-called super delegates, which are chosen by party insiders instead of voters.

Super delegates, as a percentage of the total, constitute a de facto compromise between the era of the bosses in the 19th century and the 20th-century progressive movement that produced primaries. Many Sanders supporters still viewed the system as insufficiently democratic (small d). They were especially angered by certain e-mail messages, released by Wikileaks, that revealed a pattern of behind-the-scenes plotting on the part of the Democratic National Committee in behalf of Ms. Clinton. This revelation led to the resignation of committee head Debbie Wasserman Schultz, and probably caused many Sanders supporters to stay home on Election Day, even though Sanders did endorse Ms. Clinton in the end. Republicans also faced a battle for the nomination from within and outside the mainstream. Having lost two consecutive elections with traditional candidates, many grass roots Republicans were eager for a change, even if it meant acknowledging the failures of the last Republican administration under George W. Bush. When billionaire Donald Trump entered the fray, he won key primaries by dismissing former Florida Governor Jeb Bush, the favorite in the race, as "low energy Jeb," and criticizing Jeb's brother George for mismanaging the Iraq debacle. Trump promised to "clean the [Washington] swamp," seizing on widespread dissatisfaction with Congress, a strategy that also helped him eliminate Senators Marco Rubio (FL) and Ted Cruz (TX), two presumptive swamp denizens. Ohio Governor John Kasich, a moderate, wasn't handicapped by any identification with Washington politics, but entered the race too late to offset Trump's momentum. Primary voters weren't deterred by Trump's most extravagant suggestions, that former President Obama had been born in Kenya and thus had been ineligible to run for president, and that Ted Cruz' father had participated in John F. Kennedy's assassination. Instead they welcomed Trump's call for a wall to be built from the Gulf of Mexico to the Pacific Ocean, the better to deter illegal immigration from south of the border.

In the end Trump succeeded in segregating his primary opponents as RINO's, insufficiently tough on immigration and too willing to cooperate with Democrats on trade issues, although he preferred using phrases like "low energy Jeb" and "lying Ted" (Cruz). Once he reached the White House after defeating "lying Hillary" Clinton in the Electoral College, Republicans who had opposed Trump for his campaign tactics, and whom Trump had derided in response, suddenly became his allies.

There were exceptions. Senators Bob Corker (R-TN) and Jeff Flake (R-AZ) criticized the president publicly, but recognizing that their career paths had turned downward as a consequence of their perfidy, announced their intentions to resign. House Speaker Paul Ryan, at best a lukewarm supporter of President Trump, likewise said he was stepping down. All three are excoriated regularly on Breitbart as apostates, along with Attorney

General Jeff Sessions, former FBI Director James Comey, Special Prosecutor Robert Mueller, and any other registered Republican who dared to differ with the White House.

Democrats, meanwhile, remain united only in opposition to everything Trump stands for, in the same way Republicans found common ground in opposition to President Obama. The two-party system that nobody asked for survives in its factionalized condition, with each party's leaders holding the opposition in utter contempt.

Chapter 22: The Two-Party System and Big-Time Sports

Politicians of both parties have cultivated athletes, coaches, and the owners of professional sports teams for over a century, ever since (Republican) President William Howard Taft initiated a tradition by throwing out the first ball at a Washington Senators opening game in 1910. Other presidents followed suit, and (Democrat) President Franklin Delano Roosevelt strengthened the bond between major-league baseball and the White House by insisting that the game continue during World War Two despite mandated travel restrictions and the induction of many key players into the service.

In 1918, with Democrat Woodrow Wilson in the White House, the entry of the United States into the World War prompted the federal government to call for cancellation of the World Series. When doughboys overseas insisted on knowing how their favorite teams were doing, the series was played, although it was moved to early September following a shortened regular season that honored travel restrictions and a rationing of gasoline, mandated by the war. The doughboys might have received too much credit, however. In the face of their pleas, Babe Ruth, then of the Boston Red Sox, and several teammates threatened to boycott the World Series unless certain of their financial demands were met, which put ownership on the defensive. The players got their way, but a higher power might have punished them for their unpatriotic threat; the Red Sox won that World Series, but they failed to win another one for 86 years.

Since 1922, and without partisan debate, Congress has upheld the "reserve clause," an exemption that protects major-league baseball from antitrust challenges by players or competing leagues. In 1922 baseball was still recovering from the dishonor of the Black Sox scandal, in which Chicago

White Sox players agreed to throw the 1919 World Series in cooperation with professional gamblers, so Congress cooperated. Before the onset of free agency in the 1970s, this exemption allowed franchises to micromanage a player's career.

Major-league baseball and professional football have survived political arguments over the years, at least before Colin Kaepernick first decided to kneel during the playing of the national anthem. The Cleveland Indians and Washington Redskins have been cited by liberals for insensitivity toward Native Americans in retaining their nicknames. Both teams, along with the Atlanta Braves, have stubbornly refused to change, and most fans support them, almost as if this were still the 19th century and Andrew Jackson and William Henry Harrison were winning elections as revered Indian fighters. The Indians (Cleveland), and libertarian-minded folks who see nothing wrong with teams evoking Native American images, have long argued that the name and mascot were adopted not to ridicule anyone, but to honor the first Native American in major-league baseball, Lou Sockalexis, a Penobscot Indian and exceptional all-around athlete who played for Cleveland near the end of the 19th century. The team's prior surname was "Spiders," so "Indians" might have sounded less threatening.

When liberals point out that Dartmouth College and Stanford University dropped the surname "Indians" years ago, they ask, "Shouldn't Cleveland and Washington follow their lead?" Conservatives reply, "That's political correctness. What else would you expect from a liberal college campus?" This argument mirrors a cultural divide between small-town America, which loves football for its own sake and tends to regard political correctness as a product of East Coast/West Coast elitism, and academia, which likes the money football brings in but labors to remain politically correct, meanwhile pompously calling players they recruit merely to play football "student athletes." Supporters of the Florida State Seminole team use a tomahawk chop gesture to cheer their team on, which so far hasn't been outlawed by school administrators. Fans of the Atlanta Braves also the tomahawk-chop, as if to intimidate both the opposition and any silly liberal from up north who dares to scold them for insensitivity.

In defense of political incorrectness, it might be fair to point out that nobody has yet complained to the city of Dallas, to Oklahoma State University, or to the University of Wyoming for their use of the surname "Cowboys." No doubt that's because cowboys are always the good guys, and every redskin except Tonto is a bad guy.

As of this writing the issue of players kneeling during the national anthem remains an undercurrent to the games themselves and to the political season, which happens to parallel the football season even though professional team owners wished it didn't. President Trump continues to gain political mileage by decrying Kaepernick's act as unpatriotic, while defenders of the players and civil libertarians insist the controversy isn't about "The Star-Spangled Banner" at all, but about police misconduct. The National Football League, which wishes the controversy would disappear behind a goal post somewhere, tries to accommodate the players, team owners, politicians, and football fans by adopting changing rules that don't settle the question, but at least succeed in punting it out of bounds.

The truth is that football and other sports, both college and professional, have bigger fish to fry than people who kneel during the national anthem. The #MeToo movement has focused attention on alleged acts of physical abuse by athletes, coaches, and even team doctors, against women and even young boys, accusations that were unheard of 50 years ago, but which seem to create a new headline in the sports section of the paper every day.

When an accusation is made against a player or coach of a high-profile team with a fanatical following, inevitably the accuser's credibility is measured inversely with the success and popularity of the player's team, regardless of the circumstances. It might not be a coincidence that men associated with perennial college football powers have attracted the most negative publicity on account of alleged sexual misconduct, regardless of whether the credibility of those accusations justified the greater focus.

Quarterback Jameis Winston was a Heisman Trophy winner who led the Florida State Seminoles to victory over Auburn in a championship game at the Rose Bowl. He also dealt with accusations of rape by a Florida State coed. Winston admitted to a sexual relationship with the woman, but insisted it was consensual. Perhaps because of Winston's success on the gridiron, the university failed to aggressively pursue the woman's allegations, and the matter ended up in civil court (criminal charges were not filed, because of the absence of evidence to support the charges).

After being drafted by the Tampa Bay Buccaneers, Winston was accused by a female Uber driver of fondling her improperly at a fast-food restaurant drive-thru. The National Football League took the charges more seriously than Florida State had, the result being that Winston was suspended from the first three games of the 2018 season. After first denying the woman's account, Winston declared that he was giving up drinking, a tacit admission of guilt. Football-crazy Florida seems more concerned with his team's record, however, and the fact that Winston, after returning from his suspension, was costing his team games by having too many passes intercepted. The Ohio State University, no less of a football power than Florida State, has been the locus of two separate scandals, one involving a U.S. Congressman that became a partisan spitting contest in Washington. A team doctor who attended to members of the wrestling team was accused of multiple acts of improper sexual contact in the guise of medical treatment. The school and the state's attorney general promised to investigate thoroughly, even though the doctor in question had died. Rep. Jim Jordan (R-OH), who founded the Freedom Caucus in the House of Representatives, has been accused of knowing about the accusations and doing nothing. Jordan and his supporters deny the accusations and allege that the charges against him are part of a Deep State conspiracy funded by Democrats.

While Ohio State was still reeling from the negative publicity surrounding the doctor, coach Urban Meyer of the Buckeyes' football team was accused of ignoring reports that his assistant, Zach Smith, had physically abused his wife in 2015. Smith happens to be a grandson of legendary coach Earle Bruce, Meyer's one-time mentor. Meyer denied knowing of Mrs. Smith's charges at first, then later conceded that he'd heard rumors, but that his wife wasn't sure that Mrs. Smith had really been abused, thus he didn't act on the rumors. Meyer accepted the same three-game suspension without pay from Ohio State that Winston had received from the National Football League, which begs the question, "Is there no quantifiable difference between improper sexual conduct itself, and hearing about someone else's alleged misconduct and remaining silent?"

Michigan State University was roiled by 150 accusations of sexual impropriety by women against a team doctor, Larry Nassar, a scandal that led to the resignation of the university's president. The scandal became partisan after former Republican Michigan Governor John Engler was named interim president of the school and charged with investigating the women's charges and settling claims against Michigan State. Large financial settlements were made, but Engler's handling of accusations made by one claimant were too equivocal, in the opinion of Senators Maggie Hassan (D-NH) and Richard Blumenthal (D-CT), who saw fit to criticize Engler harshly. A non-partisan observer might be justified in asking, "Would these Senators have criticized a member of their own party who happened to be in Engler's position?" Also, "What did the Senate Republicans have to say regarding Engler?"

The most toxic scandal involving a perennial football power involved Jerry Sandusky, a former star player and at the time the scandal broke, assistant football coach at Penn State University. Sandusky was accused of fondling young boys in the shower while serving as a counselor at an off-season camp, accusations that persisted over a period of years and reached the ears of legendary Penn State Coach Joe Paterno, Sandusky's boss and friend. Paterno did report what he had heard to his immediate superior, the athletic director, but otherwise did nothing. In the end Sandusky was convicted in court and sentenced to prison. Paterno resigned, said he wished he'd been more proactive, and died less than a year later. Penn State's football fortunes, which matter far more to the team's passionate fans than any legal hassle, took a temporary drop but are now on the rebound.

Television ratings of college and professional football have been lower during September 2018 than in previous years. It remains to be seen if the public is reacting to the various sex-related scandals cited here, or to President Trump and his condemnation of national anthem kneelers. Regardless of television's problems, Ohio State and Penn State have no problem selling 100,000 tickets to every game.

CHAPTER 23: THE TWO-PARTY SYSTEM AND THE SUPREME COURT

As this is written, the Senate Judiciary Committee, chaired by Charles Grassley (R-IA), is striving to deal with a stunning eleventh-hour accusation that threatens the expected confirmation of Judge Brett Kavanaugh to the Supreme Court, filling a vacancy created by the retirement of Justice Anthony Kennedy. Dr. Christine Blasey Ford, a college professor from California who, as a teenager, lived in the Maryland suburbs near Kavanaugh, alleged in a letter to her Congressional representative that at age 15 she was assaulted at a party by Kavanaugh, who was then age 17, and by Kavanaugh's friend and contemporary, Mark Judge, both of whom she said had been drinking heavily. The letter reached Senator Dianne Feinstein, ranking Democrat on the Judiciary Committee, who declined to release its contents to oblige Dr. Ford, who had requested anonymity. When media sources obtained the accuser's identity and brought it public, Kavanaugh unequivocally denied the allegations. Judge remembered nothing, and said such behavior was atypical of his friend Brett.

The case could be described as a perfect storm. It combines the worst abuses of high-echelon partisanship with the influence of the #MeToo movement respecting sexual abuse. It asks 100 Senators in the year 2018 to determine the validity of allegations that had lain dormant for over three decades, in the face of Kavanaugh's explicit denial and Ford's vagueness about the time and place the alleged assault took place. It balances the Republicans' desire to fill the seat with a conservative prior to the mid-term elections, lest a Democratic majority after November rejects the nomination, against the Democrats' desire to postpone a vote on Kavanaugh until an investigation reveals the truth or falsity of Dr. Ford's allegations. Dr. Ford has asked for an FBI investigation, but one wonders how any investigation could uncover the truth after 36 years, when the accuser is unsure of when or where the attack took place, the accused says it never happened at all, and the only possible witnesses have no recollection of any such happening. If Kavanaugh and Judge were drunk at the time, as alleged, it's easy to imagine that neither has any recollection of the night in question, so any search for the truth would be quite fruitless.

Christine Blasey Ford is a woman of unblemished reputation who has come forward in the face of death threats, and has agreed to testify before the Senate under certain conditions, one of which is that Kavanaugh himself may not be in the room when she testifies. Judge Brett Kavanaugh owns an equally spotless reputation, although even before the current "he said/she said" debate began, Democrats were objecting to Kavanaugh due to his partisan work on behalf of the George W. Bush administration regarding alleged torture of terrorist suspects, and his apparent sympathy for reduced limits on presidential power. Kavanaugh had also helped Special Prosecutor Kenneth Starr investigate allegations of sexual impropriety that led to the impeachment of Bill Clinton, which adds a dollop of irony to the charges against him in 2018.

Comparisons to the 1991 confirmation process involving Justice Clarence Thomas and the woman who accused him of sexual harassment, Anita Hill, are inevitable. In both cases, a long-suppressed accusation of sexual misconduct came forth at the last minute. When defenders of Thomas and Kavanaugh ask, "Why didn't (Hill and Blasey Ford) come forward before this?" women's advocates reply, "You don't understand the conflicted emotions women go through. If you were a woman, you would understand," a reasonable statement, but one unhelpful in searching for the truth. Republicans reasonably ask, "What is to prevent any woman from coming forward at the last minute with a phony claim, politically motivated, one that can't be proven true or false because of the time lag?" Democrats reply, "What woman would expose herself to death threats and attacks on her reputation, just for the sake of influencing a Supreme Court nomination?" Both rejoinders make sense, so how does one choose between the two, separately from one's partisan inclinations?

The parallels between 1991 and 2018 even extend to the fact that both accusers later became college professors. Liberals argue that educated women of stature would be unlikely to invent a story for political purposes, conservatives answer that college professors are wedded to a left-wing ideology that prevails on all college campuses, and that only women of stature would contrive a story, because a good reputation gives any claimant greater credibility. If the partisan divide in Congress needed any further exposure, the Kavanaugh matter has provided it. Every Senator is ready to vote along party lines, with the possible exceptions of Susan Collins (R-ME) and Lisa Murkowski (R-AK), who have expressed doubt about Kavanaugh's commitment to women's reproductive rights, and wonder if a Justice Kavanaugh would vote to overturn Roe v. Wade. Kavanaugh has declared Roe v. Wade to be a "settled matter," but has otherwise equivocated on abortion questions, not surprisingly given that he was raised as a Roman Catholic.

Collins has a well-deserved reputation for thoughtfulness and independence from partisanship, but she has come under attack on liberal websites, especially by women bloggers, for seeming to show sympathy for Kavanaugh's plight. As a female, she is expected by many women's advocates to surrender objectivity in favor of loyalty to her gender. As a Senator, her calling is presumably gender-neutral. Collins is therefore in the eye of the perfect storm.

President Trump had little to say about the controversy at first. When he finally joined the debate, he poisoned the well by insisting that if the 15-year-old Christine Blasey had really been assaulted as she now claims, her parents would have seen to it that justice was served. Ergo sum, she must be lying about it. The president apparently couldn't intuit that a teenaged girl might be so traumatized by a sexual assault that she feared telling anyone, even her parents. Trump's words raised the temperature of the debate beyond the boiling point, which seemed to many observers to have been his intention.

In a thoughtful editorial in The New York Times, David Leonhardt wrote that whatever the outcome of the current brouhaha, the Supreme Court itself has lost face with the public by pretending to be non-partisan when it is anything but. Before Justice Kennedy (a Republican) retired, pressure was brought to bear on him to resign before the November elections, so that President Trump could appoint a conservative replacement while the GOP maintained control of the Senate, thus guaranteeing confirmation. The same Republicans who want Kavanaugh confirmed without undue delay, were happy to delay the nomination of Merrill Garland by President Obama in 2016, for no better reason than to give a Republican president the chance to nominate a replacement for the late Justice Antonin Scalia.

Leonhardt laments the current situation and the few remedies available. The Founding Fathers never anticipated political parties in the first place, let alone the blatant partisanship that prevails today. The first Chief Justice, John Jay, served for fewer than six years, during which time the Supreme Court heard only four cases, none of which had any partisan aspect. Jay lived until 1829 and could have served until then, but he must have viewed court service as an act of citizenship, because he resigned his seat early and returned to private life. Later he returned to politics. Even the most controversial Supreme Court rulings in history never inspired the kind of partisan division that surrounds the Kavanaugh nomination process. The Dred Scott decision (1857) upheld the Fugitive Slave Act and the rights of slaveholders, and was therefore greeted with horror north of the Mason-Dixon line and with satisfaction in the South. The division was geographic rather than partisan, although it accelerated the growth of the new Republican party and led to Abraham Lincoln's election in 1860, which was facilitated by a rift within the Democratic party. After the Emancipation Proclamation, new Constitutional amendments guaranteed citizenship for people of color.

Plessy vs. Ferguson (1896) addressed the reality of inferior educational facilities for minorities. It did so with what history has regarded as an unrealistic and half-hearted ruling, that segregated schools were acceptable provided only that they provided an "equal" education for minority children. "Separate but equal" was accepted as a compromise without unusual rancor, albeit a growing realization that "separate but equal" was really "separate and unequal" led to the unanimous Brown vs. the Board of Education decision (1954), which outlawed school segregation. Major civil rights legislation followed a decade later.

Roe v. Wade (1973) recognized a woman's right to privacy under the 14th Amendment and extended that right to allowing women to make unilateral decisions about aborting a pregnancy within the first two trimesters, meanwhile leaving states in charge of regulating late-term abortions. Although a landmark decision, the subsequent controversy was based more on religious and moral questions than on partisan division.

Prior to the firestorm over Robert Bork's failed nomination in 1987, and the furious partisan rancor that arose from the Clarence Thomas and Brett Kavanaugh matters, the only intense partisan battle involving the Supreme Court concerned not any one decision, but Franklin D. Roosevelt's effort to "pack" the court with added justices who might advance his New Deal initiatives in the late 1930s. Republicans cried bloody murder, gained Congressional seats in the 1938 mid-terms, and FDR backed down. If social media had existed during that era, we can imagine how the debate over the court would have proceeded.

ANGRY DEMOCRAT (on RawStory): Don't those x#$#^%*@ Republicans know FDR won the last election in a landslide?

ANGRY DEMOCRAT IN SUPPORT: Ditto. Those Republican creeps oppose everything he tries to do for working people.

ANGRY REPUBLICAN (on Breitbart): That %n#*&r#* in the White House thinks he's King Franklin.

ANGRY REPUBLICAN IN SUPPORT: I give you an upvote. He and Eleanor have no regard for Constitutional government.

Full disclosure: The author's maternal grandmother, although she was FDR's third cousin, was an angry Republican at that time who couldn't stand the man, and disliked Eleanor even more fervently.

Her grandson could never comprehend how such a warm and loving presence could harbor such animus toward a public servant, let alone someone she was related to by blood.

Leonhardt is saying that however the Kavanaugh debate turns out, the Supreme Court itself will have been injured. Justices will be pressured to retire in time for an even more conservative (or more liberal) justice to be nominated, or pressured to remain on the court out of fear that a conservative (or liberal) would be the replacement. Nominees will continue to be questioned about their political views during the vetting process. If a nominee responds (appropriately), "I can't comment now on an issue that might come before the court," said nominee will be accused of evasiveness (for partisan political reasons). Every future decision made by that individual, if he or she is confirmed, will have been seen afterward as politically motivated by half the country.

Inevitably, young lawyers who dream of someday climbing the ladder to the highest court in the land will discover that their prospects depend less on legal acumen than on fealty to one party or the other. With every passing day, the Supreme Court increasingly functions in behalf of a two-party system that nobody asked for.

Chapter 24: The Two-Party System and the 25ᵀᴴ Amendment

The 25th Amendment to the Constitution was added in 1967. Its purpose was to clarify (and simplify) the order of succession within the executive branch. Like a dinner entrée to which an indigestible ingredient had been added, the amendment has recently entered the news in ways not anticipated in 1967. First, the history.

Prior to the amendment's inclusion it was understood that the death of a president elevated the vice president to the office. At least, this was understood only after Vice President John Tyler, who was sworn in as president after the death of William Henry Harrison in 1841, overcame Congressional objections to the effect that Tyler was only "acting president."

A Constitutional crisis was avoided. But what if Tyler had died in office? There was no second vice president in reserve. Congress established an order of succession that elevated first, the president pro-tempore (longest-serving member) of the Senate to the presidency, and in the event of his death, the Secretary of State, and then other cabinet officials. This wasn't entirely satisfactory, because the longest-serving Senator was likely to be the oldest (and maybe a bit dim at that stage of things). In any event, a Senator had been elected only by the citizens of one state. The various secretaries who stood next in line, meanwhile, hadn't been elected by anyone. More recently the Speaker of the House has been designated as second in line behind the vice president.

Tyler survived until the end of his term, as did Millard Fillmore, Andrew Johnson, Chester A. Arthur, Theodore Roosevelt, Calvin Coolidge, Harry Truman, and Lyndon Johnson, all of whom had been vice president when the president he served under died in office. For the rest of the deceased president's four years in each instance, there was no vice president to take over if needed. Fortunately, all the "accidental" presidents finished the deceased president's term.

The 25th Amendment was first employed merely six years after its adoption. It was needed again the following year. Vice President Spiro T. Agnew resigned in 1973, after being charged with financial misconduct dating back to his days as governor of Maryland. President Nixon nominated Representative Gerald R. Ford as Agnew's replacement, and Ford was confirmed. A year later Nixon resigned under threat of impeachment, Ford became president, and he in turn nominated former New York Governor Nelson Rockefeller as vice president. Rockefeller was likewise confirmed. The 25th Amendment had functioned well.

The devil is always in the details, or so it's said. In the process of clarifying the order of succession to the presidency, the authors of the 25th Amendment opened a can of worms that might or might not fit inside the Capitol dome. A dubious section of the amendment reads as follows: "Whenever the vice president and a majority of EITHER THE PRINCIPAL OFFICERS OF THE EXECUTIVE DEPARTMENTS [presumably, they mean Cabinet officers] OR OF SUCH OTHER BODY AS CONGRESS MAY BY LAW PROVIDE [what law, and who decides between the principal officers of the executive departments and that other anonymous body?], transmit to the president pro tempore of the Senate [oh, seniority, again?] and Speaker of the House [assuming the two are on speaking terms] their written proclamation that... [the president is unable to serve, the vice president will become president, and will nominate a new vice president, etc., etc.]."

This convoluted wording disguised a legitimate objective, i.e., to keep government operating if the president were incapacitated. In 1919 President Woodrow Wilson suffered a paralytic stroke, and for months communicated with Congress and the public only through his wife and attending physician. Vice President Thomas Marshall, who stood ready to assume the office if Wilson had died, was nowhere in evidence. This might have been at Wilson's insistence, because Marshall had been rendered politically invisible for six years. Nothing catastrophic occurred during the president's illness, but the 25th Amendment was designed in part to deal with a recurrence of presidential disability, reasonably enough.

But the definition of "presidential disability" was left to the judgment of the "principal officers" and "members of a non-specific body," as described above, who aren't identified with greater specificity, or with any pecking order. According to the wording of the amendment, the final decision as to whether a president is disabled or not could be left to the vice president, and/or to a majority of (again) principal officers of unspecified executive departments, or to the collective wisdom of an unnamed body provided by a nonexistent law, all as delivered in writing, one copy each, to the oldest guy in the Senate (provided he's awake) and to the Speaker of the House, either of whom could be the president's best friend or mortal enemy. Is that clear?

If the president has a stroke and is bedridden, as with Woodrow Wilson, that would appear to constitute a disability calling for action under the 25th Amendment. But what if a president simply behaves erratically, or is drinking heavily? Is a president who engages in extramarital affairs, and thus is subject to possible blackmail, to be considered unable to perform his duties? What about a president who won't cooperate with independent government agencies?

Upon taking office President Trump was confronted with allegations that Russians had interfered with the 2016 presidential election in his behalf. Congress called for a special prosecutor to investigate possible collusion between individuals in Russia and members of Trump's campaign staff, the objective of which (allegedly) had been to cast aspersions on Hillary Clinton. Because the president's appointee as Attorney General, Jeff Sessions, was conflicted by his own connection to Russian interests and properly agreed to recuse himself from participating in any investigation, Deputy Attorney General Rod Rosenstein assumed oversight of Special Prosecutor Robert S. Mueller's work. Meanwhile, FBI Director James Comey, whose investigation of candidate Hillary Clinton's use of a private server to transmit e-mails (some of which included classified information) while she was Secretary of State coincided with the election campaign itself, incurred President Trump's wrath and was fired.

Almost from the outset President Trump and his closest allies regarded Mueller's investigation as a "witch hunt." The president ranted and raved about the "reckless" behavior of the FBI and CIA, even though Comey's decision to reopen the investigation of Ms. Clinton's e-mails, just days before the election, probably contributed to her defeat in the Electoral College. The president spared no one in his anger, prompting the resignation of a series of appointees while leaving others in fear of their jobs. Mueller indicted several people connected to Trump's campaign, although it wasn't clear how closely the charges pertained to the president himself. Meanwhile the press published stories leaked from within the White House that called President Trump's mental state into question. These in turn shifted the focus (from President Trump's perspective) away from Mueller's investigation and onto the source(s) of the leaks themselves.

It didn't come out until the summer of 2018 that Deputy Attorney General Rosenstein had been so alarmed by President Trump's volatile behavior in 2017 that he was recorded on tape as speculating, perhaps only sarcastically, on the possibility of gathering support within the government for exercising the 25th Amendment and removing the president from office. This in turn engendered speculation that the president was considering firing Rosenstein and appointing a replacement who would agree to fire Special Prosecutor Mueller. The ongoing melodrama inspired parallels to Watergate, when President Nixon ordered Attorney General Elliot Richardson to fire Special Prosecutor Archibald Cox, after which Richardson refused to do so and resigned.

Denials followed, and the Rosenstein story took a back seat, at least temporarily, to the furor over Christine Blasey Ford's accusations against Judge Brett Kavanaugh, accusations that were followed by other new claims of sexual misconduct on Kavanaugh's part from the 1980s. Left unresolved, of course, were the manifold ambiguities surrounding the language of the 25th Amendment itself.

How "crazy" can a president get before he's removed from office? Who, ultimately, makes the decision? Could the decision ever be separated from partisan politics? Do we want to find out? Do we need a new amendment?

Chapter 25: Partisanship And Deep Pockets

In the 19th century, when politicians conducted campaigns for the presidency from the front porch of their homes somewhere in the American heartland, candidacies didn't require a lot of money. Supporters circulated handbills detailing the nominee's past success at killing Indians, or his valiant Civil War service, or his political background. Very few voters ever set their eyes on a presidential candidate.

The dawn of the 20th century brought change. Automobiles and airplanes now allowed candidates to travel to areas of the country that railroad trains couldn't reach. A candidate who visited every state could claim to represent the entire electorate. But cars and planes burn gas, which burns money, and money must come from somewhere. Once a nomination was settled, the financial resources of the party establishment could be applied against its candidate's needs. If several candidates vied for the nomination, however, the national committee was loath to favor one over another with dollars, lest it engender the same criticism the Democratic National Committee encountered for using "super delegates," those chosen by party leaders, and for otherwise privately supporting Hillary Clinton over Bernie Sanders in 2016. The primary system that had originated at the start of the 20th century, meanwhile, had taken the battle for the nomination (partially) out of the hands of political bosses, but giving the nominating process over to the voters multiplied the aggregate costs involved to the aspirants. Who would pay for a primary campaign that might last a year or more?

At mid-century television entered the picture, and politics changed for all time. Never again would a dying president run successfully for reelection, as Franklin D. Roosevelt had done in 1944. The TV camera spoke in a new and distinct language, and image superseded substance. Richard Nixon salvaged his 1952 vice-presidential campaign with the "Checkers" speech, but his unshaven countenance in 1960 was no match for John F. Kennedy's movie-star looks and Ivy League self-assurance. Lyndon Johnson's supporters portrayed Barry Goldwater as a conduit to nuclear holocaust in 1964, punctuating this portrayal with ads showing imaginary mushroom clouds looming behind frightened children. In 1968 Nixon's political comeback was enabled by shocking telecasts from the Democratic National Convention in Chicago, where outside the arena, protesters battled with police, temporarily shifting the focus away from Vietnam and creating an us vs. them political universe (not unlike the current environment). The chaos enabled Nixon's "Silent Majority" to register its disgust with threats to law and order. In the space of eight years, television had caused Nixon to lose one presidential election and helped him to win another.

Nixon's resignation following Watergate, and his subsequent pardon by Gerald R. Ford led to a temporary interregnum for the Democrats, who won in 1976 with Jimmy Carter. But the big money remained with Republicans, who seized upon soaring inflation and ballooning interest rates and elected Ronald Reagan in 1980. Reagan thrilled every disciple of limited government and laissez-faire economic policy by declaring that government couldn't be the solution to the country's woes, because government itself was the problem. The former star of B-movies in Hollywood charmed the electorate by describing the country as a "shining city on a hill," and aided by a stock market boom that began in August 1982, was reelected overwhelmingly in 1984 over former Vice President Walter Mondale. The 1980s became a Wall Street decade, one that provided Republicans with the money and political momentum to overcome the Iran-Contra scandal.

The scandal dominated President Reagan's second term in office. The United States, through its intelligence network, sold surplus weapons to Iran (via Israel) and clandestinely and illegally transferred the profits from the weapons sale to Nicaraguan rebels known as Contras, who were then fighting a socialist regime and (an elected) leader, Daniel Ortega, that Republicans disliked. The Contras used tactics that amounted to terrorism, but Reagan insisted on calling them "freedom fighters." The obvious conclusion was that one man's terrorist is another's freedom fighter.

Vice President George H.W. Bush, a former head of the Central Intelligence Agency, somehow managed to convince voters he'd been "out of the loop" during the scandal, a claim that defied credulity given his close identification with spy agencies and their covert operations. Bush was himself elected president in 1988. Crucial to his election success was a televised ad highlighting the crimes of recidivist criminal Willie Horton, who had been released from prison in Massachusetts during the governorship of Michael Dukakis, Bush's opponent in 1988, only to commit another violent crime.

Perhaps more crucial to Bush's victory was the abandonment in 1987 of the Federal Communication Commission's Fairness Doctrine, which since 1969 had required broadcasters to present balanced coverage of partisan issues. In theory, at least, the doctrine would have required television stations presenting the Willie Horton commercial to offset its impact with a reminder that the program under which Horton was released from prison had been instituted under a Republican governor. Then, voters could have decided for themselves whether Horton's release should have become a political issue, or not. The debate over the Fairness Doctrine was in fact a proxy for a larger battle for political control of the airwaves. Republicans had complained for years about "liberal" control of the media, and with the Fairness Doctrine no longer an obstacle, they applauded an opportunity to "get even" with liberals.

Fox Network debuted in 1986, its entry timed perfectly to benefit from repeal of the Fairness Doctrine. Fox professed objectivity, using phrases like, "We report, you decide," but from the outset, nothing it reported could be mistaken for balanced journalism. Its audience, primarily males age 50 and over, welcomed it as an antidote to what many viewers saw as a uniformly left-wing broadcasting universe, one geared toward political correctness and identity politics. As if to punctuate its distinctly Republican orientation and acknowledge its adversarial role in the new left/right battle for network supremacy, Fox brought Roger Ailes aboard as CEO in 1996, the same Roger Ailes who had led George H.W. Bush's successful election run in 1988 and is now regarded as a pioneer in the art of political skullduggery.

Under Ailes, Fox consistently won the ratings battle over CNN and the major networks, which divided the "liberal" audience. Fox chose an "issue du jour" every morning, then presented it from a right-wing perspective through a broadcasting team led by Bill O'Reilly, Sean Hannity, Tucker Carlson, and Neil Cavuto. In 2018 Fox still leads the pack, even though Ailes (who died in 2017) and O'Reilly were forced out by credible charges of sexual harassment by former employees, accusations that paralleled the ascendancy of the #MeToo Movement. Its political advertising is always slanted in favor of Republican candidates, which preserves its "older white guys" target audience and has helped the GOP maintain control of Congress and the White House.

Barack Obama found a way to at once counteract Fox Network and a money-in-politics burden for Democrats, one that has since been exacerbated by the Supreme Court's Citizens United decision, allowing unlimited corporate donations to candidates. In 2008 Obama's campaign sought small donations ($5 and $10) from on-line sources, a strategy cocky Republicans sneered at as climbing Mount Everest in baby steps, but which succeeded and remained as a template for subsequent campaigning at the state and local levels. The idea is simple yet ingenious; most people can afford a few bucks, and every donor becomes part of the Democrats' team going forward and a target for further donations. That said, it remains to be seen if the small-donation model will survive its current overuse by candidates who flood the inboxes of frustrated users.

It's reasonable to wonder how a candidate for Congress 2,500 miles away could ever expect financial help from people who might or might not even know the name of their own Congressional representative. Not only do these candidates expect support, they demand it several times a day, addressing voters they'll never meet by their first names in a grotesque exercise of faux bonhomie. Between demands for daily contributions come urgings to sign Michelle Obama's birthday card, or a plea to thank Ruth Bader Ginsburg for not resigning her seat on the Supreme Court (!). These requests are approximately as welcome as a late-night telephone call from someone (on a recorded line, of course) pleading the cause of the endangered lemur, now facing extinction in the dark jungles of Madagascar.

CHAPTER 26: THE WAR ON CHRISTMAS AND OTHER POLITICAL WARS

Nothing separates the two major parties more paradigmatically than so-called political correctness. Originally used in literal terms to define the appropriate context in which to discuss a political issue, it has been redefined by satirists on the political right. The phrase is used as a rejoinder to claims of insensitivity on the part of mainstream Americans (white males, essentially) toward minorities and other groups identified as victims.

As part of its ongoing campaign against political correctness, Fox Network reported that a "war on Christmas" had been declared. Fox wasn't referring to the Christmas story, as told in the gospels of Matthew and Luke. No war was declared against the Baby Jesus Himself, or against Mary, Joseph, and the Wise Men. Shepherds tending their flocks by night weren't soldiers in the war. The battle was not being fought in Bethlehem; the theater of war was the consumer universe, and the specific target was anyone who conspicuously avoided saying "Merry Christmas" and substituted a more secular holiday greeting.

The exact time in history when saying "Happy Holidays" became preferable to "Merry Christmas" can't be identified, but the motivation for the changeover remains clear. The retail industry depends heavily on the Christmas shopping season, which begins before most Americans have digested their Thanksgiving turkey. At midnight, "Black Friday" begins, and stores from coast to coast open their doors to voracious shoppers seeking the bargains of a lifetime, even at the cost of a good night's sleep. These bargain hunters include Christians who will be celebrating the birth of Jesus a month later, but also number among them Jews, Unitarians, Muslims, agnostics, atheists, and others who like bargains but think their religious beliefs, and whether those beliefs intersect with their shopping habits, are nobody else's damn business.

As if to acknowledge that Christmas shopping is separate from Christianity's celebration of the Nativity, retailers replaced signs urging everyone a merry Christmas with others wishing shoppers happy holidays. Sales clerks were instructed to use the more neutral phrase, and sales catalogues were revised accordingly. A greeting card in December from a non-Christian friend was more likely than not to avoid any religious connotation. "Greetings of the Season" became familiar. Because Jews celebrate Chanukah in December, and African-Americans of various faiths observe Kwanzaa at the end of December, using "Happy Holidays" or "Season's Greetings" in lieu of "Merry Christmas" became more inclusive and less likely to offend.

Just as the battle over the Fairness Doctrine served as a proxy for political control of network broadcasting, so the war on Christmas became a weapon in the larger battle over political correctness amid a culture war. Fox Network was happy to point out, and chide sarcastically, the trend on college campuses toward identifying all Caucasians as "privileged" individuals. Whites were always reminded to "check your privilege" before voicing any political view that might offend a member of an identity group. The fact that a given student whose skin happened to be white might have grown up in a poor or broken home, and was anything but privileged, didn't matter. White people were privileged, and it was important for them to recognize the fact.

The central issue for Fox Network in the war on Christmas wasn't Christmas, it was political correctness. To the extent that Fox demonstrated that "p.c." can be taken to unreasonable lengths, it proved its point.

The Founding Fathers wanted to keep church and state separate. The Constitution forbids state-sponsored religion while it protects the free exercise of all religious beliefs. But prominent leaders of the Christian right like Pat Robertson and Franklin Graham tend to equate morality with the original meaning of political correctness, i.e., whatever is acceptable to discuss in the public sphere. To them, the Fairness Doctrine shouldn't apply to on-air questions that bear upon religion, because to fundamental Christians, their view of morality is an absolute. Any balancing view, advanced for secular reasons, must necessarily be less than moral. For example, if abortion is murder, any discussion of a woman's reproductive rights is invalid, as said discussion collides with an opposing moral imperative.

In one respect it isn't surprising that a spat over how to wish someone a joyful holiday could have morphed into a "war" on Christmas. Article II Section 2 of the Constitution assigns to the legislative branch (Congress) the power to declare war. This prerogative was affirmed in 1973 by the War

Powers Act, passed by Congress over President Nixon's veto. But since the last actual declaration of war, which followed the Japanese attack on Pearl Harbor in 1941, the United States has engaged in military action in Korea, Vietnam, Cambodia, Lebanon, Grenada, Kuwait, Kosovo, Iraq, Afghanistan, and Syria, without once declaring war. The word "war" has stood for armed strife between combatants historically, but that usage complicates an interventionist foreign policy that insists on intruding upon the affairs of sovereign countries overseas without the need to declare war. Paradoxically, "war" has come to stand for non-military initiatives, wherever the executive branch needs rhetorical reinforcement for its objectives. But any phrase beginning with the words "war on" should be viewed skeptically.

The "war on terrorism" justified the invasion of a sovereign foreign country that had nothing to do with the terrorist attacks on 9/11/2001, but the validation of which derived from those attacks. At least Shock and Awe was justified in the minds of politicians who approved the invasion and turned away from evidence of torture that they euphemistically called "enhanced interrogation techniques." The war on terrorism also led to illegal governmental spying on private citizens. The never-ending "war on drugs" has succeeded only in elevating the cost of addictive drugs at street level, a cost that converts addicts into dealers and subjects them to 20 years-to-life prison sentences upon conviction, even as a violent criminal in the adjoining cell serves less than half that long. The preface "war on," when attached to a societal malady, dates to President Johnson's self-proclaimed War on Poverty, which either (to Democrats) lifted America's underclass to a decent standard of living once and for all, or (to Republicans) set in motion a permanent dependency on government for millions who might otherwise be supporting themselves in the workforce.

Editor's note: It did both, but don't tell anyone, because both parties use one version or the other for a theme.

Between 1861 and 1865, Americans fought a real war, one which resulted in more casualties than any other in our history. But even that effort fell victim to semantic quibbles over its name. Most history students and educators call it The Civil War, albeit "civil war" is a generic term that applies to any internecine conflict. Southerners prefer to use The War Between the States, which in fact better describes the struggle. But that usage tends to mitigate accusations of treason against Confederates that persisted for decades in the form of "bloody shirt" politicking by Republicans, while erroneously portraying the war as merely a four-year neighborhood spat that got out of hand. Whichever term one prefers, it should be noted that veterans of the war on both sides made peace with their erstwhile enemies long before politicians addressed questions that survive in 2018 CE, questions like, "Does it honor Southern tradition to display the Confederate battle flag, or is it simply a dog whistle to summon racists?" The right answer, of course, is, "It depends on the motivation of whoever chooses to fly it," but that answer satisfies neither side in today's polarized milieu.

Other symbolic relics of the antebellum era that persisted into the 20th century, but couldn't be resolved through political action, have been adjusted according to public opinion. It is no longer permissible for Caucasian performers to don blackface on stage, as Al Jolson once did. Interracial marriage, which was proscribed by law and custom as recently as the mid-20th century, is now taken for granted. Stephen Foster's lyrics in "My Old Kentucky Home" have been modified. Where once we sang, "...'tis summer, the darkies are gay," now "people" substitutes for the patronizing "darkies." No change is yet contemplated for "gay," but eventually someone will insist on converting the lyric to "joyful." The abiding lesson in this area of the culture war is that good will among neighbors will always accomplish more to resolve disputes than will spitting contests between partisan politicians in Washington, DC, or fake moralizing by television pundits.

Chapter 27: The Two-Party System and the Supreme Court

The mood in the United States as this is written can be described with a variety of adjectives. Words like "dark," "gloomy," "hostile," and "feverish" come to mind. One would infer that turnout for the 2018 mid-term elections should burgeon in proportion to the electorate's sense of urgency. But a New York Times analysis casts doubt on such conclusion.

Dr. Michael McDonald, a political scientist at the University of Florida, runs the United States Election Project, which has assembled data on turnout from 1789 forward. Dr. McDonald notes that the late 19th century, when the United States was less wedded to the two-party system than it is today, represented the peak of voter interest. Turnout exceeded 80% in some years. Even as late as 1914, mid-term elections drew over half the electorate to the polls, but that percentage has not been approached since. Among countries with developed economies, voter participation in the United States places us 26th out of 32.

Dr. McDonald points to West Virginia as a dramatic example of increased apathy among voters. In the presidential election year of 1952, turnout in the Mountain State was 77%. By the mid-term elections of 1998, the number had dropped to 29%. Times reporter Sabrina Tavernise interviewed middle-class West Virginians who portrayed the state as a once vibrant home to politically engaged workers. That condition has evaporated, replaced by a belief that activism by West Virginians inevitably yields to the entrenched power of "coal money." Editor's Interrogatory: Coal money, in the year 2018 CE?

Lula Hill, a hotel owner who first voted in 1952 but has since given up trying to make a difference, cites Washington politicians for blame. "All they're doing is slinging mud at one another," she laments. Significantly, Ms. Hill refrains from blaming either major party for the current state of affairs in Washington. But if neither party is responsible, it might follow that neither party is in a favorable position to remedy the problem.

Whereas the willingness of voters to exercise their franchise once had little relationship to economic class or educational background, that is no longer the case, according to Jonathan Nagler of New York University, who authored "Who Votes Now" in 2014. Nagler writes that twice as many college-educated voters go to the polls today, as do adults lacking a high-school diploma. Historian Alexander Keyssar of Harvard University, author of "The Right to Vote," cites a class division in the country, wherein large blocks of disengaged citizens have lost all sense of empowerment.

In a New York Times column written after the explosive testimony of Christine Blasey Ford and the response from Judge Brett Kavanaugh, but prior to the vote that confirmed Kavanaugh's appointment to the Supreme Court, David Brooks stopped just short of blaming the two-party system for hearings that, according to a recent poll, found 69% of Americans describing as "a national disgrace." Brooks' piece, titled "A Complete National Disgrace," cited what he called "the unvarnished tribalization of national life." Brooks conceded that efforts he and like-minded individuals and organizations had undertaken in recent years, not specified but aimed at reducing political polarization and promoting healing, have been a "complete failure."

At first blush, the realities Brooks lamented would seem to contradict the fact of steadily declining voter participation. If the public is split down the middle into tribes (we'll call them Hatfields and McCoys for illustrative purposes), shouldn't the mutual enmity between them lead to greater participation in the democratic process? Shouldn't every Hatfield and every McCoy be camped outside the voting booth before the polls open, eager to teach those hateful people on the opposing side a lesson?

The present author's answer is, "Most voters aren't named Hatfield or McCoy, and don't engage in tribal warfare." If one assembled together every non-affiliated voter, every third-party registrant, and all moderates within the two major parties into a single political unit, it would constitute a decisive majority of the electorate. Just as most citizens wouldn't want to involve themselves in any dispute between warring families in the Appalachian Mountains named Hatfield or McCoy, most voters would rather not have to choose sides between extremists named "Republican" and others named "Democrat." So, rather than make such an unpalatable choice, or trying to determine which of two unappealing candidates is the lesser of two evils, many voters just stay home.

Maybe it does make sense, after all. A citizen's call to duty at the voting booth is frequently appended by the familiar warning, "If you don't vote, you have no right to complain later." Are non-participant voters less than civic minded? Are they unpatriotic? Not if one acknowledges that the lesser of two evils, by definition, is evil. And if both candidates represent evil, complaining about the winner's platform is defensible, whether one has voted or not.

Political activists have become conditioned to reaching out to, and contributing money to, whichever major party more closely mirrors their hopes and aspirations. Every day of the week a new poll, scientifically conducted, reflects the most up-to-date public opinion, meaning both parties always know where the voters' toast is buttered. Why then, are fewer and fewer voters identifying themselves as either Democrats or Republicans, and why has voter turnout continued to decline since 1914?

The answer might be, "Because the two major parties continue to let *their own people* down." This isn't immediately evident to pollsters or to the media, because the leaders of both parties blame the opposition for every failure. This gets the leaders off the hook and helps them retain power, aided further by a seniority system that rewards entrenchment at the expense of merit. But the blame game leads to negative voting ("I'd never vote for _____") and to voter apathy.

Any discourse on low turnout is indivisible from the reality that many eligible voters are denied the franchise during the registration process. This phenomenon was glaringly evident in 2000, when the Republican-controlled Florida Department of State systematically excluded thousands of first-time registrants, predominantly minority citizens who would have been expected to vote Democratic, on technical grounds that included minor discrepancies on their applications. In the most flagrant example of Florida's discriminatory practices, an African-American named James Johnson was denied the right to register as a one-time felon (Florida bans even ex-felons who have completed their prison sentence from registering, although that is now about to change). Johnson denied having ever committed a crime, but the voting official pointed to a list showing "James Johnson" as a former felon. Mr. Johnson had the misfortune of owning a common name. He couldn't prove a negative, so he was denied the right to register.

Other voters who have registered are interdicted for a variety of reasons. Possibly their photo-ID doesn't match their appearance (the photo might be 20 years old), and the voting official suspects fraud, or the original signature from their registration differs from the script at the polls. Maybe the voter's correct address is called into question. In all such cases, voters are provided with provisional ballots, to be tallied subject to review of the questionable circumstances. History has shown, however, that most provisional ballots are never counted.

President Trump would have Americans believe that because millions voted illegally ("voter fraud"), Hillary Clinton tallied almost three million more votes in 2016. He appends the assertion to his anti-immigration stance and the need for a border wall. His claim has long since been investigated thoroughly, and debunked, but half the country still believes it. Seldom discussed, because the issue is technical in nature and therefore defies oversimplification by politicians, is the question of "electoral fraud," whereby electronic voting machines and regional tabulators can be programmed to flip votes from one candidate to another. There remains little doubt that John Kerry carried Ohio in 2004, won in the Electoral College, and should have been inaugurated as president, but that eleventh-hour electoral hijinks at an out-of-state (Tennessee) tabulating site allowed George W. Bush to remain in office. As discussed in an earlier chapter, only the Libertarian and Green parties cared enough about democracy to challenge the result.

Republicans focus on voter fraud, Democrats complain about unfair registration practices. Neither talks about electoral fraud, except privately and without partisan emphasis, because complexity doesn't translate well into campaign tactics. But allegations about unfair voting practices have an enervating effect on the public mood, and inevitably, upon voter turnout.

CHAPTER 28: THE TWO-PARTY SYSTEM AND MOTHER NATURE

Calamities affecting hundreds of thousands of Americans should be divorced from partisan politics. It is a measure of the toxicity that infects the two major parties in 2018 that Hurricane Michael, which struck the Florida panhandle with 155 mph winds in October 2018 and caused loss of life and historic property damage, should engender sniping between candidates for the Florida governorship.

Playing politics with natural disasters is a recent phenomenon, and ironically arose following good-faith efforts by government officials to prepare for them. No one remembers that Benjamin Harrison was president during the Johnstown Flood of 1889. Nobody blamed President Theodore Roosevelt for the earthquake and fire that devastated San Francisco in 1906. The Dust Bowl of the 1930s exacerbated the Great Depression and forced tens of thousands of farming families to move from the prairies of mid-America to California, but Franklin D. Roosevelt's popularity wasn't affected. The 1980 eruption of Mount St. Helens in Washington State, following a series of earthquakes, cost 57 people their lives, but resulted in no political harm to President Jimmy Carter.

Somehow, hurricanes are different. They can become political footballs, especially when a government agency that has been created to deal with natural disasters fails in its duty.

After the Federal Emergency Management Agency (FEMA) was created in 1979, then elevated to cabinet-level status in 1996 (by a Democratic president in both cases), its makeup has been challenged by Republicans as a parking place for political patronage (not without justification). As a government agency created under Democrats, FEMA was subjected to severe budget cuts by President George W. Bush in 2001. In response to the terrorist attacks of 9/11/2001, Bush created the Department of Homeland Security; in the process, he downgraded FEMA by making it a branch of the DHS. As if to punctuate the downgrading, a lawyer with a Republican pedigree but no background in dealing with emergencies, Michael Brown ("Brownie" to the president, who often assigned affectionate nicknames to people), was appointed head of FEMA.

Then Hurricane Katrina struck New Orleans and its environs in August 2005, and never since has any natural disaster escaped an aftermath of political gamesmanship. An underfunded FEMA was slow to respond to the emergency. Meanwhile, President Bush was photographed in an airplane, flying over New Orleans en route to the West Coast and gazing downward with a puzzled look on his face. For his part, FEMA Director Brown looked lost, and when President Bush was quoted as saying, "You're doing a terrific job, Brownie," the erstwhile lawyer became grist for comedic wisecracks on late-night television and the Internet. Bush himself became a target of ridicule for demonstrating that the Peter Principle applies equally to those responsible for hurricane preparedness.

Many New Orleans residents were relocated to Houston. The president's mother, Barbara Bush, herself a Houston resident, applauded the move, awkwardly suggesting that those displaced were better off in out-of-state hotels than in their own homes. New Orleans folks who stayed behind, whether from choice or necessity, were reassured by Mayor Ray Nagin, a Democrat, that they would be "taken care of." Nagin was planning to run for reelection in 2006, and he reminded voters that New Orleans was a "chocolate" city (heavily African-American), thereby converting a natural disaster into an exercise in identity politics. He won the 2006 election, but things went downhill for Nagin after that. He's currently serving a ten-year prison sentence, following his 2014 conviction on corruption charges.

The Florida governor's race in 2018 pits two surprise primary winners against each other. Democrat Andrew Gillum is mayor of Tallahassee, which received an indirect hit from Hurricane Michael. As the hurricane approached the Florida panhandle, Gillum suspended campaign activities and remained on the home front, and asked his Republican opponent, Rep. Ron DeSantis, to put politics aside until the hurricane passed. DeSantis did help emergency workers load supplies to be delivered to victims of the storm, but he failed to suspend negative television ads that portrayed Gillum as a socialist. His campaign claimed to have asked stations in the affected areas (only) not to show them, but that these requests had arrived too late. For his part, DeSantis dismissed criticism by saying, "It is what it is." The irony of the situation is that Hurricane Michael caused such extensive power outages that the negative ads couldn't have been viewed in the Florida panhandle, anyway.

If the Republican party thinks the weatherman is a partisan Democrat, they might have a point. Hurricane Maria devastated Puerto Rico in September 2017, resulting in almost 3,000 deaths and catastrophic property damage. President Trump lauded FEMA for its response to the disaster, his boast being based in part on erroneous claims that the death toll had been only 64, not the actual total, as revised months later. Stung by partisan criticism that the White House had deliberately understated the casualties in the immediate aftermath for political advantage, the president suggested that the revised number was wrong. He claimed, without providing evidence, that the higher figure included deaths since 2017 that were unrelated to the hurricane. He punctuated his revisionist argument by suggesting that the governor of Puerto Rico and the mayor of San Juan had been neglectful during the storm.

Five years before FEMA came into being, Senator Quentin N. Burdick (D-ND) introduced the Disaster Relief Act of 1974. It streamlined procedures for delivering federal aid in the event of a hurricane, earthquake, volcanic eruption, etc. It passed without a single dissenting vote in either branch of Congress and was signed into law by President Nixon in May 1974. In 1988 the Robert T. Stafford Disaster Relief and Emergency Assistance Act incorporated FEMA's responsibilities into a revision of the 1974 act, which also passed without partisan wrangling. In the event of a major disaster, the president may declare it as such upon the request of the governor(s) of the affected state(s), provided the governor in question has first declared a state of emergency in the affected state.

In 1974, even amid heightened partisan tension in Washington due to Watergate, there was nothing remarkable about a bill that was first introduced by a Democrat enjoying unanimous bi-partisan support in the Senate and House, and then being signed by a Republican president. In 2018 members of the two major parties agree on nothing. A typical on-line argument in the wake of a major hurricane like Michael might go as follows:

Democratic Blogger: "Don't those #@++%$ Republicans understand that global warming increases the temperature of sea water and makes hurricanes more powerful?"

Republican Blogger: "Those *%$*@#@# liberals are at it again, blaming acts of God on politicians." Democratic Blogger: "Global warming is no act of God, buster. Have you read Al Gore's book, An Inconvenient Truth?Republican Blogger: "Is that the book where Gore claims to have invented the Internet?"

And so it goes, ad infinitum, in the brave new world of the 21st century. Aldous Huxley never anticipated it, but George Orwell might have.

CHAPTER 29: THE TWO-PARTY SYSTEM AND GENDER WARS

When the United States of America came into being, there were no political parties and women played no visible role in public life. Betsy Ross supposedly designed the first flag, but she was never rewarded with the right to vote or hold office. Abigail Adams was a trusted adviser to her husband, John Adams, and raised John Quincy Adams, but was never granted any formal education. Dolley Madison ran the Executive Mansion for two presidents and reportedly saved George Washington's portrait when the British set the building on fire in 1814, becoming a national heroine by her efforts. But she died in poverty, decades before presidential wives were granted their first pension.

No female was accepted into any college or university until 1837, and none earned a degree before 1849. The 19th Amendment to the Constitution, guaranteeing women the vote, wasn't ratified until 1920, fully four years *after* Jeannette Rankin had become the first woman elected to Congress. No woman became head of a Fortune 500 company before Katharine Graham, at the *Washington Post* in 1972. The Equal Rights Amendment, first introduced in 1972, still awaits ratification by three-quarters of the states, although following its adoption by Illinois in 2018, it is only one state short at this writing.

Democrats are more often identified as women's rights advocates than Republicans, especially since Donald Trump's election in 2016. But it would be folly to assume that partisanship either retarded or advanced the growth of the women's movement, which most historians agree began at Geneva, NY, in 1848, led by Elizabeth Cady Stanton and Lucretia Mott.

Throughout the 19th century women's rights were generally subsumed into larger issues. Mott was an abolitionist first and a woman's advocate second. Stanton is best remembered as a suffragist, but was an abolitionist in her own right, a spokesperson for women in the workplace and the divorce court, and an early temperance advocate. Catharine Beecher, oldest daughter of Reverend Lyman Beecher and sister of Harriet Beecher Stowe and Henry Ward Beecher, focused on educational opportunities for young women but wasn't otherwise political. The temperance movement was closely allied with women's rights, in that physical abuse of women was identified with mistreatment by alcoholic men, so it isn't surprising that the 18th Amendment (Prohibition) and the 19th (Suffrage) were ratified a year apart.

Still, it's difficult to connect any specific advance by women with either major party, at least before the 1990s. Progressive Democratic icon Eleanor Roosevelt was on record before 1920 as being opposed to women's suffrage, while Republican Warren Harding endorsed the 19th Amendment and was elected president in 1920 with the aid of women's votes. Franklin Roosevelt did advance the women's movement by appointing the first female Cabinet official, Frances Perkins, as Secretary of Labor, but it was Ronald Reagan who nominated the first female Supreme Court justice, Sandra Day O'Connor.

Bill Clinton was the first president to emphasize gender in his appointments, no doubt owing to the influence of Hillary Rodham Clinton. As First Lady Ms. Clinton was authorized to design a national health insurance program, a departure from custom in that presidents' wives typically assumed less weighty responsibilities. The effort failed, in large part because Ms. Clinton refused to honor custom and share her plans with Congress. The First Lady also had influence on the president's choice for Attorney General, as evidenced by his nomination of three successive women to the post, these after first considering Hillary herself for the honor. Janet Reno was confirmed after two earlier nominees, Zoe Baird and Kimba Wood, had been forced to withdraw due to personal conflicts that were unrelated to gender issues. Clinton did nominate the first female Secretary of State, Madeleine Albright, and became the first Democrat to introduce a female Supreme Court justice, Ruth Bader Ginsburg.

Unfortunately, Clinton's affirmative action toward women failed to negate the less than chivalrous dialogue of his legion of supporters, one of whom chose to characterize Paula Jones, who had accused the president of sexual abuse, as "trailer trash." No one close to the president apologized for the defamatory statement, even in the face of press criticism. This invited fair-minded people to ask, "If Paula Jones were really 'trailer trash,' why was the governor of Arkansas cheating on his wife with this class of woman?" Not surprisingly, Ms. Jones responded with a lawsuit against President Clinton, a suit that led to his perjured testimony about his relationship with

Monica Lewinsky, and then to his impeachment. Clinton's acquittal in the U.S. Senate saved his presidency. But his exposure as a tomcat compromised his administration's self-image as a women's advocate.

By an accident of history Hillary Clinton, after serving in the Senate and as Secretary of State for President Obama, ran for president in 2016 and found herself opposing Donald Trump, who had been accused of sexual affairs with several women. Trump had also been caught on tape boasting that he had gotten away with grabbing a woman by her genitals. According to a Wall Street Journal article from January 2018, Trump lawyer Michael Cohen paid $130,000 to adult film actress Stephanie Clifford (aka Stormy Daniels) in October 2016, in exchange for her (signed) promise not to discuss an affair she claimed she had with Trump in 2006, while Mrs. Trump was in a recovery mode following the birth of their son.

If anyone other than Hillary Clinton had been Donald Trump's opponent in 2016, it's fair to conclude that individual would have won the election. But 52% of Caucasian *women* voted for Trump, even in the face of his cavalier attitude. They looked past Trump's tendency to judge women according to their physical attributes only, and they forgave his insulting remarks toward women who had somehow offended him, always couched in language that referenced their appearance. But as the tolerant wife of a known sexual predator, Ms. Clinton couldn't wax indignant toward Trump about sexual matters without sounding hypocritical. She asked voters to "make history" (by electing the first woman president), but to the extent that they considered gender in casting their ballots, voters evidently decided that a misogynistic male candidate was no worse than a female opponent who had overlooked misogyny in her own spouse.

The #MeToo movement hasn't yet helped either major party gain at the expense of the other. For every Republican celebrity or politician accused credibly of sexual misconduct, there's a Democrat somewhere being cited for the same. Sex always sells, so television will never tire of covering the latest accusation against a public figure, with left-leaning networks like CNN and MSNBC emphasizing allegations against conservatives in politics or broadcasting, while Fox Network prefers to highlight liberals. If politicians weren't ranked somewhere between used car salesmen and fortune tellers in terms of public acceptance, voters might be less willing to accept a president who treats the opposite sex in such a brazen manner. But with an approval rating somewhere around 40%, with Congress at 12%, Donald Trump is simply part of the swamp he promised to clear during the election campaign, but hasn't yet succeeded in draining.

President Trump is an underrated political strategist. From the internal chaos in the White House, as described by Robert Woodward in his best-selling book, *Fear*, a pattern has emerged of clever focus-shifting from a potentially threatening issue to one in which Trump can seize the initiative. The media are happy to pursue any new story angle, so the strategy works.

The #MeToo Movement, having been re-energized by the nomination of Brett Kavanaugh to the Supreme Court and the perceived mistreatment of his accuser, Dr. Christine Blasey Ford, clearly threatened Republican prospects for the November mid-terms. Undaunted as always, the president simply announced that his administration is considering a change in its official recognition of sexual identity, i.e., one's genital structure at birth becomes that individual's permanent gender identification. Under the change in policy, a sexual change (in either direction) at any future point isn't recognized by Washington.

Transgender people might well be enraged by the decision, but Trump no doubt reasoned, "They aren't going to vote Republican, anyway." Meanwhile the president has reconnected with his base of Christian conservatives, who view sexual issues through a religious prism, not as matters of gender bias or individual rights. From an argumentative standpoint, he has "moved the goalposts," turning a struggle between women and men into one setting heterosexuals against bisexuals. Experts in the genetics field concur that one's sexual identity can be separate from one's genital structure at birth. Politically, this can be dismissed as "fake science," a version of "fake news" within the current universe.

The fact that President Trump might well abandon the whole idea after the elections doesn't seem to matter to the media. The president knows that the press, and especially television, will always chase any controversial new story, especially one in which an identity group is affected. Nobody's mind will be changed, but the networks will sell a lot of sexual enhancement products to viewers whose libidos have been stimulated by the story.

CHAPTER 30: PARTISANSHIP VS. NON-PARTISANSHIP

This chapter invites readers to use their imagination. Is it possible for the government in Washington to conduct the people's business effectively under the current two-party structure, or is an entirely new paradigm necessary?

Whenever an Op-Ed appears in a newspaper that laments the intense partisanship in Congress, the writer typically waxes sentimental about the "old days," a time when leaders put aside party loyalty and worked together on an urgent matter facing the country.

Times have indeed changed, but the "old days" were more recent that the phrase suggests. A crisis like the terrorist attacks of 9/11/01 demanded unity, so the Patriot Act came into being with bi-partisan support. A respected senior figure like Republican Senator Bob Dole, who had lost the use of one arm in World War II, worked with Democrats to pass the Americans with Disabilities Act in 1990. President Bill Clinton put partisanship aside to pass welfare reform legislation, which at the time had been unpopular with most Democrats but was a priority of a Republican-dominated Congress.

In 2018 such bi-partisan cooperation is difficult to imagine. The Affordable Care Act was passed by Congress without a single Republican vote. The recent tax bill, featuring a large cut in corporate tax rates and a doubling of the standard exemption, passed with zero support from Democrats. Is it realistic to believe that not one single Republican could conclude that covering millions of Americans who could not otherwise buy health insurance due to preexisting conditions, was in fact a desirable social advance? Only if one ignores the prior claim of Republican leader Mitch McConnell that his party's overriding goal (which superseded the public interest wherever necessary) was making Barack Obama a one-term president. How is it that every Democrat ignored the potential for accelerated economic growth from a large tax cut, instead focused only on perceived inequities between economic classes within the bill? It makes sense if one accepts that Democrats wanted to deny President Trump a political victory at any cost, and further that party leaders used leverage against any member who threatened to render an independent judgment.

Party loyalty is enforced in various ways. A member who strays from the party line will find it hard to obtain financial support for the next campaign. Sometimes party leaders will encourage opposition to the disloyal rascal from within the party at the next primary. The same traitor to the cause, who hopes to serve on, say, the influential Ways and Means Committee or Appropriations Committee, might instead end up on the less desirable Native American Affairs Committee, even if he or she represents an urban district somewhere and had never once met a Native American. If party leaders aren't sure whether a representative is on board for favored legislation, the party Whip is summoned to remind the wayward miscreant of the penalties for voting one's conscience.

The word "whip" is capitalized in the previous paragraph for effect, and because it's an official position in both parties. A Whip ranks just behind the party leaders in both houses, and in the Senate behind the president pro tempore of the party in power. Its genesis coincided roughly with the end of the Victorian Era, arguably because before Queen Victoria's death in 1901, the word picture it evoked, that of a politician cracking a whip in the direction of a colleague, might have offended accepted standards of Victorian delicacy. Possibly Her Majesty had nothing to do with it, and only the progressive turn-of-the-century political resurgence stimulated both parties into more aggressive tactics.

Republicans in the House named their first Whip in 1897, and Democrats followed in 1900. The Senate, with a more chivalrous self-image than the House, waited until 1913 (Democrats) and 1915 (Republicans) before establishing the position.

Sometimes being a party whip can lead to bigger (but not necessarily better) things. John Sparkman leveraged his years as Democratic House Whip into the vice-presidential nomination in 1952. Erstwhile whips Carl Albert (OK), Tip O'Neill (MA), and Nancy Pelosi (CA) became House Speakers, having first proven their mettle as persuaders. On the Republican side, Leslie Arends (IL) whipped people from 1943 until 1975, a longevity record that might never be broken. Newt Gingrich (GA) was rewarded by becoming Speaker of the House, and one-time GOP whip Dick Cheney (WY) was appointed Secretary of Defense in the Bush 41 administration, then was elected vice president in 2000 after first nominating himself for the position without the need for a whip.

If one isn't quite cruel enough to be the party's whip, subordinate whip roles are available in both parties. Democrats introduced the role of Chief Deputy Whip in 1955, and apparently liked the idea so much that they created multiple chief deputy whips. If nothing else, this demonstrated that it's possible to have more chiefs than Indians in a national party's leadership, especially if one has never served on the Native American Affairs Committee. The Democrats' first Chief Deputy Whip was Hale Boggs (LA), who did so well that he later became Majority Leader. He also served on the Warren Commission, where Boggs (officially) agreed with its conclusion that Lee Harvey Oswald acted alone in the murder of John F. Kennedy. Someone on the commission must have cracked the whip to gain unanimity, because in private Boggs did not believe that Oswald had acted alone.

Republicans were more circumspect and waited until 1981 before creating the subordinate job. In the GOP there is only one Chief Deputy Whip at a time. The first was 33-year-old David F. Emery of Maine, who lost his job not through ineptitude as a young whippersnapper, but because his constituents at home voted him out of office. Emery was last seen as Deputy Commissioner of Administrative and Financial Services in Maine, a job he quit after 16 months, possibly because Governor Paul LePage wouldn't allow Emery to be *Chief* Deputy Commissioner of Administrative and Financial Services.

Maine is a quirky state politically; bless its Downeastern heart. In 2012 it elected an Independent, Angus King, as Senator (previously King had served as Maine's governor). Independents don't have a whip position of their own in Congress (it's almost a contradiction in terms), but because King and Sen. Bernie Sanders (I-VT) must caucus with one party or the other (both chose the Democrats), they remain available for a whipping at any time.

Maine's other Senator, Republican Susan Collins, responded to the call of party leaders and voted to confirm Judge Brett Kavanaugh to the Supreme Court. Republican Whip John Cornyn (TX) applauded, but Collins got whipped by angry women from coast to coast who couldn't reconcile her vote for an accused sexual abuser with her ongoing support for a woman's right to choose.

Senator Collins' self-proclaimed role model is the late Margaret Chase Smith (R-ME), the first woman to have served in both the House of Representatives and Senate. Ms. Smith was honored for her independence and willingness to challenge Republican orthodoxy, most dramatically by her opposition to the tactics employed by Senator Joseph R. McCarthy (R-

WI) at the height of Cold War tension in the 1950s. One cannot conceive of Margaret Chase Smith being hounded by a Republican whip at any time.

The reader is invited to consider the effect on civil discourse if a whip were used in deliberative circumstances outside the halls of Congress. Imagine a jury contemplating the fate of an accused felon; several jurors are skeptical about the prosecution's case, but the whip (appointed by the jury foreman, presumably) intrudes and reminds the heretics that unanimity is paramount, especially if everyone wants to get home in time for dinner. A conviction follows in due course. Or, consider a meeting at a church, wherein elders are deciding which of several applicants to call as a replacement for the retiring pastor. An impasse results. Every elder has a personal favorite, so a whip is chosen by lots who proceeds to browbeat fellow parishioners into accepting his or her personal choice.

It is a supreme irony of today's politics that every candidate for office is portrayed by the opponent as being enslaved to party leaders. Republicans cry, "[Democratic candidate's name] was handpicked by Nancy Pelosi." That's bad, of course, and probably not the case. Democrats reply, "Don't vote for _____, who's nothing more than a stooge for Mitch McConnell." True or not, the message is clear; voters should be entitled to elect someone to represent their interests, free from partisan obligations. And, members of Congress should be free to vote their conscience, even if the party whip returns to the leadership having failed in his solemn duty.

Of course, once such a candidate is sworn in, party leaders are quick to enforce discipline. If their initial efforts to deprive the new representative of independent thoughts fail, the newcomer will run afoul of the party whip. Well, at least the chief deputy whip.

Chapter 31: The Two-Party System Makes Strange Bedfellows

In *Conscience of a Conspiracy Theorist* (Algora, 2011), the present author prefaced comments made in an academic article by former Harvard University law professor Cass R. Sunstein, who later headed the Office of Information and Regulatory Affairs in Washington during Barack Obama's presidency. The book's central theme was that so-called conspiracy theories, while they often do reflect paranoia on the part of the theorist, are a natural response to governmental deceit. His statements showed that Sunstein was less concerned about governmental lies than about the skepticism they engender, because in his article he suggested that "government agents (and their allies) might enter chat rooms, online social networks, or even real-space groups and attempt to undermine conspiracy theories by raising doubts about their factual premises, causal logic or implications for political action." In other words, if the government is lying about something, the one thing that matters is preventing people from knowing the truth, or even theorizing about why the lies are being told.

That the United States has lied to its citizens repeatedly, unapologetically and without embarrassment, is not in doubt. The Central Intelligence Agency overthrew the leader of Iran, Mossadegh, in a 1953 coup, and lied about it until the late '70s, when a retired CIA agent revealed the truth in a memoir, reinforcing Iranians' long-held suspicions and contributing to the subsequent hostage crisis. It removed Jacobo Arbenz of Guatemala from power in 1954 through a second coup, and it lied about that. Both Mossadegh and Arbenz had been popularly elected, but their politics didn't suit certain Cold War imperatives. The CIA conspired to assassinate Cuba's Fidel Castro almost from the day he came to power in 1959, and used Lee

Harvey Oswald's murderer, Jack Ruby, to deliver weapons to anti-Castro Cubans. The CIA persistently denied any connection to Ruby or to Oswald himself, only to have its deceit exposed by the discovery of a 201 -file it had maintained on President Kennedy's accused assassin.

As early as 1963 former President Truman condemned the covert operations of the spy agencies, reminding Americans that he had created CIA simply to act as a meeting place for diverse intelligence reports, and nothing more. During the 1970s the Rockefeller and Church hearings detailed the extra-legal conduct of those same spy agencies. Undaunted, they have expanded their activities to include drug smuggling, torture, maintenance of secret prisons, and kidnapping of suspected terrorists or people with knowledge about terrorists.

President Trump competed for the Republican party's nomination in 2016 against former Florida governor Jeb Bush, among others. He derided Bush during the primary campaign as "low-energy Jeb," and made critical reference to his brother George W. Bush's presidential leadership, specifically his decision to invade Iraq and mismanagement of the aftermath. Since taking office Trump has been highly critical of the country's spy network, targeting the FBI most often, but the president's critical remarks seem to have been motivated by self-interest rather than any desire for reform. If anything, the CIA and FBI have drawn sympathy from Trump's verbal attacks.

President Trump's political allies include Alex Jones of Infowars, who represents the breed of conspiracy theorist that Professor Cass Sunstein and millions of Americans find dangerous, although Sunstein's article at Harvard made no distinction between Jones' tactics and honest skepticism of governmental truthfulness. Jones has developed a wide following through flights of fancy that include an allegation that the school shootings in Newtown, Connecticut in 2012 were staged, and that the children involved were "crisis actors." Jones persisted in the face of contrary evidence, even to the extent of revealing personal information about the parents of one victim, an act that has led to a lawsuit from the family and the banning of Jones from several social media organizations.

It isn't necessary to sympathize with Alex Jones personally to recognize that the rise of the Tea Party, and no less Donald Trump's election to the presidency, manifest a deep division in the body politic that began decades before Trump first thought about running for president. When Trump refers to a "deep state" in Washington that conspires to undo his initiatives, one cannot dismiss the notion without gainsaying everything we now know about recent history, and about the mendacity of spy agencies that purport to advance American ideals but in fact behave beyond the control of civilian leadership.

Cass Sunstein left his post at the Obama administration in 2012. In a recent article syndicated by Bloomberg News, he lamented the partisan division in the country in 2018, apparently without recalling the article he wrote at Harvard that suggested that conspiracy theories, in and of themselves, threaten governmental function. He saw no contradiction, apparently, between the rise of blatant hostility between political parties and his own writings, specifically his postulate that government should respond to conspiracy theories by invading the sites that give birth to them.

Sunstein's 2018 article, titled "Skip Party to Meet in the Middle," doesn't discuss the issues surrounding conspiracy theories. Instead he advanced his own conspiracy theory by referencing a report from More in Common, an organization he described as "an international initiative, seeking to reduce social divisions, [that] describes seven American tribes." Without identifying these tribes or the tribal nation to which they belong, the report Sunstein relies upon offered distinctions between Americans in terms of "group identity, such as nationality, ethnicity, gender and other factors [unspecified]," as highlighted by responses to certain questions. These questions also probed the responders' "belief in personal agency" and moral foundations of their judgments, such as the extent to which they believe in authority and purity (?); and several other items (also unspecified).

Sunstein proceeds to a discussion of "partyism." He doesn't define the term with specificity, but it's impossible to argue with his comment that "... partyism means that Republicans show automatic hostility and aversion to Democrats, and vice versa," or with his parenthetical addendum, "Partyism is significantly more pervasive among Republicans than Democrats." Sunstein then cites familiar political questions that have resisted compromise, viz. gun control, abortion, climate change, and immigration, and argues that the inability to reach consensus on these issues is inseparable from the fact that the two parties despise each other.

Very true. But how does one reconcile Sunstein's call for placing harmony over partisanship with his previous suggestion that government should penetrate the private deliberations of political groups in order to isolate (presumably destructive) conspiracy theories? The fact is, the word "government," under the two-party system that nobody asked for, stands for whichever party is in power at a given time in history. If challenging that government (meaning the party in power) on matters of truthfulness represents a conspiracy theory to anyone who represents the government from within that party, as it did to Sunstein himself, then any such challenge will necessarily become a test of credibility, and therefore not available for compromise. Democrats will assume Republicans are lying, Republicans will assume Democrats are lying. In fact, that's currently the case, as exemplified by the political ads circulating as we speak.

President Trump has been vilified, not without justification, for inventing the phrase "fake news." He uses the term very broadly, to include any news item, however truthful and fact based, that reflects badly on him personally. But whatever the president means by the term, the lies that have spewed forth from Washington, DC since the end of World War Two deserve to be categorized with even stronger verbiage than "fake news." References to a "deep state" cannot be divorced from the lies themselves or the damage they have caused to the government's standing with the public.

CHAPTER 32: NOBODY IS ALLOWED TO BE AN INDEPENDENT

According to an article by Philip Bump in the *Washington Post* dated January 11, 2016, titled, "The Growing Myth of the Independent Voter," (according to Gallup polling) 42% of American voters identify as independent rather than as a Democrat or a Republican. Bump adds that "...this has been the case for a while now, so (the percentages given) aren't by themselves earth-shattering." In the same Gallup poll 29% of interviewees identified as Democrats, 26% as Republicans. The present author recognizes that the numbers don't add up to 100, but please bear with us.

The article then proceeds to take the numbers apart. It arrives at the conclusion that only a small portion of the 42% who identified as independent were truly independent. Most leaned one way or the other, it seems, as was (supposedly) affirmed by statistics taken from the 2012 presidential election, when 90% of "Democratic-leaning independents" voted for President Obama, while 78% of "Republican-leaning independents" voted for Mitt Romney.

Casual readers might have failed to notice that Bump used the above percentages to arrive at a premise that isn't otherwise validated in the article, i.e., that most people who claim to be independent are really closet Democrats or closet Republicans. By using ex post facto logic, the writer never allowed for the likelihood that true independents might vote for a Democrat or a Republican without "leaning" that way, for a number of many reasons for doing so.

The Gallup numbers represent a *national cross-section of voters.* According to the U.S. Constitution, however, the Electoral College leaves it to the *individual states* to conduct all elections, including presidential elections, according to the states' own guidelines. It's very common for a given third-party candidate with limited funding to appear on some state ballots but not on others, simply because each state has its own requirements for listing.

A true independent voter in a state without a third-party candidate on the ballot, therefore, is left with a choice to make... 1) leave the presidential line blank, or 2) vote for whichever major-party candidate is perceived as the lesser of evils. Many Americans vote out of a sense of civic duty, and therefore would prefer #2, because option #1 represents an abandonment of that duty. In no way, shape or form should any "lesser of two evils" vote be construed as one cast because the voter leaned toward one major-party or the other. No independent voter should be assumed to "lean" toward one of the major parties, merely for refusing to leave the presidential line blank on Election Day in favor of exercising a right of citizenship.

What the *Washington Post* article represents is nothing more than establishment thinking, with a dollop of amateur psychology added. But anyone can play the amateur psychology game, too (see the following).

WaPo can abide a spirit of bi-partisanship within the voting public, because bi-partisanship is an everyday fact of life in Washington. Non-partisanship is a different breed of cat. A pursuit of non-partisanship suggests that the current political system, with its bi-partisan framework, has failed the public (is this wrong to suggest?). It implies that the two major parties have used bi-partisanship as a cover, while putting their own selfish interests ahead of the public interest (who would argue with that?). Above all, the non-partisan ideal relies on a presumption that mature adults in Congress should be capable of discussing, and possibly compromising, a sensitive issue without some party boss inflicting political damage therefor.

The *Washington Post* is part of the media that President Trump has described as an "enemy of the people." That's too harsh. We need a free press. But *WaPo* is a (Fortune 500) business first and a media outlet second. For them to concede that a plurality of American citizens regards the current two-party structure as antediluvian and ineffective, even if true, would reduce the paper's own standing in Washington. Inside the Beltway, individual politicians are often criticized. That's part of the game. But the system in which they function may not be criticized, because the *Washington Post* is a willing extension of that system. Calling for major reform editorially would be a self-destructive act on WaPo's part. It would lead to reduced circulation and reduced advertising revenues. Shareholders would revolt.

So much of the paper's political commentary is devoted to the daily spitting contest between Mitch McConnell and Chuck Schumer, or Democrats and the White House, that for *WaPo* to say editorially, "All these people are wrong, their tactics are hurting the country, and the public recognizes it" would be an abandonment of *WaPo's* core audience, meaning politically involved citizens who not only lean toward one party, but openly despise the other one. The national trend described by Gallup, with 42% of the public now describing itself as independent, doesn't apply inside the Beltway. The closer one gets to Washington, DC, the less likely one is to be above partisan politics.

In 1992 H. Ross Perot was a victim of the same establishment thinking. His independent candidacy for president drew 19% of the popular vote nationwide. It would have drawn more, but for the fact that the national media treated Perot as a caricature of himself, by highlighting his idiosyncratic personal mannerisms and his predilection for using a variety of (sometimes confusing) charts to support his arguments. His non-partisan approach to government and practical ideas were relegated to the background. His inexperience in government was emphasized, his great success in business deemphasized. As a volunteer for the Perot campaign that year, the present author can assure readers that most of the Perot voters he encountered would not have "leaned" one way or the other if Perot had not run. Almost all were equally disgusted with both parties, and especially with the negative tone of the campaign. Sound familiar today?

Why did a political newcomer from Texarkana, Texas do so well without media support in 1992? He was running in the first presidential election after the Clarence Thomas/Anita Hill debacle that reduced a Supreme Court nomination to the level of gutter politics. That was a turnoff. Voters still remembered the "Willie Horton" ads from four years earlier, and how the press had chased Gary Hart and his then current mistress aboard a yacht until Hart was forced to exit the race. The 1988 campaign had been the first in years in which negativism was the dominant characteristic throughout, the result being a public backlash four years later against both major parties.

The media applaud themselves for achieving "balance" in their coverage. If the scales balance between Democrats and Republicans in terms of volume and fairness, the media assume they've done their job. But what if the scale itself is broken? Achieving balance should take a back seat to repairing the scale, should it not? If 42 percent of the electorate sees itself as independent, while the two major parties enjoy 29 percent and 26 percent support, how honest is it to say that most of the 42 percent are only pretending to be independent while secretly favoring one of the other two parties? That's not analysis. It's making a wish the mother to a thought.

A future chapter will be devoted to speculating on possible independent candidacies in 2020. A candidate for president running without either Democratic or Republican support will have to overcome a multiplicity of handicaps. A lack of money is the most obvious problem for anyone who's less than independently wealthy. Less obvious is the fact that newspapers and television networks profit handsomely from portraying politics as a *mano a mano* contest between two bitter rivals. They typically lean toward one party or the other, but the media lean toward profits first. The party and candidate opposite to their editorial preference is always an integral part of the profit-making scheme, like the "bad guy" in professional wrestling. But an outsider who challenges the system as corrupt and ineffective is poison to the media, because the media are complicit in that corruption. Anyone like Ross Perot, then, must be kept subordinate.

An independent or third-party candidate in 2020 must have money. More than money, he or she must first be savvy to the workings of the media. Calling it the "enemy of the people" won't work, because that phrase has been patented. Understanding what makes television and the press tick is vital, however.

Donald Trump already knows the television part, because without his television career as an introduction, he'd never have run for president in the first place. Assuming only that he's still in office and running for reelection in 2020, his opponent will have to be his equal with the media.

CHAPTER 33: "JUDGE NOT, LEST YOU BE JUDGED NON-PARTISAN"

The furor over Brett Kavanaugh's nomination and eventual placement on the Supreme Court was almost entirely partisan. Only one Senate Republican, Lisa Murkowski (AK) voted against, and just one Democrat, Joe Manchin (WV) voted in favor. The raw partisanship exhibited by Senators surprised nobody. Residual anger over previous nominations, especially the refusal of Republican leaders to even consider President Obama's nomination of Judge Merrill Garland in 2016, made an impasse inevitable. The eleventh-hour entry of Dr. Christine Blasey Ford into the fray, and the fierce debate over her credibility and over Kavanugh's response to her allegations, changed nobody's mind, with the possible except of Murkowski's. If Dr. Ford had never come forward, the final vote would have been virtually identical. Her appearance merely made Congress look pathetic.

Lost in the debate over Judge Kavanaugh was a larger question. "If justice is to be free of all bias, whether it be racial, religious, gender-based, or political, why are judges ever subject to Democrat/Republican identifications in the first place?" A corollary question is, "Should judges have to meet a political test before they may sit on the bench?" Another is, "If a judge is elected following a campaign in which partisan issues intersect with legal issues (that often happens), would a later verdict by said judge be subject to appeal based on political bias, as had been demonstrated during the campaign?" Finally, "If a given candidate for a judgeship is unaffiliated politically, along with almost half the population, should he or she have to register with one of the major parties in order to get on the ballot?"

Not every election to the courts is necessarily partisan. The following conduct elections for state judgeships on a purely non-partisan basis: Arkansas, Georgia, Idaho, Kentucky, Minnesota, Mississippi, Montana,

Nevada, North Carolina, North Dakota, Oregon, Washington, and Wisconsin. Interestingly, these states are predominantly rural and small-town in character. Local matters typically take priority over national politics. One would expect to find elections in these areas, for mayors, comptrollers, sheriffs, and school administrators, to likewise be non-partisan. If your next-door neighbor is running, does party identification matter to you?

Michigan and Ohio are hybrid states. They do allow partisan identification during the campaign. On Election Day, though, ballots carry the name of neither party, so a voter for whom partisanship extends to the courtroom is tasked with remembering what happened during the campaign. For example, the question might be, "Is that candidate who promised to get tough on jaywalkers and loiterers a Democrat or a Republican?"

The six most heavily populated states subject all judicial candidates to a test of partisanship before appearing on a ballot, and these states also specify them as Democrats or Republicans on Election Day. Big cities have common problems; crime and law enforcement, drug traffic, guns, poor schools, racial conflicts, and poverty are all identified with national politics, in that the federal government often becomes involved in remediating them. It follows logically that any movement to remove partisanship from the election process in California, New York, Texas, Florida, Pennsylvania or Illinois would encounter resistance from the governors and mayors in those states, all of whom gained power through the two-party system, and many of whom are candidates for national office at any given time.

When one examines the history of governors who became presidential candidates, one finds that more heavily urbanized and populated states produce the majority. Since the dawn of the 20th century, the pattern has been consistent. Woodrow Wilson reached the White House from the state house in New Jersey, Franklin D. Roosevelt from New York. Adlai Stevenson had been governor of Illinois. Ronald Reagan led California, George W. Bush was governor of Texas, and Mitt Romney governed Massachusetts. Jimmy Carter from Georgia was the exception.

If one asks, "Has the two-party system contributed to a smoother administration of justice, anywhere?" only the most intense partisans would answer in the affirmative. If the question were, "Do Democrats or Republicans make better judges?" the response would follow partisan lines.

In less partisan times than the present, recommendations from the American Bar Association sufficed to establish qualifications for judicial candidates. The ABA was founded in 1878, under a constitution that sought "the advancement of the *science of jurisprudence* [!], the promotion of the administration of justice, and a uniformity of legislation throughout the country [!!]."

If the association has ever explained what it meant by the "science of jurisprudence," the explanation is lost to history. No doubt it connects in some way with the ABA's central mission, which is to establish academic standards for law schools. They were a rare sight in 1878 and certainly needed help from someone. But what really catches the eye in the ABA's founding document is its desire to bring about uniform legislation.

Therein lies the rub. For longer than anyone can remember conservatives have complained about liberal judges who "legislate from the bench." You can't blame the critics, when the American Bar Association included a desire to influence legislation as part of its constitution, which article runs counter to the separation of powers principle intrinsic to the Constitution. Giving the ABA the benefit of the doubt, in 1878 there was relatively little need to emphasize a separation of powers between the executive and judicial branches. Most lawyers had begun as apprentices to a senior attorney who might never have attended law school. In the beginning, the ABA's membership looked like that of an exclusive country club, with no female members before 1918 and no African-Americans until 1954. Who, before 1918, would have challenged an organization whose personnel structure was identical to the federal government's, and identical to the makeup of every major corporation in the country?

Ben Sasse (R-NE) is a member of the Senate Judiciary Committee. While a Republican and proud conservative, Sasse has been a frequent critic of President Trump and has gained a reputation as an independent thinker. When it comes to the American Bar Association, however, Sasse's views conform precisely to orthodox Republican doctrine.

In a speech on November 16, 2017, Sasse was quoted as follows: "The American Bar Association cannot make liberal arguments to the Supreme Court and then walk across the street and seriously expect that the hundred members of this body, in the United States Senate, will be treating them like unbiased appraisers." Sasse emphasized that the ABA is well within its rights to hold any opinion on any issue. But he then proceeded to cite "friends of the court" briefs the association had offered on matters involving the 2nd Amendment, Christian organizations on college campuses, the death penalty, same-sex marriage, and immigration. In every instance the ABA had taken a position favored by liberals. Thus, Sasse maintained, the bar association cannot profess political neutrality.

His argument would have been all the stronger, and even more satisfying to conservatives, had Sasse cited the founding document of the

ABA, specifically the clause calling for uniformity of legislation. Not every Republican holds an identical position on gun control, the death penalty, or same-sex marriage. But all stand for the separation of powers, and for the principle that judges should never legislate from the bench.

The present author has appeared for jury duty three times, once each in New York, Connecticut, and Florida. He has been selected to serve every time. No political opinion was ever advanced by any attorney or judge inside the courtroom, either during the jury selection process or the actual trial, let alone that any of the judges sought to preempt a legislator's responsibility. Yet the issue persists in the political realm, and divides Democrats and Republicans down the middle of the aisle.

Rhetorical question for the American Bar Association: "Would your leadership be willing to disavow its stated goal of bringing about uniformity of legislation, however innocuous that objective must have sounded in 1878, if the disavowal would mean that politics would leave the courtroom once and for all?" If the ABA is truly a liberal organization masquerading as politically neutral, it would be in the association's best interests to deprive Republicans of one of their pet issues. But it would mean entering the political realm to accomplish that goal, which in turn would affirm Republican arguments that the ABA is a political organization at heart.

CHAPTER 34: THE TWO-PARTY SYSTEM IS BAD FOR ONE'S
HEALTH

As this is written, four days before the 2018 mid-term elections, health care has become a potentially decisive issue in determining the makeup of Congress. Republicans control the White House and both houses, so one would expect that their ongoing criticism of the Affordable Care Act (Obamacare in their lexicon), rhetoric that helped them gain control of the Senate and add nine House seats to their majority in the 2014 mid-terms, would stand them in good stead with the electorate four years later.

Maybe not. Democrats have defended the ACA successfully by reminding the public that before its passage, folks with pre-existing conditions had great difficulty in finding affordable health insurance. Since most Americans, even those in good health themselves, at least have a friend or relative with a troubled health history or birth defect who can't qualify for coverage through the free market, the question of fairness has now superseded other considerations in the public mind. Should someone born with, say, a defective heart valve be permanently excluded?

The Affordable Care Act was passed in 2010 on a straight party-line vote. Republicans in Congress had openly declared their intention to limit President Obama to a single term, and the ACA had the potential for defining his presidency. So, the GOP decried the advance of "socialized medicine," perhaps forgetting that Medicare had been around since 1965. Medicare is socialized medicine if nothing else is, but as a successfully administered program, it has enjoyed the unanimous approval of a large voting bloc with a history of turning out at the polls...senior citizens. Medicare is now categorized as an entitlement, and even the most strident opponents of socialism know that repealing an entitlement is the third rail of national politics.

Civil libertarians and Constitutional hardliners within the GOP focused their attention on one clause in the ACA that bothered them the most, i.e., the "mandate" for everyone to buy coverage or else pay a penalty for refusing to do so. Democrats argued that absent the mandate, only sick people would buy coverage, and since private insurers were being utilized in the plan's implementation as an accommodation to Republicans (and some Democrats), it would mean premiums would have to reflect the negative morbidity factors involved, and thereby would be unaffordable for almost everyone. A mandate was the only available solution to the dilemma.

Legal challenges eventually brought the question of the ACA's viability to the Supreme Court, where Republicans assumed their ideological majority would prevail. But Chief Justice John Roberts, a conservative, disappointed the GOP by ruling that the mandate to buy coverage was effectively a tax, and therefore passed Constitutional muster in the same way any tax passed by Congress would. His vote proved to be the difference, and the Affordable Care Act survived.

Undaunted, Republicans vowed to press the issue until they were able to replace the ACA with their own health plan. They tried in 2017 with the support and encouragement of President Trump, but the GOP lost again when the late Sen. John McCain, whose relationship with the president had deteriorated due more to personal issues than to policy questions, rose from a sickbed and cast the deciding vote against the plan.

The question of coverage for preexisting conditions had been central to the debate over Medicare in the 1960s. Candidate John F. Kennedy made "medical care for the aged" a linchpin of his 1960 campaign, stressing the point that retirees typically lose their group health plans upon retirement, or at least the same benefits they had enjoyed. Because seniors frequently have a health history that precludes them from buying coverage at any affordable cost after they retire, if at all, and because younger voters wanted their parents and grandparents protected, Medicare became an added benefit to Social Security recipients, and part of President Lyndon Johnson's Great Society initiative.

In 1965, providing health insurance to seniors wasn't seen as discrimination against anyone under 65, because most in that demographic group were covered under group plans, either at work, through an association, or from a labor union. Those that were not otherwise protected were usually able to buy private coverage. But back then, corporations offered generous benefits as a hiring incentive, which included free hospitalization, major medical plans, and defined benefit pension plans, all of which became dinosaurs amid the late 20th-century globalization trend in business. Defined benefit pensions were replaced by 401-K plans, and the vacuum created by vanishing group health insurance has led to pleas for Congressional remedies.

Polls have consistently shown the public to be in favor of the Affordable Care Act, by almost two to one. No substitute plan that fails to cover preexisting condition will satisfy the majority, assuming the polls are accurate. This has forced Republican candidates in 2018 to proclaim their own support for coverage for everyone, but their ongoing opposition to obligatory participation has meant that policies offered under a GOP umbrella, to be affordable, will be inferior. And their late-in-the-game discovery of preexisting conditions as an issue unto itself has been greeted with media skepticism, given their vehement opposition to the ACA from the outset. President Trump's claim that Republican plans will cover preexisting conditions, and that Democrats' plans will not, was greeted with derision, deservedly so.

One Republican candidate for office who replied to the question, "What can a poor person without coverage do in an emergency?" with the response, "Go to the emergency room," was severely criticized in the media. The very fact that emergency room treatment is required of hospitals by law, irrespective of a patient's financial status, is largely responsible for exploding costs. Hospitals simply pass the cost of treating the indigent on to those who can pay (or to their insurers).

However the mid-term elections pan out, the political dynamic surrounding health care has shifted. Exploding costs of health insurance, and especially of prescription drugs, have neutralized long-standing ideological objections to socialized medicine. An effective argument has been advanced that the heavy promotional outlays by private insurers, and even by private hospitals, which are designed to persuade the public to shift their allegiances but also contribute to the exploding costs for everyone, would be obviated by any government control. Another point to consider is that damage suits for negligence, that often result in multi-million-dollar settlements because of runaway inflation in health care costs, would be moderated, because regardless of who was or wasn't negligent, accident victims would have unlimited availability of care at negligible expense. Litigators who live off huge damage awards and advertise their services with phrases like "for the people," would be the only losers. The effect would be not unlike that of "no fault" automobile insurance, in terms of keeping accident and health matters out of the courtroom.

There are other questions that should be asked, however. If everyone is covered for everything (Medicare for All), will there be enough doctors, nurses, and hospitals to handle the increased demand? Would delays result with respect to certain surgical procedures, as has happened in Canada and other countries with socialized medicine? If a doctor chooses not to participate in Medicare for All because its allowance for a service is too low, would that not exacerbate any shortage of doctors that exists?

What about cosmetic surgery? What about alternate forms of medicine, like chiropractic and podiatry? Is oral surgery considered dentistry, and if so, is it excluded? Are annual physical examinations covered? Periodic eye and hearing tests? What about flu shots and other preventive procedures?

Under Medicare for All, presumably Veterans Administration hospitals would close, because every veteran could opt for the nearest public or private hospital instead, which would be more convenient in most cases. Would the system be able to handle the added demand, or would new hospital construction be required? Could a V.A. hospital be reconstituted as a public facility? Would extended care facilities and nursing homes be covered under Medicare for All?

The above questions could be resolved, provided only that the two major parties find a way to place the public interest ahead of their selfish interests. At the end of the day, Medicare for All will become reality if enough voters go to the polls with the mind-set that health coverage is a human entitlement, regardless of health history or ability to pay.

Ronald Reagan, a conservative icon, allowed for a "safety net" to protect the masses. Reagan's safety net included food on the table, clothes to wear, and a roof over one's head. In the 21st century, will the safety net include free health care for all?

CHAPTER 35: THE MAN WHO UPSET THE TWO-PARTY DUOPOLY

In 1998 Minnesota voters went to the polls to elect a governor. The list of candidates included two sons of former vice presidents of the United States who had also been U.S. Senators, and one son of a former Minnesota governor and U.S. Secretary of Agriculture, all running under the Democrat-Farmer-Labor banner. The Republican candidate was a former Democrat-Farmer-Labor party member who switched to the GOP and was later elected to the U.S. Senate.

There were several minor-party candidates in the race, one of whom was a retired professional wrestler and actor. All among the latter group were regarded as potential spoilers, at best.

Hubert "Skip" Humphrey III had a perfect pedigree for politics. In 1948 his father and namesake stunned the Democratic National Convention in Philadelphia when, as the ambitious young mayor of Minneapolis and Senate candidate, he spoke out passionately in favor of civil rights, upsetting a delicate philosophical balance within the party between progressives and states-rights hardliners. Democrats in 1948 were still divided on segregation, so much so that J. Strom Thurmond of South Carolina led a breakout group of Southerners and ran for president as the Dixiecrat candidate. Humphrey's advocacy attracted nationwide attention on coast-to-coast television, and his Senate campaign succeeded. In 1964, after having lost the 1960 nomination for president to John F. Kennedy, Humphrey was elected as Lyndon Johnson's vice president. In 1968, following a turbulent year that saw the murders of Martin Luther King, Jr. and presidential aspirant Robert F. Kennedy, and a Democratic convention in Chicago that took place amid violent clashes between the police and Vietnam War protesters that were televised coast to coast, Hubert Humphrey was nominated for president.

He lost to Richard Nixon in a close race. When Humphrey died in 1978, his widow Muriel inherited his Senate seat, as if to preserve a family legacy. Now, in 1988, their son was running for governor.

Theodore "Ted" Mondale's father, Walter F. "Fritz" Mondale, has a strikingly similar and equally impressive (liberal) political resume. He was a two-term U.S. Senator from Minnesota, vice president under President Jimmy Carter (1977–1981), and a defeated presidential candidate in 1984. Mondale made history when he chose for his running mate Rep. Geraldine Ferraro, who became the first woman to appear on a presidential ticket. Ted Mondale sought to keep a family tradition alive as Minnesota's governor.

The 1998 contest in Minnesota involved several interconnected personal relationships. Mike Freeman, the third legacy candidate in the race, had worked as an advance man for Walter Mondale's 1972 Senate reelection campaign. His father, Orville Freeman, ran Hubert H. Humphrey's successful 1948 Senate campaign before serving as Minnesota's governor in the 1950s, and later served as Secretary of Agriculture in President Kennedy's Cabinet, a position he maintained throughout President Johnson's tenure.

Norm Coleman, the former Democrat and in 1998 the mayor of Minnesota's capital city, St. Paul, was the Republican candidate in the gubernatorial race. He was favored to win, if only because three well-connected members of the opposing party could be expected to divide the Democrat-Farmer-Labor vote.

Representing the Reform Party was Jesse Ventura, a former wrestler, actor, and motorcycle enthusiast who had served as mayor of Brooklyn Park, Minnesota from 1991 to 1995. Born James George Janos in Minneapolis in 1951, Ventura entered the Navy after graduating from high school, serving as an underwater demolition team member, but without seeing combat in Vietnam. Later he turned to wrestling, where he dubbed himself Jesse "The Body" Ventura.

Ventura had limited money to spend, so he toured the state, connecting with the public face to face while garnering generous television coverage, where his experience in front of a camera served him well. A self-proclaimed fiscal conservative who was liberal on social issues, Ventura admitted to a limited understanding of certain complex questions. Instead be asked voters to avoid "politics as usual." When the ballots were counted, Ventura shocked the pundits, if not himself, by winning with 37% of the vote, against 34% for Coleman and 28% for Humphrey.

The Minnesota governorship became the signature achievement of the Reform Party. Ventura left the party a year after being inaugurated governor, bothered by internal squabbles among the party officials, and became a

Libertarian. In 2003 he decided not to seek reelection, citing the effect that media criticism had had on his family. A wrestler expects to be booed by half the crowd and can laugh it off afterwards. Politics can invite more permanent hostility of the personal sort, that one lacking experience in the political game might be unprepared for.

Ventura's next stop, remarkably enough, was Harvard University, which hired him in 2004 as a fellow in the John F. Kennedy School of Government. If the elite Ivy League school, situated adjoining the city that bills itself without false modesty as the Athens of America, had ever before employed a mere high-school graduate as an instructor, that individual has not been publicly identified. If nothing else, by hiring Ventura Harvard was displaying an open-mindedness toward advancers of conspiracy theories, a posture that ran directly counter to the views of former Harvard law professor Cass Sunstein, as cited in an earlier chapter. Sunstein had suggested in a position paper at Harvard that a government beset by conspiratorial rumors should invade the sites were the ideas germinated, the better to counteract them. Now the same Harvard University was hiring as an instructor, a man who found it easy to imagine the worst from government and vocalized his suspicions.

As described in the preface to the present author's 2011 book, "Conscience of a Conspiracy Theorist," while at Harvard Jesse Ventura invited as a guest lecturer one David Fetzer, a former Marine-turned-college professor at the University of Minnesota-Duluth, whose field was the philosophy of science. Fetzer was there to discuss the Kennedy assassination with Ventura's class. A recognized ballistic expert, Fetzer had concluded from his research that the Warren Commission's conclusion, that Lee Harvey Oswald, acting alone, murdered John F. Kennedy, was impossible. Ventura was surprised at the time to find a gathering of older men in the lecture hall, dressed in business suits and clearly not college students. Several of these men interrupted Fetzer's comments with accusations that regardless of his qualifications. or the merits of his argument, the ex-Marine was *unpatriotic* for encouraging a distrust of government. In other words, if Washington covers up the cold-blooded murder of a president, anyone who points this out must be a disloyal citizen.

No doubt the experience at Harvard motivated Jesse Ventura to author a series of books that call the United States government to account. "*American Conspiracies: Lies, Lies and More Dirty Lies that the Government Tells Us*," which he co-authored with Dick Russell, was brought out by Skyhorse Publishing in 2010. In 2013 Ventura, Russell, and David Wayne combined on "*They Killed Our President: 63 Reasons to Believe There Was a Conspiracy to Assassinate JFK*," also published by Skyhorse. Through these books and others, and through his publicized quotes, Ventura has become identified in the public's mind as that most loathsome of characters, the conspiracy theorist. More recently the phrase has come to connote people without the stature of a David Fetzer, those who instigate wild theories to advance a self-serving political agenda or even to sell merchandise to gullible followers.

The phrase, which was created by the CIA to paint the agency's critics in a negative light, has become associated with President Trump and his followers, with good reason. The president uses his Twitter account to advance unproven but politically advantageous rumors, such as his claim that the caravan of Hondurans marching toward the Southern border of the U.S. was infested with Muslim terrorists, and separately that the refugees seeking to cross the border were hired by George Soros as a political tactic. These conspiracy theories are welcomed by the same dissident faction that elected Trump, the group that chants "Make American Great Again" and "Lock Her Up" (meaning Hillary Clinton), at the intermittent rallies the president conducts for no evident reason, wherever he can count on a welcoming throng of sycophants. One conspiracy theory with a factual basis is that some of these sycophants have been hired by Trump's own people to fill out the crowd.

The same conspiracy-loving faction interpreted the president's campaign theme, "Drain the Swamp," in no small part as a clarion call against governmental deceit. Trump's rudeness toward people and his tendency to make himself the matrix of every political question, should be separated from the fact that Washington, DC, as a political bastion, deserves every calumny voiced against it. Washington is a swamp. The president's approval rating has hovered around 40%, placing him among the least popular chief executives in history. But Congress stood at 12% as of October 2018 (pending an update), suggesting that the dog-whistle phrase, "Drain the Swamp," has a factual basis with the public.

In the meantime, the Republican Party has become "Trump's party," with nearly everyone falling in line, including a number of prominent Republicans who had earlier condemned his tactics. This holds true, notwithstanding the fact that Trump repeatedly abridges the so-called 11th Commandment, as attributed to President Reagan, "Thou shalt not speak ill of a fellow Republican."

CHAPTER 36: PARTY-SWITCHERS DON'T HURT THE DUOPOLY

It's time for a quiz. What do the following prominent American political figures, living and dead (here listed in alphabetical order), have in common?

- Treasury Secretary/Chief Justice Salmon P. Chase

- U.S. Senator Norm Coleman (Minnesota)

- Texas Governor/Treasury Secretary John B. Connally

- Vice President Hannibal Hamlin

- U.S. Senator Jesse Helms (North Carolina)

- U.S. Senator Trent Lott (Mississippi)

- New Mexico Governor Susana Martinez

- Texas Governor Rick Perry

- California Governor/President Ronald Reagan

- Secretary Of State Condoleezza Rice

- U.S. Senator Richard Shelby (Alabama)

- U.S. Senator J. Strom Thurmond (South Carolina)

- President Donald Trump

- 1940 Presidential Candidate Wendell Willkie

Next, what do the following have in common?

- U.S. Senator Lincoln Chafee (Rhode Island)

- Treasury Secretary/Chief Justice Salmon P. Chase

- First Lady/U.S. Senator (New York)/Secretary Of State Hillary Clinton

- Florida Governor/Congressman Charlie Crist

- Journalist/1872 Presidential Candidate Horace Greeley

- Congressman/New York City Mayor John V. Lindsay

- U.S. Senator Wayne Morse (Oregon)

- U.S. Senator Arlen W. Specter (Pennsylvania)

- U.S. Senator Elizabeth Warren (Massachusetts)

Give up? The first list incorporates prominent Republican politicians who started out life as Democrats. The second grouping lists Democrats who were previously Republicans. Salmon P. Chase (1808–1873) makes both lists because he left the Democratic Party to become a Republican, and later he switched back to the Democrats.

A broader list of party-switchers would include Presidents Martin Van Buren, Millard Fillmore, and Theodore Roosevelt, who left the Democrats, Whigs, and Republicans, respectively to run as third-party candidates. Vice President Henry A. Wallace left the Democrats to run as a Progressive in 1948, and throughout history certain third parties have attracted favor from politicians disenchanted with a major party.

President Ronald Reagan is an especially interesting case study whose political evolution demonstrates how inadequately the two-party system reflects the breadth of mainstream thought in the United States. Reagan was an extreme liberal in the beginning (1941), when he joined the Screen Actors Guild. He rose through the ranks of the organization, which for all intents and purposes was a labor union seeking a larger share of the profits of movie studios. Following a series of work stoppages, the last in 1960, Reagan, as the guild's guiding light, succeeded in negotiating residual payments for actors whose films were later shown on television. He achieved this in the face of fierce resistance from moguls who had been spoiled by the "studio system," wherein an actor was the property of a studio and subject to its dictates in all regards.

Within a year after this success, Ronald Reagan had transformed himself into an extreme right-winger. When John F. Kennedy ran for president in 1960 on a platform that included what he called "medical care for the aged," Reagan was still helping the Screen Actors Guild. But in 1961 Ronald Reagan began denouncing plans for Medicare as socialism, and warning of the dangers of socialism to Americans' daily way of life. He actively supported Barry Goldwater's 1964 presidential run; three years later he was elected as California's governor. Reagan was 65, a normal retirement age for business executives in Corporate America, when he campaigned for president in 1976, losing the nomination to President Ford after a spirited fight, and he became the oldest man elected to the presidency four years later. The Ronald Reagan who led the Screen Actors Guild had vanished from the Hollywood hills.

He will be remembered as the president who said government can't solve problems, because government itself is the problem, and for his hatred of Marxist-Leninist ideology. But his sunny personality and optimistic outlook served to neutralize these negative views with the voting public.

Heavy military-industrial outlays, often made with little regard for reasonableness of costs, marked his eight years as president, and evidenced Reagan's two-sided view of governmental activism. Where fighting Communists was concerned, he most assuredly saw government as the solution to a problem. This earned him the everlasting gratitude of the military-industrial complex, the same unit that an earlier Republican president had warned the country about, as the stocks of companies in the defense industry soared to unprecedented heights in the 1980s thanks to new government contracts. Reagan's rigid anti-Communist ethos led to the illegal transfer of weapons to Iran, the profits from which were redirected to Nicaraguan Contras, whose cause fit his political agenda perfectly.

How legitimate is a two-party system that allows for the same person to adopt polar-opposite political philosophies, and succeed in advancing the cause of both within twelve months' time? Ronald Reagan was a likable man, unquestionably patriotic, but his political success, in the face of a Jekyll & Hyde ideological transformation, suggests that labels like "Democrat" and "Republican" can be nothing more than self-serving conveniences.

Ronald Reagan and Donald Trump, two men with diametrically opposite personality profiles, nonetheless have much in common as politicians. Both began as liberal Democrats and became conservative Republicans. Both were divorced, having had children with more than one wife, and both first gained fame and popularity through an entertainment medium. The children of both men leveraged their family names to good advantage in their own careers, albeit Reagan's daughter Patti Davis, his son Ron Reagan, and Trump's daughter Ivanka Kushner are well to the left of their fathers politically.

If Presidents Reagan and Trump had first been conservative Republicans who morphed into liberal Democrats, would their political fortunes have been different? Probably not, if they were elected president through the force of their respective personalities, as is probably the case, more than any ideological criterion. Not if the celebrity status that derived from their earlier movie and television exploits immunized them against political opponents who might have emphasized the fungibility of their views.

Donald Trump was the first man to reach the White House with neither political or military experience. Like Ronald Reagan, he was an entertainment celebrity before running for office relatively late in life. In that regard Trump and Reagan enjoyed the same advantage as military heroes like Ulysses S. Grant and Dwight D. Eisenhower, neither of whom ran for president as an ideologue or extreme partisan. Republicans were delighted to affix the GOP label to Grant and Eisenhower, but given their heroic status, Democrats would have welcomed them in a heartbeat. Both parties emphasize winning elections over ideological purity, though they carefully disguise that pragmatism when appealing to special interest groups for money and votes.

If either major party nominates a celebrity whose popularity transcends ideology (for example, if Oprah Winfrey were nominated by the Democrats in 2020), what effect would such a nomination have upon fundraising? If raising money necessarily involves appealing to potential donors on an ideological basis, or because a party mistakenly believes its target for contributions is a loyal partisan ("We are at a turning point in history, Robert, and we're counting on good Democrats like you [sic] to donate today "), would a celebrity candidate whose views might conflict with the party's platform positions turn people off? Would a platform even be necessary for an Oprah Winfrey?

At some point in the not-too-distant future the public is likely to decide that the two-party system no longer represents a consensus position in American thought, even in the aggregate. The fact that more voters identify themselves as independent than as either Democrats or Republicans suggests we're close to that point. Someone might soon create a third party, devoid of rigid thinking and one that endorses only candidates for office who have a prior connection to the public through the media (like Oprah Winfrey). The present author welcomes suggestions for naming such an imaginary party. It can't be the "Hollywood party," because that would merely reinforce the image of show business as an extension of the Democrats. Maybe the "Citizen's Media" party would work. #Send suggestions for naming a third party via the publisher. The winning entry will receive a "Go Perot" button, one in perfect condition that hasn't been worn since 1992, and a provocatively posed photograph, suitable for framing, of Jesse "The Body" Ventura.

CHAPTER 37: THE MID-TERMS SETTLE NOTHING

This volume will be published in 2019, when the 2020 presidential race will have already begun, and in the wake of what turned out to be an indecisive mid-term election in 2018. As polls had indicated, Democrats seized control of the House of Representatives, while Republicans increased their majority in the Senate. For all the advance hoopla that the mid-terms received, nothing was settled. Democrats boasted that it was a "blue wave." Donald Trump hailed it as a GOP triumph and a validation of his presidency. It was neither of the above.

Democrats set out to take advantage of their House majority, and the resulting subpoena power, to further investigate the president's dealings with Russia, and to look at his tax returns. As of this writing there is nothing to suggest that the extreme polarization in the country will abate, and every indication that the 2020 presidential campaign will be nasty in the extreme.

Post-mortem analysis of the vote focused on turnout, but always in terms of the two-party duopoly. It was as if registered Democrats and registered Republicans, who together comprise a bare majority of the electorate, were the only ones whose votes mattered. Such a narrow approach is consistent with media presumptions that independents aren't truly independent, but "lean" one way or the other, as discussed skeptically in an earlier chapter. This observer is waiting eagerly for the first example of any Democrat or Republican voter who is said to "lean independent."

Any thought that bi-partisan nastiness might vanish following Election Day disappeared quickly. The author's home state of Florida, which had been dubbed "Flori-duh" by out-of-state liberals after the 2000 presidential election debacle, again became the focus of a nasty post-mortem fight predicated on voting issues. Democrat Andrew Gillum conceded the gubernatorial race to

Republican Ron DeSantis, only to have "uncounted" votes appear in Broward County that reduced the margin between the candidates to less than half a percentage point, forcing an automatic recount. Other votes (including provisional ballots and votes from military personnel overseas) were still to be counted, so Gillum withdrew his concession (legally, concessions are never binding, so the withdrawal was a formality).

The Senate race between incumbent Democrat Bill Nelson and Republican (Governor) Rick Scott is even closer. Governor Scott leads by 18/100ths of a percentage point, pending the tally of uncounted votes from Broward County and elsewhere.

A Scott spokesperson immediately criticized Sen. Nelson for requesting a recount, adding with barely veiled compassion, "It's a sad way for his career to end," as if to suggest that the recount could not possibly change the outcome. Republican leaders, including Sen. Marco Rubio, boldly suggested that election officials in Broward County (next door to Palm Beach County, where the "hanging chads" controversy in 2000 arose) were fraudulently trying to deprive Scott of a fairly-earned Senate seat.

Brenda Snipes, Broward County Election Commissioner, argued that because the ballots in her region were five and six pages long, the process of tallying them was necessarily slow. Dr. Snipes' explanation was widely dismissed, except by older Democrats throughout the state who remembered the disenfranchisement of tens of thousands of eligible voters, mostly Democrats, by Republican Secretary of State Katherine Harris in 2000. Poll watchers (including the present author) who personally witnessed electronic vote flipping and a deliberate shortage of election machinery throughout Democrat-leaning districts by state officials in 2004, have understood ever since that heavily Democratic Broward County, while it has real issues handling elections, is far from the most serious problem in Florida.

Both sides rushed to file lawsuits in defense of their positions, which will probably mean that in the end, courts, not hyperbolic rhetoric from partisans, will administer justice. Anything is preferable to mindless hyperbole, but already the media are referring to Florida's current problems as a nightmarish replay of Bush v. Gore in 2000.

Next door to Florida, Georgia is undergoing its own electoral controversy as this is written. Republican Brian Kemp, Georgia's Secretary of State, declared victory over Democrat Stacey Adams in the race for governor. Kemp had earlier rejected calls for his resignation as Secretary of State, requests that cited the clear conflict of interest involved. A Secretary of State is empowered to rule on the eligibility of voters, while maintaining overall supervision over the counting of votes. Ms. Adams, an African-American seeking to break a color barrier in the state, is insisting on a recount, claiming enough uncounted votes in her favor to change the result.

Mr. Kemp eventually resigned as Secretary of State, but made it clear his resignation was given only so he could arrange his transition to the governor's office. Without prejudging the eventual outcome in Georgia, can any fair-minded person, regardless of political leanings, argue that a person running for office should be in position to decide who is eligible to vote there? Should that same person be supervising the vote counting? Isn't that a bit like putting a fox in charge of guarding a chicken coop?

Would not a first step toward cleaning up elections in the United States be passing a federal law, to the effect that persons running for office may not be involved in the electoral process? Such a law would necessarily supersede the sole authority of states to run all elections, as set forth in America's founding documents, and therefore would face opposition from Constitutional purists. But election disputes, however they are resolved, exacerbate the polarization of the electorate, turn voters cynical toward the process, and depress turnout. The two-party system that nobody asked for has proven incapable of running honest elections, as manifested by allegations from both sides of the aisle that the opponent can't be trusted.

Further evidence isn't needed of wrongdoing. It's only a small leap of logic to presume that if Party A thinks Party B is rigging an election (Party A has made that clear), then Party A will fight fire with fire and rig the election itself.

This is not to suggest that individual states haven't make good-faith efforts to improve elections. "Motor-voter" registration means the owners of newly registered cars are automatically eligible, but that doesn't help seniors and handicapped folks who rely on public transportation. Voting by mail helps reduce lines on Election Day, but it offers no remedy for lost ballots and can leave voters in doubt that their ballots had been counted. "Photo-ID" voting can leave one's identity (and eligibility) in question, for example if the photo doesn't match the voter's current appearance, which is often the case ("When did your hair turn orange, Mr. Trump?"). A discrepancy between the handwriting on the original registration document and the signature provided on Election Day (a common circumstance), might cause problems. Electronic voting machines, which were thought to revolutionize the process as recently as 20 years ago, have proven to be so easily hackable that most states have reverted to paper ballots or other non-electronic methods.

When conflicts such as those cited above arise, generally the voter is provided with a provisional ballot. That's fair enough. Statistically, though, most provisional ballots are never counted, so the outcome of any election can be questioned on that basis.

Under the two-party system, only officials appointed by Republican or Democratic administrations are put in charge of conducting elections. It all depends on who won the previous election. This means that regardless of the personal reputations of the officials themselves, any election dispute thereafter will inevitably become tainted with accusations of partisanship and cheating. In the 21st Century, given instant communication and social media that lack a verification filter, any accusation of malfeasance, even one lacking a sound foundation, can be taken as fact. The response will be immediate, and no more likely to be fact-based.

The spitting contest continues. Please, someone fix this.

CHAPTER 38: THOSE INSCRUTABLE FLORIDA VOTERS

Florida is typically labeled a "purple" state by the national media, while describing a pivotal state that is neither Democrat blue or Republican red. "Lavender" might be more accurate.

Democrats outnumber Republicans in Florida. Still, heading into November 2018 the GOP controlled the governorship and both branches of the legislature by wide margins (lobbyists have more control than either party, but that's an issue for a separate book). A benign explanation for this seeming contradiction would be that Democrats are more likely to vote for a Republican than a Republican voter will choose a Democrat. Another might be that most independents "lean" and vote Republican. Either rationale might be right, but it's at least as likely that voter suppression efforts, some lawful and others questionable, have worked to the disadvantage of Democrats and canceled out their overall registration advantage over Republicans.

The current brouhaha over the gubernatorial and Senate races has focused attention on Broward County's historic failure to count votes quickly and effectively. Given the heavy Democratic registration advantage in Broward, Republicans from as far away as the White House are crying "voter fraud" in 2018. But for years, Republicans have taken advantage of Florida's strict registration procedures, which probably have had a greater effect on election outcomes than vote fraud. Either way, Florida gives partisans on both sides plenty to complain about.

The most restrictive voting law in Florida, one favoring Republicans, is about to be overturned. The same Sunshine State voters that elected Rick Scott as governor twice, that gave him a solid Republican legislature to work with, and probably just elected him to the Senate in favor of a four-term Democrat incumbent, Bill Nelson, nonetheless approved Amendment Four to the state constitution, which allows convicted felons to vote after serving their prison sentences (with murder and sex-related crimes excepted). A 60% vote in favor was needed, and the measure attracted 64% approval. The Florida legislature, whose members can have difficulty ordering a ham sandwich from the delicatessen, immediately began debating how to implement the will of the voters procedurally. Apparently, it was expected that the amendment would fail, because nobody in Tallahassee has any idea how to enforce the public's will on an amendment to the state's constitution.

Since felonies are committed disproportionately by minority individuals on a statistical basis, this outcome is welcome news to Democrats. The precise number of new voters isn't known, but an estimate from representatives of the Sentencing Project and the American Civil Liberties Union, both of which supported the amendment, is that 1.4 million new voters have been created. As POLITIFACT reminds us, this total is greater than the populations of Wyoming, Vermont, North Dakota, South Dakota, Delaware, Rhode Island, Maine, and New Hampshire. The vote came too late to help Democrats in 2018, but it could become the decisive factor in 2020, given Florida's history as a pivotal state in national elections. The vote on the amendment proves only that in Florida, nothing can be taken for granted on Election Day.

This author voted in favor of Amendment Four. As a matter of simple equity, once a felon has paid for a crime with time served and been released or paroled, no further punishment is warranted. When the ex-felon finds a job, taxes will be deducted from every paycheck, so to continue denying voting privileges to that individual would constitute taxation without representation.

The effect of the amendment's passage might go far beyond a matter of fairness, however. In 2000 a strong national voting drive brought new registrants to the polls in Florida and elsewhere. As cited in an earlier chapter, Florida's Secretary of State, Katherine Harris, helped George W. Bush (brother of her boss, Governor Jeb Bush) win the election by effectively disenfranchising thousands of eligible voters, including one James Johnson, a first-time would-be registrant who had never committed a crime but who mistakenly appeared on a list of ex-felons. Credible accusations were made in 2000 that teams of ruffians from out of state had been imported into Florida to harass African-Americans, threatening them that the Internal Revenue Service would be auditing tax returns (or investigating a failure to file) in the case of all first-time registrants. It was nonsense, but many frightened folks fell for it. Amendment Four, as important as it might prove to be, cannot remedy this type of harassment, which is reminiscent of Jim Crow-era tactics throughout the South, aiming at keeping people of color away from the voting booth. Florida, despite its heavy concentration of retirees from up north, is still part of the South, and true to its contradictory profile, is more southern, culturally, in the northern reaches of the state.

Broward County's problems in 2018 involved more than registration issues, and more than possible election fraud that was in fact alleged by candidate Rick Scott, and fellow Republicans Marco Rubio and President Trump. The evidence suggests that ineptitude on the part of Dr. Brenda Snipes' office, rather than outright fraud, might have cost Bill Nelson his Senate seat. In a bizarre echo of the "butterfly ballot" debacle that found Democrats in neighboring Palm Beach County voting for third-party candidate Pat Buchanan instead of Al Gore in 2000, Broward's ballots in 2018 resulted in over 20,000 people who had cast votes for Democrat Andrew Gillum for governor, and who had voted overwhelmingly for Democrats in Congressional and state legislative races, not voting for any candidate in the Senate race. It seems that the Senate candidates, Nelson and Rick Scott, were listed in a corner of the ballots in Broward County, not immediately visible to the naked eye. For senior citizens with failing eyesight or other cognitive handicaps, they were difficult to notice.

As an illustration of how Broward County creates its own problems on Election Day, their ballots totally omitted the name of one Democrat who was running unopposed, according to an inscrutable local regulation that lists candidates in competitive races only. This might have added to the confusion. How someone would be able to vote for a write-in candidate of his or her own choosing, when the absence of any candidate's name on the ballot suggests that nothing is at stake, is left to the voter's imagination.

Election disputes constitute a perfect storm in the current political environment. Regardless of how the disputes in Florida and Georgia turn out, the side that loses will cry foul. In fact, the crying has already begun, together with lawsuits by candidates on both sides, asking courts to order ballots counted or not counted, or voting machines impounded. A poll worker in Broward County, recently fired, filed an affidavit to the effect that she had witnessed ballots being tampered with.

President Trump has demanded that all recounts and challenges end immediately, and that Election Day tallies be accepted as final. The president lacks the Constitutional authority to intervene in state-controlled elections, and probably knows it, but the media are drawn to his tweets like moths to a flame.

On the Internet, sentiment is divided exactly according to partisanship. Liberal sites feature accusations of voter suppression, not surprisingly given Florida's history, and in the case of Democratic gubernatorial candidate

Andrew Gillum, an African-American, the rhetoric includes cries of racial bias. A more legalistic argument, supported by Democrats in Congress, calls for Governor Rick Scott to recuse himself from any involvement in the recount process in the Senate race, as one with a direct stake in the outcome. Conservative bloggers insist that fraud began during the recount process, and that Broward County officials are pretending to find votes that they themselves are creating out whole cloth. Given Broward County's history, conservatives' arguments cannot be dismissed out of hand.

It's conceivable that Senator Nelson will be declared the winner after all the recounting is done, have courts confirm his victory, yet Rick Scott could assume the Senate seat. Impossible, you say? No. The Constitution allows the Senate itself to become the final arbiter of any election dispute. With Republicans in the majority there, if the leadership were to decide Nelson won by fraud (whether evidence of fraud exists or not), and Mitch McConnell keeps every GOP Senator in line, the election infrastructure and the courts would have been overridden and Scott would be seated. This is a real possibility. There is no middle ground in Congress, and no trust between leaders of the two major parties. Lost is any sense that a solution to election disputes lies anywhere outside the two-party system, for example with a non-partisan election commission under the aegis of the League of Women Voters.

On the contrary, Tampa Bay Times columnist Daniel Ruth, who normally reserves his sardonic humor for the sake of ridiculing whichever party is in power at the time in Florida, instead now blames third-party candidates and their supporters for close elections that turn out badly in his mind. In a recent column Ruth called Libertarian and Green Party candidates "sad sacks," while using own peculiar brand of epithetical language to slander third-party voters as "dumber than a sack of mold spores."

Ruth probably wouldn't admit it, but by disparaging third-party candidates he's tacitly arguing that the best candidate in any election must be either a Democrat or a Republican. This begs the question, "How then, in the name of Ross Perot did we end up with Donald Trump as president, and with such a dysfunctional Congress?" My letter to the paper, which was printed, asked that very question.

Daniel Ruth is effectively advancing the "Don't throw your vote away (by choosing a third-party candidate)" line of thinking, with casual insults added to the mix for the sake of entertainment. Third-party candidacies typically draw a small fraction of the total vote, with an occasional glaring exception like Jesse Ventura in 1998, who stands as a role model for future long-shot office seekers. But Ruth's argument, however one judges its merits, serves to strengthen the two-party system at a time in history when both parties are focused on destroying each other. Thanks for nothing, Daniel Ruth.

It's not an exaggeration to argue that the two-party system in the United States has become a 21st-century version of the Hatfield/McCoy feuds of the 19th century. Daniel Ruth won't choose sides. He doesn't blame either family for the ongoing feud. No, it's all the fault of the people next door, those sad sacks who want to restore peace and comity to the neighborhood.

Chapter 39: Gerrymandering And The Courts

Elbridge Gerry of Massachusetts was vice president of the United States in 1813 and 1814, having joined President James Madison on the Democratic-Republican (anti-Federalist) ticket when Madison ran for reelection in 1812. That had been a busy year for Mr. Gerry, who earlier in 1812, while serving as governor of the Commonwealth of Massachusetts, rearranged a Congressional district in such an unorthodox fashion that on a map, the district was said to resemble a salamander.

Public disapproval of this act led to his defeat for reelection later that year. It was the apparent end to Gerry's long political career, only to have President Madison seek him out as his running mate.

Gerry's political opponents decided the controversial district had been "Gerrymandered," an accusation that failed to prevent his nomination for vice president (Vice President George Clinton had died in April 1812, leaving the office vacant). It might have hurt the feelings of self-respecting salamanders, who probably would have preferred that creators of the term use "garden snake" or "tadpole," except neither creature's name combined well with "Gerry" in forming a portmanteau. The American Society for Prevention of Cruelty to Animals hadn't come into being in 1812, and it's doubtful that they'd have come to the defense of a lowly salamander in any event. Besides, the issue of cruelty took a backseat to the fact that someone had mispronounced Mr. Gerry's name, changing the hard-G of Gerry to a soft-G, resulting in a word that sounded like "Jerrymandering."

Back in the day, when Elbridge Gerry had been helping James Madison and others design the Constitution, it was decided to leave questions about how to allocate Congressional representation within a state to the states themselves. The raw number of representatives per state was always based on population, as determined by the most recent census (in 1810 when Gerry was governor), but how they were distributed *within* the state was up to the governor and/or the legislature.

Remember, the Founding Fathers didn't anticipate political parties. George Washington, who loathed the very idea, was about to take office as the states pondered ratifying the Constitution. We can forgive the men who sweated out that summer in Philadelphia, then, for not intuiting that partisan politics would someday become integral to any conversation about the size or shape of "districts" within a given state. Salamanders? Rectangles? The Constitution, in fact, didn't require the establishment of districts at all. The Founding Fathers would have rested content if every Congressional representative had been an "at large" legislator.

Elbridge Gerry might have been the first state official to recognize that birds of a political feather will often flock together. In Massachusetts, for example, Puritans and free thinkers might have chosen to live apart from one another, but remain within their own tight cliques. As the two-party system developed in the 1820s, a clever political observer could have reasoned that to design a political district wherein like-thinking citizens ("liberals" for the purposes of illustration) monopolized the area, would operate to the advantage of the opposing faction, because the population of liberals in the other districts would have been diffused. "Conservatives," as their opponents, would therefore have benefited from the heavy concentration of liberals in a single district. Obviously, if every representative were at large, neither side could take advantage.

In a 21st-century context, we can replace the hypothetical "Puritans and free thinkers" with realistic examples, like "African-Americans and whites" or "Hispanics and Anglos." If African-Americans of voting age represented 20% of the population of a given state, but 80% of them were crowded into the largest city in the state, then the population distribution elsewhere in the state would be 96%-4% in favor of whites. African-Americans overwhelmingly vote Democratic, so in this example Republicans would be delighted to concede one or more districts in the city in exchange for controlling five or ten elsewhere in the state. In this example, the percentage of Republicans in Congress from the state would necessarily become greater than the overall percentage of Republicans of voting age in the entire state.

Identifying gerrymandering as a strategy is easy. Combatting it politically is much harder. Because the U.S. Constitution left everything up to the states (as it did with the Electoral College), districting and redistricting became intra-state questions. They remain so. Every 10 years a new census determines how many representatives a state is entitled to, but only state officials will determine their allocation within the borders. If state officials are partisan (in 2018 that's almost a given), then Congressional districts can look like salamanders, or octopi, or armadillos.

The devil is in the details. "State officials" can mean the governor (as it did with Elbridge Gerry in 1812), or the legislature, or in the event of a turf battle (the governor might be dealing with a legislature controlled by the other party), state courts. In any state where the governorship, legislature, and courts operate under single-party rule, it becomes next to impossible for the opposing party to effectively challenge all gerrymandering of districts. In Florida a few years back, this author was waiting for a reply to a second letter he'd sent his Congressman on a matter that concerned him (his first letter had been ignored altogether), when he came to realize that the neglectful Congressman _____ had been redistricted out of the author's area. A new Congressman _____, who had been voted into office by citizens of a different precinct years before, had now been gerrymandered into the author's district. Meanwhile, _____ still lived within his old jurisdiction, which was several hours drive away. He soon afterward announced he would not be running for reelection, probably because nobody in his new district knew who he was. At that point it was clear my letters would never be answered.

Gerrymandering is like negative advertising during election campaigns. Nobody likes it. The media condemn it editorially. But it works. It serves a political purpose, so it continues. Occasionally a judge will rule against the creation of a certain district, but that provides only temporary relief. Each act of gerrymandering is a separate legal matter. Lawyers charge a lot, so challenging abusive practices can become a cost issue. It's often prudent to wait for the next election in the hope that a new governor, a new legislature, or new court appointments will provide an opportunity for change. In the interim, it's an issue to raise against the party in power, but other issues typically sound more exigent.

The only permanent solution to this dilemma would be a Constitutional amendment that eliminates Congressional districts altogether. Every member of Congress would become a member at large. This would end gerrymandering for all practical purposes. But it would have the disadvantage of separating many citizens from their representatives geographically, especially in huge states like California and Texas, and it would mean that the most effective legislators would receive the most mail, hear the most complaints, answer the most questions from the media, and seek relief from the harassment by running for the Senate.

CHAPTER 40: THE NEW POLITICAL LANDSCAPE

Democrats were expected to take over the House of Representatives in the mid-terms, and Republicans were favored to maintain control of the Senate. Both succeeded, albeit the precise makeup of both branches of Congress will depend on the outcome of inevitable election disputes, some of which have already turned into courtroom battles.

One distinct new pattern emerged, however, that is likely to influence how the 116th Congress does business. It has implications for the 2020 presidential election and beyond, as well. With several races yet to be decided as of this writing, at least 121 women will serve in the House (about 28% of the total), versus 107 in 2018. The Senate will include 23 women. Virtually all the newcomers are Democrats, including the first African-American woman to serve in the House from Massachusetts, Ayanna Presley, and Alexandria Ocasio-Cortez, a Hispanic from New York City, who at age 29 will become the youngest member of the new Congress. Ms. Ocasio-Cortez has heralded her arrival in Washington by engaging in a verbal exchange with Donald Trump, Jr., boasting of her ambitions as an activist, and otherwise becoming a convenient target for conservative bloggers to aim at.

Two Muslim women were elected to the House, Rashida Tlaib in Michigan and Ilhan Omar in Minnesota. Given President Trump's scapegoating of Muslims as terrorists, some of whom he alleged had wormed their way into the cavalcade of refugees from Honduras hoping to cross the U.S.-Mexican border, it will be interesting to see how the presence of these women affects relations between Congress and the White House.

One of the first questions to be answered when Congress convenes in January is, "Who will be Speaker of the House?" Nancy Pelosi (D-CA) is the former Speaker and current Minority Leader, and she has made it clear she expects to resume her leadership duties. But Ms. Pelosi will be 80 years old in 2020, and already she faces a faction within Congress that seeks younger leadership. Her second-in-command in the House, Steny Hoyer, and the Democratic leader in the Senate, Charles Schumer, are also in their late 70s. Questions of age aside, the fact that at least 14 more females will be serving in the House in 2019 should work to her advantage, although Ms. Pelosi has consistently emphasized her effectiveness as a legislator, and especially her success at raising money for the party, while deemphasizing gender as a qualifier. More than a few of Ms. Pelosi's supporters have argued that objections to her continuing leadership are gender based, because objections about age haven't been raised against Sen. Schumer or Rep. Hoyer. This has kept supporters of other potential House Speakers on the defensive. One potential challenger has already stepped aside, suggesting that Ms. Pelosi's supporters are in charge.

Ms. Pelosi's history as House Speaker, and her recent comments regarding the possible impeachment of President Trump, strongly suggest she would discourage her fellow Democrats traveling down that road in 2019. She would have Democrats focus instead on the party's legislative imperatives, at least until Special Prosecutor Robert Mueller issues his final report. These priorities include preserving the Affordable Care Act and coverage for preexisting conditions, maintaining funding for Planned Parenthood, protecting the interests of immigrants, gun control, the environment, and defending public education. All Democrats have been vocal about the need to protect Robert Mueller's ongoing investigation of possible Russian interference in the 2016 election, which is possibly an urgent matter given that President Trump has fired Attorney-General Jeff Sessions, removed Deputy Attorney-General Rod Rosenstein from oversight of the investigation, and installed in Rosenstein's stead a controversial figure, Matthew G. Whitaker, who is on record as believing that Mueller is on a witch hunt and that the investigation should be terminated. A Constitutional argument has already arisen over the legality of Whitaker's hiring in the absence of Senate confirmation, with attorney/pundits weighing in on both sides of the argument on television and in the blogosphere.

A preponderance of those Democrats who seek a younger leader than Nancy Pelosi also favor more aggressive action against President Trump — some favor impeachment, but all have called for using their new subpoena power to conduct investigations into his business dealings and those of his family members, especially where Russia is concerned, and inspection of his tax returns. Whoever becomes Speaker will have to balance this sentiment against the risk of becoming a "do-nothing" Congress in terms of constructive legislative achievement, and the further risk that jeopardizing Trump's presidency will impede cooperation with Republicans in Congress on legislation, and still further, give the GOP an issue to run on in 2020.

The Logan Act was passed in 1799. It bars American citizens from negotiating with hostile foreign countries, in that such contact would preempt the executive branch of government's diplomatic sovereignty. Jared Kushner, President Trump's son-in-law, is at once a presidential adviser and a real estate mogul who is known to have met with a Russian diplomat, and separately with a banker from Moscow. The Mueller investigation is reportedly looking into whether these meetings constituted violations of the Logan Act or other law. Because nobody has ever been convicted of violating the act (only two individuals have been prosecuted under it, unsuccessfully, both in the 19th century), a Trump-controlled Justice Department would hardly use it against a member of the president's own family. It's also unclear whether Russia qualifies as a hostile foreign country under the Logan Act, given that ordinary diplomatic relations exist between the countries. Non-partisan observers will note a political role reversal, in that the former Soviet Union was the bugbear of anti-Communist zealots, including most Republicans, throughout the McCarthy Era and the Cold War. Now, Russia has now become the devil incarnate to Democrats who highlight President Trump's seeming "bromance" with Vladimir Putin.

If the influx of women into Congress serves only to "lower the temperature" on Capitol Hill, it will be a welcome development, regardless of one's political leanings. Women are widely regarded as less confrontational than men (with notable exceptions, such as Ms. Ocasio-Cortez), and presumably are more amenable to peaceful negotiating and compromise, two lost arts that have surrendered to polarization. If this occurs, the improvement could be short lived, should several women in Congress who are regarded as potential presidential candidates decide to start their campaigns early.

Senator Kamala Harris of California (born 1964) is the daughter of an Indian mother and Jamaican father who divorced when she was age 7. She and her younger sister were raised by their mother. Before being elected to the Senate in 2016, where she assumed the seat formerly held by Barbara Boxer, who retired, Sen. Harris was California's Attorney-General, and before that a district attorney in San Francisco. She is junior in the Senate to Dianne Feinstein, with whom she once clashed over her refusal to seek the death penalty in a case involving the murder of a San Francisco policeman in 2004. Where a run for the presidency is concerned, Sen. Harris has said she "isn't ruling it out." The media, of course, treat anything short of a Shermanesque denial as a tacit acknowledgement of one's candidacy.

Senator Amy Klobuchar of Minnesota (born 1960) has a similar personal profile to that of Kamala Harris. The older of two daughters whose parents divorced, she became a lawyer after graduating magna cum laude from Yale in 1964 (B.A., Political Science), and from University of Chicago's law school. First employed by a private law firm, she was elected Hennepin County (Minneapolis/St. Paul) Attorney, then elected to the Senate, first in 2006. Klobuchar has been reelected twice by comfortable margins. She's earned a reputation as an effective legislator who will cross the aisle to work well with Republicans. Is she a candidate for president? She says she's happy serving her Minnesota constituents and is not a candidate, but the New York Times has opined that she's the most likely female to enter the White House.

Senator Kirsten Gillibrand of New York State (born 1966) is also a child of divorced parents, and a former attorney who graduated from Dartmouth College and UCLA's law school. Her maternal grandmother set an example for young Kirsten Rutnik by founding the Albany (N.Y.) Women's Democratic Club and becoming prominent in the powerful (Albany Mayor) Erastus Corning political machine. First appointed in 2007 to the Senate seat vacated by Hillary Clinton when Clinton became Secretary of State, Gillibrand retained the seat by winning a special election in 2010, then was reelected in 2016. Outspoken on matters involving sexual harassment and misconduct, she facilitated Al Franken's exit from the Senate, which earned her mixed reactions from her colleagues. Ms. Gillibrand has openly expressed interest in becoming president, hoping to "restore integrity" to the White House.

Senator Elizabeth Warren of Massachusetts (born 1949) is also a lawyer, having matriculated at the University of Houston and Rutgers (Newark) Law School. A specialist in legal issues surrounding bankruptcy, Warren taught law at a good number of schools, including Harvard University. Hugely popular in Massachusetts, Warren has attracted attention as an outspoken critic of big-city banks and corporate corruption in general. Her one year at Harvard (1992), however, became shrouded in a controversy that didn't arise until years later.

Warren was born in Oklahoma, to a mother who passed on to young Elizabeth a family tradition that they were descended from Native Americans. She identified herself as a Native American when she applied at Harvard, but otherwise refrained from making the association publicly. When, as a Senator, she began to criticize President Trump aggressively, he referred to her mockingly as "Pocahontas," chiding her for using her supposed ancestry as an entry ticket to the Harvard faculty and challenging Warren to take a

DNA test, meanwhile volunteering to make a generous donation to charity if the test revealed Native American blood. Eventually Senator Warren took the test, which only added to the controversy, because while it suggested a very small amount of Cherokee inheritance, current members of the Cherokee Nation said they didn't consider Elizabeth Warren a "tribal" member. Trump, meanwhile, reneged on his promise to donate to charity, insisting Warren take a new test, to be administered by Dr. (?) Donald Trump. As an experiment the present author asked Democrats in his Community College political classroom to name their first choice as presidential nominee in 2020, regardless of gender. To his surprise the most votes went to former First Lady Michelle Robinson Obama, who like the women cited above is a professional lawyer who graduated from Princeton University and Harvard Law School. Mrs. Obama has never expressed interest in the presidency, but media speculation about the possibility arose after a poll suggested she would defeat President Trump easily. She has become more vocal on public issues since leaving the White House in 2017, famously commenting, "When they (Republicans) go low, we (Democrats) go high," thereby identifying herself as less confrontational than openly partisan Democrats who detest Trump and won't shy away from confronting him at his own level of combat.

Oprah Winfrey (born 1954) is a fabulously wealthy actress, television host and executive, book reviewer, and outspoken advocate for philanthropic causes. She is believed to be the richest African-American woman in history, despite being born to an unwed teenage mother in Mississippi, and herself being impregnated at age 14. Winfrey has used her public platform to advance LGBT rights and other progressive causes, gaining enough political visibility to be included with Michelle Obama and former Vice President Joe Biden on a list of Democrats who, according to the same poll, would defeat President Trump by wide margins in 2020. She has adamantly denied being interested in the presidency, but Winfrey's outspokenness on issues keeps the speculation going. Skeptics point to the fact that as a candidate who gained prominence via television, she would be meeting Trump on his own turf, opposing a man who enjoyed blockbuster ratings by firing people. This is a potential disadvantage that Oprah Winfrey is smart enough to have long since recognized. Her denials of interest are no doubt honest.

Other women whose names have arisen concerning a possible nomination in 2020 are Hillary Clinton, who won the popular vote in 2016, and Maggie Hassan, newly elected Senator from New Hampshire. Men figuring to enter the large field include Bernie Sanders, Joe Biden, John Kerry, Ohio Senator Sherrod Brown, Connecticut Senator Chris Murphy, New Jersey Senator

Cory Booker, and New York Governor Andrew Cuomo. Presumably, any of these who shows up in Iowa and New Hampshire for no apparent reason during 2019 will be signaling to the world that they're aiming for the top.

CHAPTER 41: POSSIBLE THIRD-PARTY CANDIDACIES IN 2020

Pertinent to the theme of this book, suggestions follow as to possible alternatives to President Trump and to whichever Democrat opposes him in 2020. These are entirely the author's selections, among prominent Americans whose personal histories transcend partisanship. It is taken for granted here that the president will survive a possible impeachment effort, will run for reelection, and that he would easily overcome any primary challenge he might face.

In 2016 Independent Bernie Sanders sought the nomination as a Democrat. The author's criterion for inclusion in the following grouping is that the candidate not seek major-party status, instead run independently, possibly under a reform banner, as Ross Perot did in 1992. The author believes Sen. Sanders would not run, except as a Democrat, and if denied the nomination, would endorse the voters' choice.

Former New York Mayor Michael Bloomberg has flirted with the idea of running for president in the past. He deflected talk of a candidacy while mayor (2001–2014), but in 2016 was said to be considering a run. He decided against it and endorsed Hillary Clinton, but that has not quieted rumors that he retains interest.

According to estimates Bloomberg is the 11th richest man in the world. He has promised to give away at least half of his estimated net worth of $5.1 billion. His empire embraces media, financial services, and software; not that he needs further validation of his business acumen, but Bloomberg is a graduate of Johns Hopkins and Harvard Business School. Politically, Bloomberg offers something for everyone. A Democrat for most of his adult life, he became a Republican when he ran successfully for mayor in 2001, was reelected as a Republican in 2005, then switched to an independent status before his reelection in 2009. He left office in 2014, and rejoined the Democrats in 2018, a change that heightened speculation about his plans for 2020.

Michael Bloomberg might lack charisma, but his resume establishes him as a man of rectitude and competence, and one who was even more successful than was President Trump in business. His most obvious handicap is one he shares with Bernie Sanders and Joe Biden; Bloomberg will be 78 on Election Day in 2020. Were he to run as an independent or reform candidate, it isn't clear which major party he'd draw away the most votes from. That uncertainty should exempt him from accusations that he was running as a spoiler, and likewise exempt his supporters from suggestions that their votes would be wasted.

Russ Feingold (born 1953) served three terms as U.S. Senator from Wisconsin (1993–2011). A registered Democrat, he sometimes clashed with the leadership of his own party and established a reputation for independence, as exemplified by his work with Sen. John McCain in passing the McCain-Feingold Act, advancing the cause of campaign finance reform. He voted against funding the invasion of Iraq, and he was the only Senator to vote "no" on the Patriot Act. He has refused to accept "soft money" political contributions, and as a man without a party, would need a flood of small contributions from the public for a credible campaign in 2020. Feingold is a deficit hawk who personifies the ideal of non-partisanship, and so would appeal to independent voters, Democrats dissatisfied with the party's nominee, and even traditional Republicans who consider the national debt level obscene. Feingold is a member of Phi Beta Kappa, was a Rhodes Scholar at Oxford University, and holds a juris doctor from Harvard Law School. He would have no compunction against running without the Democrat label.

William Floyd "Bill" Weld (born 1945) was the Republican governor of Massachusetts from 1991 to 1997. He ran for the Senate in 1996 in opposition to incumbent Senator John Kerry, losing in a race that was notable for a near total absence of negative politicking, according to a pledge both candidates made in advance, and kept. Weld is independently wealthy and a blue-blood on both sides of his family; his Weld ancestry traces to the Mayflower, and one direct ancestor was among the first graduates of Harvard. Two buildings at Harvard are named for Weld's ancestors. A direct ancestor on his mother's side, for whom he was named, William Floyd, was a signer of the Declaration of Independence. His former wife, mother of his five children, is President Theodore Roosevelt's great-granddaughter. Weld is not a dynamic campaigner, but he is respected by folks on both sides of the aisle.

Politically, Weld was a moderate Republican before joining the Libertarian party in 2016. Like Russ Feingold, he is a long-standing critic of exploding federal deficits, a stance that influenced his change of parties. He served as Gary Johnson's vice-presidential running mate on the Libertarian line; they formed the first presidential ticket merging two former governors since 1948 (Thomas E. Dewey-Earl Warren). Johnson-Weld finished third with 3% of the vote. Earlier in his career Weld was U.S. Attorney for the Massachusetts District, and an Assistant U.S. Attorney-General (Criminal Division). He is a summa cum laude graduate of Harvard.

Mark Cuban is 12 years younger than President Trump, so we know they weren't separated at birth. Arguably, though, no American in public life is more like Donald Trump, in terms of their business backgrounds and bombastic temperaments, than Cuban.

Cuban owns the Dallas Mavericks in the National Basketball Association. Trump once owned the New Jersey Generals, a member of the (long-since defunct) United States Football League. Cuban, aside from being co-owner of the multi-media company 2929 Entertainment, is a "shark investor" on the ABC series "Shark Tank" and has appeared frequently on camera. Trump segued from casino and hotel entrepreneur into reality television via "The Apprentice" on NBC, where he became popular for firing people. Cuban attends Dallas Mavericks basketball games and typically spends two hours screaming at the officials, for which he has been fined repeatedly by the league. He uses social media to express anger at a variety of personal demons, as does the president. Donald Trump is equally unrestrained when dealing with the media, political opponents, and courts that rule against him. His primary outlet is his Twitter account. Both Cuban and Trump seem to enjoy fighting battles for no higher purpose than winning a fight. Cuban might be too much like Trump to present an advantageous contrast to voters.

Cuban is cited here as a possible third-party candidate in 2020 because he has demonstrated an interest in national politics and a Trump-like aggressiveness in pursuing his goals. Politically independent, his libertarian instincts derive from a fondness for author Ayn Rand, founder of Objectivism. At the same time, he has publicly equated paying taxes with patriotism, a contradiction that shows his Trump-like talent for pronouncements that conflict with his actions. In 2008 Cuban urged Michael Bloomberg to run for president, though he eventually voted for Barack Obama. He was critical of President Trump throughout the 2016 presidential campaign, taking note of his failure to acquaint himself with the job's basic requirements, though he did concede that Trump's media skills enabled his election.

If Cuban entered the 2020 race as a third-party candidate, he'd have the advantages of wealth and relative youth. Objectively, he is so alike President Trump in background and manner that he would almost certainly draw more votes away from Trump than from any Democratic opponent. He would be a true spoiler as a candidate.

Senator Angus King (born 1944) hasn't been mentioned as a presidential aspirant, but he is cited here as a true independent whose political history suggests he could draw votes from Republicans dissatisfied with President Trump and from Democrats who like his positions on health care and the environment. King is a former Democrat who caucuses with the Democrats on Capitol Hill.

Maine voters elected King to the Senate in 2012 and reelected him in 2018. Previously he served two terms as governor (1995–2003). A graduate of Dartmouth (B.A.) and University of Virginia's law school (JD), King is a strong supporter of health care legislation, having survived cancer at age 29. He has been described as a "radical centrist" and as an idealist "who wants to slash regulations, preserve the environment, avoid tax increases, establish work and educational requirements for welfare recipients, and promote public school options."

King is two years older than President Trump. That would be a drawback to a candidacy, but if the Democrats are divided in 2020 between moderates (traditionalists) and left-wing progressives, as was the case in 2016, half of the party's voters are likely to be dissatisfied with the nominee and willing to look elsewhere for a viable antidote to the president.

The Trump administration has been notable for heavy turnover. According to Bob Woodward and other sources, then Secretary of State Rex Tillerson openly referred to the president as a "moron," and was preparing to resign his post when Trump abruptly fired him in March 2018, after only 13 months on the job. Tillerson is a lifelong Republican who has never indicated an interest in running for president, but the present author assumes he is one of many who worked in the Trump administration and retain unpleasant memories of their association, a list that might well have expanded by 2020 if the White House merry-go-round continues.

Tillerson (born 1952) is a civil engineer by training who rose to the top at Exxon-Mobil in 2006. A former Eagle Scout and president of the Boy Scouts, he was close to retirement at Exxon when he sacrificed a multi-million-dollar retirement package to become Secretary of State. He would make a controversial presidential candidate, due to his long-standing business ties to Russia and the fact that at Exxon he used a faked identity when sending e-mails. He isn't a likely candidate for president, but he is included here as an example of a prominent American with personal reasons to want to limit Donald Trump to a single term as president, but who would not want a Democrat in the White House.

Tom Steyer (born 1957) is a billionaire former hedge-fund manager turned political activist who has attracted attention as the Democrat most openly committed to the impeachment of Donald Trump. A summa cum laude graduate of Yale (economics/political-science), Steyer later graduated from Stanford's business school and served on Stanford's board of trustees. Like Michael Bloomberg, Steyer has pledged to give half his net worth to charity.

Steyer has faithfully supported Democratic candidates in the past, but his steadfastness on the impeachment question highlights the reluctance of mainstream Democrats to focus on it. No doubt it will engender speculation that Steyer would be willing to run on a third-party or independent label, merely to guarantee that impeachment would be fully vetted. His relative youth, willingness to use his wealth in behalf of his goals, and the fact that he has been "outside the (Washington) swamp" for years stand in his favor. He's unknown to most in the hoi polloi, and no doubt will need generous exposure from the media to run an effective campaign. To the extent that mainstream Democrats avoid impeachment as poisonous, Steyer's contrary emphasis on it will enhance his still remote chance to become president.

CHAPTER 42: THE ELEPHANT(S) IN THE ROOM

Recent campaigns for president and Congress, as conducted by the two major parties, have focused on the issues most important to the candidates themselves, not necessarily those most important to the country's health. If a given candidate isn't sure which causes to run on, the results of multiple-choice surveys distributed by the national committee, or by the candidate's advisers, will serve as a guide.

Typically, a voter will receive an e-mail like the following: "Robert, we want to know which issues are important to you in the coming election. Please select from the following list." The list isn't prepared according to the needs of the country going forward, except maybe in the short run. It's a list comprised of questions *the party has already decided are the most advantageous for its candidates to emphasize.* In other words, it's all about winning, not about determining what the public wants. What's best for the United States of America is lost in the rush for votes.

The list might include health care, gun control, immigration, LGBT rights, abortion vs. freedom of choice, or that all-encompassing category that everyone cares about and understands, "jobs." What it will not include are issues that political "experts" have decided are either too complex for the average voter to understand fully, or too toxic to include in a survey — issues that only matter to your crazy Uncle Harry, who always ruins Thanksgiving dinner by talking about the "good old days," when a dollar was worth a dollar and people saved money before spending it. Uncle Harry's issues are the elephants in the room that no candidate wants to talk about, which is why professional politicians ignore them. They also ignore Uncle Harry.

The first elephant is our national debt. That's what the United States of America owes to individuals, financial institutions, and foreign governments in the form of U.S. Treasury obligations, better known as "T-bills," "T-notes," and "T-bonds." As of the fiscal year ending September 2018, that figure was $21,700,000,000,000 (trillion), an increase of $779,000,000,000 (billion) from September 2017. President Trump isn't responsible for most of the 21.7 trillion, but he did promise to completely eradicate our national debt by the end of his second term. Clearly, after 18 months we were still headed in the wrong direction.

Two caveats are typically offered by sincere people with an economic orientation who hope to minimize our national debt as a political issue. Most often, these apologists represent the administration currently in power. The first rationale is to consider the size of the debt in comparison to the size of the economy, as measured by the GDP (gross domestic product, the sum of all goods and services in the domestic economy). Obviously, the larger the economy the more debt it can sustain, but economists differ (surprise, surprise!) over what an acceptable percentage is. Economics is a social science, and therefore inexact, but certain numbers speak volumes.

As of 2018 the ratio of debt-to-gross domestic product is 104%, which is forecast to increase to 108% in 2019. Taken alone this percentage seems staggering, and by comparison to recent years it is even more so. For example, in 2010 the percentage was about 65%, in 2000 and 1990 it was 55%, and in 1980 barely over 30%. In 38 years, the ratio of debt to gross domestic product has increased almost three-and-a-half fold. Nobody can identify the point at which the economy will fall apart under the burden of growing debt, but most objective observers agree that such a point does exist.

Why is this issue absent from almost every political campaign? Why does it never appear on surveys of the most crucial challenges facing the country? The answer is twofold. It involves economic complexities that can't be reduced to sound bites or sloganeering, and thus is uncomfortable for politicians to deal with. And, *the explosion of debt has occurred while both major parties were in control of Congress and the White House. Neither party can blame the other, meaning it's of no use to either party as an issue.* You won't see "national debt" as an option when you answer a questionnaire from your party of choice.

Historically, Republicans considered themselves guardians of the national pocketbook. Democrats, they always claimed, were free spenders whose lust for social engineering required tax increases, after which additional social programs would be called for. There was ample evidence to support the Republicans on this score. But when Ronald Reagan won the 1980 election, debt-to-GDP stood close to 30%, and almost doubled in ten years because of huge increases in defense spending. Under Republican President George W. Bush, the ratio increased yet further, due largely to commitments to Afghanistan and Iraq. Clearly, the GOP's historical claim to fiscal conservatism no longer stood up under scrutiny. But Democrats don't focus on the national debt, either, because they campaign with an emphasis on unmet social needs in health care, education, and the environment, all of which suggest either new taxes (unacceptable) or larger budget deficits (not apt to discuss). So, the elephant remains in the center of the room.

The second caveat used to excuse the enormous buildup of Treasury debt pertains to the identity of the creditors. In other words, who owns these Treasury obligations? If most of the debt is owned by Americans or American financial institutions, so the theory goes, a high debt-to-GDP ratio is tolerable. In effect, we owe the money to ourselves, and the interest payments on the debt are circulated back into the economy.

One problem with that theory is that the Social Security and Medicare trust funds own about 30% of the debt, so the interest payments don't get circulated into the economy until they're allocated for pensions and medical care. Another is that people are living longer, and medical costs are exploding, so these trust funds will necessarily be buying increasing quantities of Treasury debt going forward.

As of September 2018, China owns $1.151 trillion in Treasury securities, and Japan owns $1.028 trillion. If China were to sell theirs (if they were angry over trade sanctions, for example), it would create a market panic. Bond prices move inversely to their effective rate of return, so sales of over one trillion would depress prices and elevate interest rates on all U.S. obligations. Because credit markets move in sympathy to one another, rates on corporate bonds and municipal bonds would also rise precipitously. The economy would fall into a recession.

Speaking of Social Security and Medicare, we can now discuss the other elephant in the room. It's at least as toxic as the national debt to Democrats and Republicans alike, so maybe this elephant belongs in the garage.

Entitlements, by definition, allow little or no wiggle room for budget cutters. When Social Security came into being in the 1930s, it was designed according to the same criteria used by life insurance companies — life expectancy tables and interest-rate assumptions. A few years after Medicare was tied to Social Security in 1965, it was decided to move Social Security into the budget, alongside welfare, foreign aid, and the rest of the socialistic infrastructure. Having been paroled from an actuarial prison, the Social Security trust fund was then available for Congressional tampering, such as indexing the monthly benefits to inflation.

Somewhere along the way cautionary sounds began to be heard from apolitical sources. People were living longer, and the ratio of retirees (recipients) to workers (those paying in) was increasing. Actuaries determined that the trust fund would go bankrupt in _____ years (disputed). Separately, Medicare outlays were increasing, because as people lived longer, they relied on Medicare more. And, overall health-care costs spiraled for other reasons, such as new and costly advancements in medical technology.

Occasionally a politician would issue a warning that Social Security would go broke, only to be overwhelmed by polls that appeared almost overnight, revealing the public's hostility toward any and all entitlement cuts. In 2005, President George W. Bush, emboldened by his reelection in 2004, introduced a plan whereby the Social Security trust fund would be replaced by a system giving future recipients (current contributors) choices among various mutual funds—thereby converting guaranteed benefits into a gigantic 401-k-type plan, and placing one's retirement security in the hands of a specified group of Wall Street's money managers. Perhaps not coincidentally, a number of these managers were connected politically to the Bush family.

The public was having none of it. Entitlements are the third rail in politics. Since 2005 no serious proposal has been offered to adapt Social Security and Medicare to future realities. In fact, the reverse is true. Democrats now seek votes by issuing threats that Republicans will tamper with both. As with our national debt, craven politicians are content to pass the problem along to future generations.

The previous chapter cited Russ Feingold and Bill Weld as deficit hawks. If either of the two were running as an independent or third-party candidate against President Trump and any Democrat in 2020, he could point out that the president has fallen far behind on his promise to eliminate our national debt, and that the Democrat (whomever they nominate) is making promises that, if kept, would only add to the deficit in the absence of tax increases. In addition to calling attention to the problem, Feingold or Weld would have to offer a realistic plan for, at a minimum, aborting the runaway debt-to-GDP ratio, either by identifying possible cutbacks in government programs or through new taxes on the highest income earners. At the same time, the candidate should address Social Security and Medicare with an equally forthright approach, emphasizing that Republicans and Democrats have been avoiding the problem out of (not very) enlightened self-interest.

The few presidential candidates who have dared to talk about the elephants in the room over the years, for example Ross Perot and Steve Forbes, have been chided as "eat your spinach" scolds by mainstream politicians and the media. They lost their races to candidates who adopted the "ostrich" approach to politics, i.e., ignore a problem in the hope that voters will pretend it doesn't exist.

CHAPTER 43: ANOTHER POTENTIAL ELEPHANT

As this is written (late November 2018) the Standard & Poor's-500 and Dow Jones Industrial averages have slipped into minus territory for the year. A potential trade war with China has been blamed by some so-called experts; others point to the likelihood that the Federal Reserve will continue to raise short-term interest rates. President Trump's willingness to ignore the finding of the Central Intelligence Agency, that Saudi Arabian Crown Prince Mohammed bin Salman ordered the murder and mutilation of journalist Jamal Khashoggi in Istanbul, has upset the international community, especially Turkey's leader Recep Tayyip Erdogan, with possible implications for the world economy.

The NASDAQ index, which is heavily weighted with technology stocks, has suffered from recent adverse publicity surrounding Facebook's involvement with Russia during the 2016 political campaign, and from the company's earlier dismissal of rumors that later proved accurate. Facebook's CEO founder Mark Zuckerberg had also faced criticism over privacy violations resulting from a massive data breach. Without predicting how this will play out, it's a given that when a leadership group in the market, like social media technology stocks suffers sharp losses, the entire market is affected.

As one who spent 28 years with Wall Street firms, the present author can assure readers that the stock market never rises or falls for any one particular reason to the exclusion of all others, no matter what one reads in the financial press or hears on television. It is equally true that no president, regardless of party, deserves credit for a strong stock market, or the blame for market weakness. But President Trump, until recently, has been touting his deregulatory actions in behalf of business, and the tax cuts a Republican

Congress passed at his behest, while boasting about market gains since his inauguration. A prolonged market correction would weaken him politically, at least to the extent that the public had given him credit for earlier market strength. Of course, President Trump would be blaming everyone except himself for the slump.

It's important to understand that President Trump's willingness to risk trade wars around the globe with new tariffs collides with the mind-set of almost every economist, including most of his own advisers. Trade wars scare Wall Street's money managers, whose performance on a quarter-by-quarter basis *relative to other money managers* determines whether they can afford to keep that summer place in the Hamptons and the Manhattan townhouse. If the current market weakness presages a major correction or a bear market, no one managing a multi-billion portfolio can afford to stay fully invested, because by the end of a given quarter, managers that earlier sold stocks and raised cash will have performed better *and will draw business away, often never to see it return.*

The same phenomenon prevails in reverse. A bearish money manager who holds, for example, a 30% cash position, waiting for stocks to decline to a comfortable buying range, will be out of luck if a market rally continues, even when stocks might seem to have risen to unrealistic (overvalued) levels. It's highly probable that the 28% gain the Standard & Poor's 500-stock index enjoyed in 2017 owed largely to institutional fears of being "left out" of a rally, and to fiduciaries paying up for stocks they considered historically overvalued.

The media underestimate the extent to which managed money dominates the market. Often one will read in the financial press, or hear on television, that "investors were nervous over (_____) and sold stocks," or "investors were encouraged by (_____) and bought stocks." The fact is, individual investors had little to do with it. The overwhelming majority of money entering (or leaving) the market at any moment derives from decisions made by portfolio managers *who are handling other people's money.* These aren't investors, rather people acting in behalf of investors, with entirely different motivations. A Wall Street portfolio manager would prefer that his client lose 10% in a quarter, while other money managers are losing 15%, versus seeing his client gain 10% in the same quarter while the competition averages a 15% gain. The fact that the client is 20% better in this example matters less than the reality of the manager's inferior *relative performance.*

The current situation in the stock market is perilous, to the extent that President Trump's opposition to free trade continues. A history lesson suggests why. By June 1930 the stock market averages had regained more than half of the losses suffered in the October 1929 crash. It was thought to have been a normal correction. Then the Smoot-Hawley Tariff (to protect domestic producers) was passed and signed by President Hoover, even though the president had objected to the tariff as conflicting with his own internationalist ideal of economic cooperation. When companies overseas responded with tariffs on American imports, the stock market averages headed downward again. The Great Depression began in earnest.

History offers no guidance concerning an economic slump that occurs while the nation is $21.7 trillion in debt (see previous chapter). In the past, during recessions the Federal Reserve Bank has injected liquidity (dollars) into the banking system through its open-market operations. In 2018 that strategy would run counter to its policy of gradually increasing short-term interest rates to guard against inflation. Further, a weak economy would tend to discourage banks from lending, so any liquidity provided by the "Fed" wouldn't reach the people who needed cash the most. Banks would tend to keep the money in reserve, or choose to use it to buy back their own stock.

Suffice it to say that protectionist tariffs would exacerbate any economic slump that might follow a stock market sell-off. It happened in 1930, when federal debt levels were a tiny fraction of $21.7 trillion, and less than 20% of Gross Domestic Product.

During a recession, tax collection revenues from individuals and corporate entities fall, proportionate to increases in unemployment and declines in business profits. That increases federal debt, because entitlements remain in place and government spending doesn't decline sufficiently to compensate. At the same time, any new tariffs will have made imports of foreign goods more expensive to American consumers and businesses. A weak dollar, which typically accompanies a recession, will make them still costlier, meaning the expected revenue benefit of the tariffs is forfeited. If, as usually happens, foreign governments retaliate with tariffs against American goods, that hurts American companies doing business overseas by neutralizing the advantage of the weaker dollar.

It's easy to imagine a snowball effect throughout the international economy from the combined effect of a stock market decline in the United States and a trade war. If China or Japan were to sell significant amounts of American government bonds to liquefy their own treasuries during a global recession, that would raise interest rates at a time when our domestic economy most needs liquidity, accelerating the snowball effect.

Such a scenario would be politically damaging to the Trump administration, obviously. Herbert Hoover's fortunes never recovered from the 1929 market crash and the Smoot-Hawley Tariff. But Democrats in 2019–

2020 would have a harder time repairing the ship of state than Franklin D. Roosevelt enjoyed in 1932. The federal debt level, relative to GDP, would be on the order of six or seven times the ratio FDR encountered. It's hard to conceive how Democrats could even gain political advantage over the Republicans, given their commitment to costly new initiatives the country clearly could not afford.

The two-party system, especially one in which cooperation with the other side is seen by party leaders as political weakness, might finally be held to account for the country's woes. Americans might just come to a belated recognition that what it had needed all along was an "eat your spinach" disciplinarian, that odd political animal one rarely finds in either of the two major parties. George Washington, who saw it all coming 230 years ago, will deserve a new monument, except it won't be built in Washington, DC.

CHAPTER 44: A RADICAL (?) IDEA FROM A RADICAL (?) CENTRIST

When incumbent members of Congress run for reelection, they win over 90% of the time. Yet Congress itself has a public approval rating of 21%, as of October 2018, which bad as it is, represents a 9% improvement over the previous year. This glaring paradox has been pointed out often, far more so that it has been satisfactorily explained.

An earlier chapter cited the fact that Congress makes its own rules, rules than serve the selfish interests of its members without benefiting the public. Examples include granting the most power to the most senior people, albeit those folks might well have begun to exhibit age-related disabilities, e.g., dementia. They include allowing a single Senator (out of 100) to place a "hold" on a nomination, even if the other 99 would have voted to confirm. Worst of all, both houses of Congress vest extraordinary power in those holding leadership positions, power that is often exercised against members who opt for the public interest over partisanship. Such disloyal rascals are sometimes brought to heel by the "whips" that both major parties employ to enforce loyalty, which fact does nothing to advance the commonweal. Whips simply advertise the true priorities of Republicans and Democrats alike.

The mandate doesn't appear in any Congressional rule book, but former Congressman David Jolly (R-FL) revealed that new representatives are told they must spend 40% of their work hours on the telephone, raising money for the party. Mr. Jolly no longer serves in Congress, his district having been gerrymandered into a Democratic safety zone, but he has been rumored to have considered running an independent campaign at some point. If he did so, no doubt he'd emphasize the extent to which dollars and cents govern politics in the 21st century.

Do any of these unpleasant facts explain why voters approve of the job their representatives are doing by a ratio of ten to one, yet disapprove of the place where these same representatives hold forth, by five to one? Probably not, because while these rules might be undemocratic and entirely self-serving to the people who operate under them, the public is generally ignorant of the rules themselves. The answer to the enigma might lie within that ribbon of highways that traverses parts of Maryland and Virginia, a heavily trafficked section of concrete called the Beltway. The problem just might be Washington, DC itself, and not the people the public sends there to conduct its business.

Washington succeeded New York City and Philadelphia as the nation's capital in 1790, when the entire country consisted of what we now call the East Coast. Virtually everything west of Pennsylvania was populated by Indian tribes that had been there a while, and possibly a stray Mongol whose ancestors had gotten lost after crossing the land bridge from Siberia a millennium earlier. Travel was painfully slow by contemporary standards, consisting of slow-as-molasses boats powered by wind or horse-drawn carriages along unpaved roads. Communication was crude, unless one owned a very reliable carrier pigeon. In forming a republican government, therefore, it became necessary for the founding fathers to situate the Executive Mansion, Capitol, and Supreme Court in close proximity to one another. Washington, connected to the Atlantic via the Potomac River and Chesapeake Bay, became a compromise location, favoring neither the money centers of the Northeast nor the agrarian South.

By the time the Federal Reserve Banking System came into being in 1913, there were 48 united states, and with the advent of coast-to-coast travel and a nationwide telephone communication network in effect, it was decided to divide the system into regional banks, which today number twelve, from Boston to San Francisco. The Board of Governors is in Washington. The author is unaware of any difficulty the Federal Reserve has encountered by the fact of its disparate locations.

But the Federal Reserve System is unique within the federal bureaucracy. All executive (cabinet) departments are located within the city limits of Washington, DC., save for the Department of Defense, which is headquartered across the river in Arlington, Virginia, in a building that couldn't quite fit inside the district.

Washington is where the Department of Agriculture has been located since its founding in 1862, even though very few crops are grown in its streets and the nearest grain storage silo is somewhere in Kansas. The Department of Energy has been headquartered in Washington since it came into being in 1977, albeit no oil has ever been discovered or refined anywhere close to the city. And the Department of Education, founded in 1979, is also based in Washington, despite wide agreement that the best schools have always been administered by people who live close to the schools themselves, unencumbered by interference from a bureaucrat located hundreds or thousands of miles away, someone who was appointed by a president who probably went to a private school.

This homogeneous arrangement can't be defended on the grounds of convenience. A text message can reach Los Angeles from New York every bit as quickly as one sent from one Washington office to another. Telephone companies offer unlimited long-distance calling for a set fee. People travel round-trip from coast to coast on the same day. There is no reason beyond tradition that every Cabinet official must operate out of a Washington, DC office. But there is a single overriding reason why they should be scattered throughout the country instead.

The letter "K" has mostly benign connotations. It stands for "thousand," as in a 10-K road race of ten thousand meters. In a baseball scorebook it means "strikeout," and "K" often appears in lights on the scoreboard when the home team's pitcher is mowing down hitters. "K-K-K Katy" was once a popular song. And "K–12" means "kindergarten-to-12th grade." So far, so good. But there's a place in Washington, DC where the letter "K" isn't benign at all. That's on K-Street, once the geographic center of lobbying in the nation's capital, the place where retired Congresspeople went to get rich by dictating terms to existing Congresspeople, and by often writing the desired legislation themselves, just to make sure every "t" is crossed and every "i" is dotted.

Most lobbying firms no longer operate on K Street, but the address lingers as a symbol of corrupt practices, primarily because former (Republican) House Majority Leader Tom DeLay used it to identify his "K Street Project," a kind of hybrid strategy initiative that combined political concessions to lobbyists (including a do-it-yourself imprimatur), in exchange for contributions to the Republican Party on a quid pro quo basis. That's Latin for "bribes."

DeLay was first elected to Congress from Texas' 22nd District in 1985, despite a checkered personal history. He had been expelled from Baylor University for criminal mischief, and his extermination company, though it was good at killing bugs, had been cited thrice by Internal Revenue for non-payment of taxes. Still, he became Republican Majority Whip in 1995, and was so successful at wielding weapons of persuasion that he became known as "The Hammer," a moniker that DeLay carried as a badge of honor.

Although frequently at odds with Republican leader Newt Gingrich, whom he considered insufficiently devout, the pious Mr. Hammer leveraged his vote-gathering talents into an election as Majority Leader in 2003. Within two years DeLay had been indicted (back in Texas) on money laundering and conspiracy charges. He was convicted and sentenced to a three-year prison term, but the conviction was overturned by a 2–1 vote on appeal.

Would the K-Street Project ever have come into being if the government's business were not conducted within a radius of several miles in Washington, DC? It's impossible to know, but it's a safe bet that if lobbyists were kept at arm's length from our elected representatives, and required to make contact only by e-mail, snail mail, or telephone, that they at least wouldn't be positioned where they could write the laws themselves.

Ask yourself this, friends. If a lobbyist who was never elected by anyone to the position is permitted to author legislation, why not extend the privilege to everyone who makes a political contribution to the party in power? Think tanks, which typically do more proselytizing than thinking, should be allowed remain in Washington, but they should be forbidden to make political contributions to anyone.

The author suggests that the government be decentralized. Geographic diversity works for the Federal Reserve System, it works for Corporate America, and the same approach would improve governmental function beyond anyone's imagination. Some changes would be more impactful than others, but the only negative effect would be upon real estate values inside the Beltway, which have risen in proportion to the corrupt influence of money on politics.

I would move the Department of Energy to Dallas or Houston. The Department of the Interior should be transferred to Denver, and the Department of Agriculture to Kansas City or Omaha. I would abolish the Education Department, although laws forbidding segregated schools must remain in effect. Other executive departments should be relocated to separate states, covering all sections of the country. Defense should stay at the Pentagon, if for no better reason than that a building of that size couldn't be replicated anywhere. Even if it could be, the cost of razing the current building would be prohibitive.

The Supreme Court and the White House should not be domiciled in same city, for two reasons: 1) The three branches of government are co-equal, and 2) All courts should be deaf to partisan politics. When a president and a Chief Justice get into a spitting contest, as occurred recently, it isn't a fair fight, because the president has the advantage of a bully pulpit. Moving the Supreme Court to Philadelphia or Boston would help. Electing a president who understands the importance of an independent judiciary would also help.

The Capitol should remain where it is. But all members of Congress should be compensated only for the time they spend doing the public's business. They should pay for their own health insurance coverage and that of their families, until every American is guaranteed the same coverage at the same cost. No member may work for a lobbying firm or think tank for a minimum of five years after leaving Congress, and no former lobbyist is eligible to run for Congress. No exceptions.

There you have it. The author offers this advice as a public service. He isn't naïve. He understands that the above changes could only accrue from a political revolution, one that divides political power according to its alignment within the adult population — approximately 45% independent or third-party, 30% Democrat, and 25% Republican. Nothing stands in the way of such a realignment, except the brute force of the two major parties themselves, and the fear of opposing them.

There is nothing to fear, but...well, you know the rest.

Chapter 45: Until It Happens...

The scenario outlined in Chapter 44 is a flight of fancy, at least until the government in Washington returns to some semblance of bi-partisanship — or better still, non-partisanship. Until a non-partisan hero emerges from the clouds to "drain the swamp" without creating a new swamp, certain urgent matters should be dealt with in the public interest, as follow:

ELECTIONS: Neither of the two major parties trusts the other. Close elections become political and legal battlegrounds, with Democrats blaming Republicans for alleged voter suppression, while Republicans accuse Democrats of voter fraud in one form or another. Both parties have legitimate grounds for their complaints, unfortunately.

It is apparent that cheating in one form or another is thought of as a necessary means to an end. "They're rigging the books, so we have to play the same game." The outcome of a close election in the 21st century often depends on which party is the better cheater. In the current environment, even a clean election that ended up close would bring accusations from the losing side. The bitterness carries over into the next legislative session, and each party blames the other for a failure to cooperate.

It bears repeating that all elections for president and Congress are conducted at the state level. No federal law serves as an oversight. Whichever party controls the state house finds itself in a position to influence voting in both subtle and not-so-subtle ways, as happened most prominently in Florida in 2000, and in Ohio and Florida in 2004. Republicans were able to limit minority turnout by preventing eligible voters from registering with questionable tactics. In many districts, voters whose signature differed from the signature on their photo-IDs, regardless of age or health considerations (handwriting can change), were given provisional ballots. In the end, most of these were never counted. As the present author observed first-hand in 2004, the Florida department of state allocated fewer voting machines than were needed to minority districts, creating long lines and forcing voters to decide between voting and returning to work on time to save their jobs. This tactic was also used in Ohio, to equally deadly effect. In Republican-dominated districts in both states, more than enough voting machines were on hand. Voting proceeded normally.

George W. Bush won the 2000 election because of manipulation of the electorate in Florida. He won in 2004 because of extra-legal tactics in Ohio and Florida, as conclusively shown by a statistically prohibitive 6-1/2% discrepancy between the tabulated vote in his favor and the exit-poll tally in favor of John F. Kerry.

Republicans have long argued that in Democratic-controlled states, voter fraud (people voting without being registered, or voting more than once) is the real issue. President Trump averred that Hillary Clinton won the popular vote in 2016 due to voter fraud. While that claim is specious at best, and although independent investigations have found voter fraud to be a very minor problem, it is nevertheless true that in 2016 California was still tallying votes a week after every other state had reported; given that California is home to the technology capital of the world, Silicon Valley, one would expect maximum efficiency from California officials, who are nonetheless habitually late to record and report votes. It is also true that heavily Democratic districts in Florida (Broward and Palm Beach counties) have been chronically slow and disorganized in tabulating votes.

To the extent that willful misconduct on the part of state officials is responsible for electoral controversies, it will continue in one form or another until the miscreants operate under a higher authority with prosecutorial powers, i.e., federal oversight. This is unlikely to occur, because a new federal law would have to be written in such a way that both Democrat and Republican grievances are assuaged. It's also likely that whichever federal official serves as a watchdog will be accused of partisanship whenever an election is whisker-close.

An exception might be a federal law that forbids any candidate to run for office in a state where that person has dominion over the election process. Democrat Stacey Adams, the losing candidate, maintained that Secretary of State Brian Kemp won the Georgia gubernatorial race in 2018 dishonestly; whether she was right or wrong, it is quintessentially unfair for any candidate to be in position to oversee the same election, especially one requiring a recount. Any member of Congress who voted against a bill to eliminate that conflict of interest would have a difficult time explaining why.

One remedy that wouldn't involve federalism questions is to make Election Day a national holiday. No voter would need to fear being fired for returning to work late because of long lines at the polling site, because going to work would be optional to begin with.

GLOBAL WARMING: In the space of two months in 2018, two separate calamities resulted in extensive loss of life and property damage in the United States, both of which have been identified with global warming. Hurricane Michael devastated the Florida panhandle and continued to wreak havoc in Georgia and the Carolinas, and massive wildfires in several areas left thousands of Californians homeless. Scientists are estimating that future hurricanes could reach unprecedented levels, and that further increases in average temperature would leave forests even more vulnerable to conflagrations.

This is hardly a newly discovered problem. The polar icecaps are melting, and natural disasters are increasing worldwide. Yet significant numbers of Americans choose to believe that global warming is a fiction, encouraged in their belief by President Trump and other politicians whose electoral base resides in the energy belt, and still others who see the issue as one promoted by liberals and academic elitists from the two coasts who enjoy feeling superior to rubes in "flyover country." The present author isn't a scientist, and he isn't competent to argue ecology with anyone. But 90% of those who are qualified to do so believe carbon emissions from fossil fuels represent a grave threat to the planet, and that alternate fuel usage will be increasingly necessary over time. A carbon tax might have enough bi-partisan support to pass Congress. It should be passed *on a trial basis*, giving all interested parties an opportunity to gauge its effectiveness. The revenue from such a tax could be applied, dollar for dollar but not beyond, toward continued research into the efficacy of alternate fuels.

GUN CONTROL: Mass killings have become so commonplace that even many ardent supporters of the 2nd Amendment seem willing to consider improved background checks on gun purchasers, longer waiting periods, and/or bans on bump stocks, those devices that convert pistols into automatic weapons. A question that remains unanswered, but might hold the key to the possibility of major reform down the road is, "Are opponents of gun control really all that concerned with the Constitutional right to bear arms (as part of a militia, as it was written), or is their opposition centered on the very profitable business of selling guns and ammunition?"

The fact that drastic measures, such as arming schoolteachers, have been endorsed by some law-enforcement professionals demonstrates the degree of public anxiety over tragedies like the Parkland, Florida shootings. If it can be taken as a given that the random killing of innocent victims, unknown to the assailant, reflects some level of mental instability on the killer's part, then would such a killer, who is likely to have taken his own life in the process, be deterred by knowing someone behind a desk could be firing back? Isn't the likelihood that a teacher who has little or no experience with weapons could accidentally shoot a student by mistake, or that the ricochet of a projectile could cause an accidental death, reason enough to reject the idea out of hand? It has been further argued, in opposition to the arming of schoolteachers, that the mere sight of a teacher holding a weapon would terrify a young child. Before agreeing with that postulate, every citizen should consider the amount of violence children are already exposed to through video games and television, and the extent to which those outlets glorify violence, on a daily basis.

Outlawing of all weapons except hunting rifles, if it should ever come to pass, will be an evolutionary process. Incremental steps such as those cited above are doable, if only our elected representatives are willing to stop running for reelection long enough to reach agreement on them, and further provided that members of Congress not care if the National Rifle Association gives them a low grade.

MONEY IN POLITICS: There is nothing more ludicrous than to hear a politician pontificate about the evil of money in politics, then to visit one's e-mail inbox to find a dozen or more accumulated demands for money from that same politician, or in behalf of some candidate 2,000 miles away the politico has endorsed. The author's own experience is that these pleas resist any and all efforts to stem their flow because the addressee has been mistakenly identified as a party loyalist. The fact that the solicitations have increased, both in volume and in their arrogant tone, proves that either 1) Flooding someone's inbox works statistically, or 2) The sender doesn't care if people are offended, if even one recipient out of a hundred responds with a donation. At the risk of beating a dead horse, the author would remind the reader that contributions to Candidate A, or to that candidate's party organization, are merely spent on advertising that tells us how awful Candidate B is, and the disastrous consequences to everyone's life should Candidate A lose the upcoming election. The Supreme Court decided in its wisdom that corporations are people, and thus exempt from any restrictions on campaign contributions that don't also apply to individuals. Because the court is dominated by conservatives following the installation of Judge Brett Kavanaugh, it's highly unlikely that the Citizens United decision will be reversed in the foreseeable future. One possibility that stands at least a faint chance of passage is a federal law to require all candidates to reveal the source of every contribution received, with no exceptions. Such a law would necessarily have to pass federalism tests, because it's a lead-pipe cinch that attorneys-general would insist that their own state's laws cannot be abrogated. Stay tuned. In the meantime, if a major corporation donates to a candidate one dislikes, one is entirely within the bounds of ethics to boycott that company's products and to let the whole world know.

MEDIA: The death of former President George H.W. Bush at age 94, and the praise from diverse sources for his courtly and statesmanlike manner, has drawn attention to the decline in civility and bi-partisan cooperation since he left office in 1993. One of President Bush's last requests was that President Trump be invited to his funeral, certainly a magnanimous gesture in the face of Trump's harsh criticism in the past of George W. Bush and Jeb Bush, and his generally uncivil political style.

Newspapers and television aren't responsible for cutthroat political tactics, but they make a bad situation worse by drawing attention to every early-morning message from President Trump's Twitter account, as if name-calling and bluster substituted for statesmanship. Like parents indulging a spoiled child, the media respond to the president's impulsive tweets with instantaneous headlines, knowing that a response in kind will probably follow from the insulted party and that their readership/audience will grow in direct proportion to the heightened level of combat. Controversy sells, even when the headlines suggest a supermarket tabloid.

The problem defies easy solutions. Freedom of the press extends to other media, and newspapers and television are private businesses engaged in competition. If one paper or network decided to ignore President Trump's tweets, another would seize the competitive advantage. But a candidate for president in 2020 would attract attention (and this author believes, respect) by politely answering, "I don't have a comment" whenever a reporter asks, "What did you think of President Trump's accusation about ____?" and then shifting the conversation in a constructive direction.

If such a reply emanated from a Republican competing with President Trump for the nomination instead of from a Democratic candidate, it would have an exponentially greater effect. Civility could triumph over rancor for a change, and the family and friends of President George H.W. Bush would know he hadn't died in vain.

Epilogue

The following will doubtless be dismissed as "fake news" by everyone in Washington, regardless of party. The author has heard from an "unimpeachable" source that George Washington and Abraham Lincoln were recently seen together in a convenience store, the same store that Elvis Presley has often visited since his rumored death. This source, who has requested anonymity, was eavesdropping, and described their conversation as proceeding as follows:

ABE: "Mr. President, I'd know you anywhere from your photographs. You're still wearing your hair long, I see."

GEORGE: "I can't believe what barbers charge these days, Abraham. I'm going to leave my hair the way it is, thank you."

ABE: "I've always wanted to ask you this question, Mr. President. Did you really chop down a cherry tree?"

GEORGE: "No, it never happened, Abraham. Why do people make up stories like that?"

ABE: "Well, sir...often to gain political advantage. Did you have enemies that we never read about in our history books?"

GEORGE: "Well, General Cornwallis certainly wasn't a friend of mine. Did that story possibly originate in England?"

ABE (laughing): "No, Mr. President. I meant, 'Did you have partisan enemies here in the United States?'"

GEORGE: "I don't think so. Mr. Jefferson and Mr. Hamilton had ideas of their own. But neither man was my enemy."

ABE: "Well, sir, my history books said you belonged to the Federalist party. Thomas Jefferson was an anti-Federalist. It's possible he spread the rumor that you chopped down the tree, but only to compliment you for having owned up to it."

GEORGE: "Damn those history books, Abraham! I never should have let them call me a Federalist. That was a mistake."

ABE: "Why, Mr. President? You believed in a strong federal government, did you not?"

GEORGE: "Damn it, Abraham! If the federal government is strong, does that mean half the people in the country want it to be something else, for the sake of their own selfish interests?"

ABE: "I don't understand, sir."

GEORGE: "It's about personal ambition, Abraham. The only way some men can satisfy their political urgings is by attacking the people in power on a partisan basis. I told Mr. Jefferson and Mr. Hamilton over 200 years ago that their rivalry would lead to disharmony based on political labels, and that the breach would continue to widen indefinitely."

ABE: "I was never ashamed of being a Republican, Mr. President."

GEORGE: "You were a Whig when you served in Congress, weren't you, Abraham? Then, after the Whigs vanished into the ether, you became a Republican, and you were elected as a Republican in 1860. But in 1864 you shifted to the Union party. You've run for office under three different party labels. And you're rated as the greatest president of all, ahead of me. Doesn't that prove that partisanship has nothing to do with success in politics?"

ABE: "I never looked at it that way, sir."

GEORGE: "Nice to see you, Abraham. I have to get back to heaven now. Give my regards to Mary."

Bibliography

Applegate, Debby, *The Most Famous Man in America*. Doubleday, 2006

Bamford, James, *The Shadow Factory. The Ultra-Secret NSA from 9/11 to the Eavesdropping on America*. Anchor Books, 2008

Barry, John M., *Roger Williams and the Creation of the American Soul*. Viking, 2012

Bleyer, Kevin, *ME the People* Random House, 2012

Borneman, Walter R., *Polk*. Random House, 2008

Clarke, Richard A., *Your Government Failed You. Breaking the Cycle of National Security Disasters*. RAC Enterprises, 2008

Dean, John W., *Worse than Watergate. The Secret Presidency of George W. Bush*. Little, Brown, & Co. 2004

Fetzer, James H., *Murder in Dealey Plaza*. Catfeet Press, 2000

Goodwin, Doris Kearns, *Team of Rivals. The Political Genius of Abraham Lincoln*. Simon & Schuster, 2005

Ivins, Molly, *Bushwhacked*. Random House, 2003

Kaplan, Fred, *John Quincy Adams*. Harper Collins, 2014

Kreig, Andrew, *Presidential Puppetry. Obama, Romney and their Masters*, Eagle View Books, 2013

Lincoln, Evelyn, *Kennedy and Johnson*. Holt, Rinehart, and Winston, 1968

Malcomson, Scott, *Generation's End. A Personal Memoir of American Power after 9/11*. Potomac Books, 2010

Mosley, Leonard, *Dulles. A Biography of Eleanor, Allen, and John Foster Dulles and their Family Network*. The Dial Press/James Wade, 1978

Nolan, Patrick, *CIA Rogues and the Killing of the Kennedys*. Skyhorse Publishing, 2013

Palast, Greg, *Armed Madhouse*. Dutton, 2006

Paul, Rand, *The Tea Party Comes to Washington*. Center Street, 2011

Potter, David M., *The South and the Sectional Conflict*. Louisiana State University Press, 1968

Raymond, Allen, *How to Rig an Election: Confessions of a Republican Operative*. Simon & Schuster, 2008

Schoenfeld, Gabriel, *Necessary Secrets. National Security, the Media, and the Rule of Law*. W.W. Norton & Co, 2010

Shlaes, Amity, *Coolidge*. Harper Collins, 2013

Ventura, Jesse (with Dick Russell). *American Conspiracies*. Skyhorse Publishing, 2010

Wilentz, Sean, *The Politicians and the Egalitarians*. W.W. Norton &. Co, 2016

Will, George, *One Man's America*. Crown Forum, 2008

Woodward, Bob, *Fear. Trump in the White House*. Simon & Schuster, 2018

INDEX

Numerals

Printed in the United States
By Bookmasters